THE TALE OF TWO CHURCHES

Rise of the Apostates

AMOS DERTES

ISBN 979-8-88751-778-0 (paperback)
ISBN 979-8-89043-845-4 (hardcover)
ISBN 979-8-88751-779-7 (digital)

Copyright © 2023 by Amos Dertes

All rights reserved. No part of this publication may be reproduced, distributed, or transmitted in any form or by any means, including photocopying, recording, or other electronic or mechanical methods without the prior written permission of the publisher. For permission requests, solicit the publisher via the address below.

Christian Faith Publishing
832 Park Avenue
Meadville, PA 16335
www.christianfaithpublishing.com

Printed in the United States of America

DEDICATION

I dedicate this book to all Christians. The book is purposed to encourage those who are striving to become like Jesus Christ, those who thirst for holiness, justice and righteousness. To you who are holding strong, I say, hang on! Remember Jesus blessed those who hunger and thirst for justice and righteousness. Jesus will fill and satisfy you but don't give in to the ways of the world. The crown is for those who overcome like Jesus did. This book is also dedicated to those who are confused, those who love Jesus Christ but are becoming disenfranchised with the current institutional church. Don't give up! Continue loving and having faith in Jesus. Keep your eyes on him. Jesus is righteous and just and he commands you to be like him. To be like Jesus should be your primary Goal. To achieve this Goal, you need the mind that was in Jesus. Seek the Holy Spirit while he can be found. When the spirit of the Lord inhabits your heart, he will mold you in the shape of the savior. Then you can be a true Christian. Don't be offended by the truth but let it change you. Don't be like the crowd who wants to be pleased. Instead, live your life to please God.

CONTENTS

Preface ix

Chapter 1: The Origin of Good and Evil in the
 Congregation of Man 1
 God divided the sons of Adam into two seeds 6
Chapter 2: The Beginning of the Congregation of Israel 11
Chapter 3: The Renaming of the Congregation of the
 saints, The new Israel, The Church 23
 The Beginning of the Church of Jesus the Christ 26
 The Church under Captivity 27
 The Church Left Roman Captivity 29
 The Two Churches in the Christian congregation 32
Chapter 4: The Elects of God and Satan's Cunning
 Imposters in the Congregations of the Church 35
 The Influence of the Seed of Evil in the Church 39
 The Antichrist Spirit in Church Leadership 42
 The Counterfeit Gospels 44
Chapter 5: As the Church Evolves to Become a Worldly
 Institution 46
 Two Manner of People in the Church 50
Chapter 6: The Reprobate in the War 54
Chapter 7: The Christian in the War 63
Chapter 8: Ignorance of Satan among the Christians 71
 The Sword of the Spirit 74
 Are You Ready for the Marriage of the Lamb? 78
Chapter 9: The Hired Hand and the True Shephard 80

Chapter 10: The Lukewarm Worshiper 92
Chapter 11: 'Tis not by Might nor by Power 100
           My Quest for the Truth 102
Chapter 12: The Person of the Holy Spirit 110
           The Holy Spirit in the Old Contract 112
           The Holy Spirit Begins the New Contract 115
Chapter 13: There is one Baptism 118
           To Produce Good Fruits 121
           The Baptism of Water: The First Step in
           Becoming a Christian 123
           The Baptism that Makes the Son of God 125
Chapter 14: Wrong Spirit, Wrong Priority 127
Chapter 15: "The Once Saved Always Saved Doctrine" 132
           No salvation without repentance 134
           Work out your own salvation 135
           The conditions to stay within God's grace 137
           This is a battle for the mind 137
           Come as You Are and Stay as You Are 139
           Save from the mouth of Hell 140
Chapter 16: Christians, the Only Resistance to Satan's
           Power in the World 143
           Human politic is Satan's diplomatic affair 144
           The Esoteric Satan and the Genuine Saint
           on Earth 144
           Satan Tempted Jesus to choose the self over
           the Father 147
           The kingdom of Satan, platform of
           unrighteousness 149
Chapter 17: Restricting the Holy Spirit 153
Chapter 18: Keep the Mass in the Dark 163
Chapter 19: Deviating from the Great Commission 170
           Disciples and Church goers 171
           The Holy Spirit is the Teacher 172
           Theologian does not mean Christian 173
           Preaching instead of teaching 176
Chapter 20: To Preach the True Gospel 180

out demons; they will speak in new tongues; they will pick up snakes with their hands, and if they drink any deadly poison, it will not harm them; they will lay their hands on the sick, and they will be made well" (Mark 16:17–18 BSB). Jesus and his disciples performed miracles to glorify the Father. He said to the Jews, *"I am come in my Father's name, and ye receive me not: if another shall come in his own name, him ye will receive"* (John 5:43 BSB).

Well, once again, Jesus has been proven right in our generation. Using the power of Satan, these workers of iniquity are performing miracles in their name as if they use their own power to perform them, and the whole world is believing them. Some of them will heal people and tell the masses that it is a point of energy in the universe that you have to tap into. That too, is a lie! The reality is that if it is not done in the name and spirit of Jesus, it is all done by the demons.

SAVE TO SERVE: FIND A MINISTRY

Once you are sanctified, you have work to do, not only charitable work but spiritual as well. James told us that faith without work is dead. You are a warrior, not a Sunday churchgoer. You should go to church because Elder Paul advised us not to abandon our assembly, which is for good reasons. The congregation gatherings strengthen your faith and help you in the fellowship with other brothers and sisters. In addition, Jesus promised his presence in the middle of the assembly in these words, *"For where two or three are gathered together in my name, there am I in the midst of them"* (Matthew 18:20 BSB).

However, if that assembly is not preaching the cross and holiness, and if it is not attracting the presence of God by embracing the power of the Holy Spirit, you need to stay clear. Wherever the name of Jesus Christ is pronounced, the Holy Spirit is there. Find a congregation that names the name of Jesus Christ in their worship and sings about his agony on the cross—a congregation that preaches holiness and the gospel of the cross of Jesus or, as Elder Paul put it, Christ crucified!

Jesus warned us to be careful, saying, *"Behold, I send you forth as sheep in the midst of wolves be ye therefore wise as serpents, and harmless as doves" (Matthew 10:16 BSB).* Remember that Apostle Paul's farewell to the Ephesians was not to tell them to prosper but instead he said to them, *"I know that after my departure, savage wolves will come in among you and will not spare the flock. Even from your own number, men will rise up and distort the truth to draw away disciples after them. Therefore, be alert and remember that for three years I never stopped warning each of you night and day with tears" (Acts 20:30 BSB).*

Seek a church managed by the Holy Spirit. As I told you earlier, Christians are in a spiritual fight. You do not fight it standing in public places, reciting long prayers. This is for the hypocrites. Instead, your battles should be fought on your knees in the secret place, as Jesus ordered you to go into your closet to pray. Be vigilant, stay strong, and be constant in the fight. Be a worshipper, an every-hour worshipper. Prayer should be a constant, a habit, and medicine for your mind and soul. Pray for an hour at least per day. You have twenty-three hours for everything else, but the first hour is for prayer. Make it a habit. The more you keep this habit, the more urgent your desire to communicate with God will become, and the longer time you will spend in his presence.

The closer you get to God, the more you can discover his goodness, his greatness, and his plan for your life. He will fill you with power, the same power Peter, elder Paul, and the rest of the apostles had to carry out the great commission. If you listen to the advice in this book and apply them, you will discover a totally new Christianity, the warrior one, which is entirely different from the bench warmer image we have of it today. Then God will be able to use you to show forth His power in this world.

Join a Ministry

Start working in one of the ministries of the church. If there is none, start one. For instance, you can start a prayer ministry at the church, where you come in and pray before every service. You can also set up a ministry where you go to the hospitals to pray for the sick. You can start a ministry where you go to the prisons to be a witness to the prisoners and tell them about Jesus. You can volunteer to be an intercessor for the unsaved in your city. You can volunteer to be a prayer warrior to undo the devil's snares for the population of your city, your unsaved family members, and church members who have not yet understood the fight.

You can also start a worship service during the week. Whatever you do, don't sit idle. Develop those spiritual muscles to grow strong in the Lord. Beloved, don't become a part of the apostate church. They are boasting all kinds of riches and fame as blessings from God when, in reality, they are hooked on Satan. When God is blessing someone, the first thing he does is bless them spiritually, not materially. Elder Paul said it this way: *"Blessed be the God and Father of our Lord Jesus Christ, who hath blessed us with all spiritual blessings in heavenly places in Christ: According as he hath chosen us in him before the foundation of the world, that we should be holy and without blame before him in love: Having predestinated us unto the adoption of children by Jesus Christ to himself, according to the good pleasure of his will, To the praise of the glory of his grace, wherein he hath made us accepted in the beloved"* (Ephesians 1:3–6 BSB).

Notice what Paul said here: **that we should be holy and without blame before God in love**". The blessing of God is a relationship with the Father, the Son, and the Holy Spirit. Everything material you receive from Him is a side gift. Pursue peace and sanctification, and once you are sanctified, you can receive the true gift, which is the perpetual presence of the Holy Spirit—the Spirit of life and truth. *"And the peace of God, which passeth all understanding, shall keep your hearts and minds through Christ Jesus"* (Philippians 4:7 BSB).

May the Lord God, Creator of heaven and earth, Architect of our salvation, Father of our Lord Jesus Christ, our Father, bless you and keep you. May He make His face shine upon you and be gracious to you. May the Lord lift up his countenance upon you and give you peace to stay firm and persevere faithfully in his Word until the great day when we see Jesus face-to-face to be with him forever. Amen!

ABOUT THE AUTHOR

Amos Dertes is an author, preacher, and worship leader. He lives in the eastern parts of the United States with his family. He is the founder and manager of Banner of Grace Ministries. In this publication, he shows that there are two churches of Christianity. He identified them as the church of Jesus Christ and that of the Antichrist. This is his first publication out of a series of books that God inspired him to write. As the voice crying in the wilderness, he is calling the church to holiness, which is the state that will bring back the Holy Ghost for another Pentecost. To learn more, please visit his website at www.BGM.org.

Printed in the USA
CPSIA information can be obtained
at www.ICGtesting.com
LVHW040904240724
786351LV00007B/143/J

  Preachers of Men's Religions and Traditions............184
  Only the Righteous will Enter Heaven...................185
  Christian only in name 186
Chapter 21: Apostasy in the Old and New Church....................188
Chapter 22: Examine Your Walk in Life......................................196
  The Great Divide: The Tare and the Wheat............198
  The Tares 200
  The Wheat...205
  Take a Stand and Repent 206
Chapter 23: The Power of Sin versus the Pentecost Power..........208
  The Intellectual Gospel vs. the Gospel of Power.....211
  Save to Serve: Find a Ministry 219
  Join a Ministry 220

PREFACE

All the nations have drunk the wine of the passion of her immorality. The kings of the earth were immoral with her, and the merchants of the earth have grown wealthy from the extravagance of her luxury." Then I heard another voice from heaven say: "Come out of her, my people, so that you will not share in her sins or contract any of her plagues. For her sins are piled up to heaven, and God has remembered her iniquities."—Revelation 18:3-5 BSB

Come out from among them, my people! Conform to holiness, and submit to the Holy Spirit to make way for the new Pentecost. There is a fundamental problem with the Christian nation. It is why your thirst is not quenched, why your soul is yearning for more. Jesus promised to turn you into a fountain of living water. Yet, the great majority of those who call themselves Christians is still thirsty. Here, I point out the flaws that are at the root of the problem. Read and you will find out the reasons why the congregations are cold and distant. I invite you on a journey of discovery where I unveil some of the great deceptions. Read and learn to come out of the crowd. Salvation is personal. Run! Run! Save yourself from the coming judgement!

CHAPTER 1

THE ORIGIN OF GOOD AND EVIL IN THE CONGREGATION OF MAN

In the beginning of the age of man, God created the physical Universe, heaven and earth. In the center of the earth, he placed the garden of Eden. In the center of Eden, God placed the tree of good and evil. Then after all was perfectly done, God Created Adam. We read in Genesis chapter 1 verse 26-31 (KJV) *"And God said, Let us make man in our image, after our likeness: and let them have dominion over the fish of the sea, and over the fowl of the air, and over the cattle, and over all the earth, and over every creeping thing that creepeth upon the earth. So God created man in his own image, in the image of God created he him; male and female created he them. And God blessed them, and God said unto them, be fruitful, and multiply, and replenish the earth, and subdue it: and have dominion over the fish of the sea, and over the fowl of the air, and over every living thing that moveth upon the earth. And God said, Behold, I have given you every herb bearing seed, which is upon the face of all the earth, and every tree, in the which is the fruit of a tree yielding seed; to you it shall be for meat. And to every beast of the earth, and to every fowl of the air, and to everything that creepeth upon the earth, wherein there is life, I have given every green herb for meat: and it was so. And God saw everything that he had made, and, behold, it was very good. And the evening and the morning were the sixth day".* God created Adam as a spirit and ordained that spirit ruler over the earth. Then He shaped a body of clay from the dust of the earth and animated it to house Adam's soul. In Genesis 2:7 (KJV) we read, *And the Lord God formed man of the dust of the ground, and breathed into his nostrils the breath of life; and man became a living soul".* Man is a spirit, born of the Holy Spirit.

As we just read, God placed Adam's body in the garden of Eden to rule. Genesis 2:7 instructs us that God did not call Adam into existence like he did for the angels. Rather, God fashioned a body with his hands and in that body of clay, he breathed his Spirit of life into him to animate his soul. Thus, Adam is a spirit, an offspring of the Spirit of God (Luke 3:38, KJV). He was assigned a soul which serves as the interface between spirit and matter. He was a mediator between worlds. The body of Adam was stationed on earth but his spirit was in the presence of God where the two could engage in eternal fellowship. The body was not meant to identify the man; rather, it was his house on earth.

After Adam came to being, God entered into a contract with him. The terms of the contract were simple. Adam would inhabit the paradise of God. He would find every provision he needed to enjoy existence to live forever. And from his sit on earth, he would rule the physical Universe. In return he would abstain from eating of the fruit of the tree of good and evil, the only thing that could sever his direct connection with the Spirit of God; the Spirit who authored his being, maintained his soul and renewed his spirit to live eternally.

In Genesis 2:15-17 (KJV) we read, *"Then the LORD God took the man and placed him in the Garden of Eden to cultivate and keep it. "And the LORD God commanded him, "You may eat freely from every tree of the garden, but you must not eat from the tree of the knowledge of good and evil; for in the day that you eat of it, you will surely die."* God commanded Adam to refrain from eating of the tree of good and evil because it was designed to keep evil at bay. As long as evil resided in the inanimate tree, Adam would have dominion over it.

However, as soon as God left them alone in the garden, Adam and his wife Eve, ate the fruit of the tree. Satan tricked Eve, who tricked Adam. He made them breach their contract with God. They consumed the fruit of the tree of the knowledge of good and evil. Satan suggested that they would be like God if they ate of the fruit of good and evil, which was a lie.

As mentioned above, Adam was already like God because he was created as the seed of God. He was a perfect being, the offspring of perfection. He was lord of the realm. He was anointed to have dominion over it. Adam had full knowledge of this fact. But the fallen cherub didn't approach Adam directly to play his ruse. Instead, he approached Eve, who was new in the garden. The woman did not contest the lie. Either because she did not know about the contract between God and Adam or she did not care. Her wish to satisfy her curiosity surpassed any respect or fear she had for her husband.

When God ordained Adam to rule, He imbued him with knowledge, the knowledge of God, the knowledge he needed to rule the physical Universe from the earth, to take care of everything in it. God gave Eve to Adam as a servant to help him, to serve him. Adam was her husband, her lord. She was made in Adam's image. This is why upon seeing her for the first time Adam stated, *"This is now bone of my bones And flesh of my flesh; She shall be called Woman, Because she was taken out of Man* (Genesis 2: 23, KJV)". God didn't create a new body from the mud to breathe into to make Eve; rather, he took from Adam's flesh, spirit, and soul to make his woman. Eve did not have the knowledge of the Spirit of life. She had the knowledge of Adam.

God gave Adam dominion over all the creatures in the garden including Eve. But Adam failed to supervised the Eve. Eve then succumbed to the suggestion of the dark prince and ate the forbidden fruit of the tree of knowledge. In doing so, she injected the evil spirit into her DNA, then seduced her husband to do the same. Thus, they introduced evil in God's Paradise. Adam and Eve surrendered the future civilizations of man to the domination of evil as a consequence.

The fruit contained the seed of evil. By eating it, Adam provided it with a fertile breathing ground to multiply. You see, evil is a spirit. It is restless. It is always seeking a place to rest. When Adam open its mind to it, it entered and made its abode in his heart. The seed of evil is the embodiment of every rebellion and disobedience.

It is at the root of all unrighteousness, injustice, pride, lie, all murderous tendencies, all greed, and all lusts. This is the seed that populated the earth in majority. However, it could not stifle the Spirit that animated Adam's body, the Spirit of God. The seed of the Spirit of God is obedience, righteousness, justice. This seed produces love, joy, peace, longsuffering, gentleness, goodness, faith, meekness, and temperance. In a few of the sons of Adam, this Spirit still exists and is in a constant conflict with the spirit of evil. This is the seed that God is seeking.

Adam's act of disobedience tore a veil in the physical realms allowing the fallen angels entrance and they invaded. They establish their government on earth. Before his transgression, Adam had dominion over this world, all of it. But after he sinned, Adam became slave of Satan. He became a subject to the creation instead of its creator. Moreover, Adam lost his communion with God. Before eating the fruit, Adam was a member of the court of heaven. He was in perfect communication with heaven. He had full access to the library of heaven. With the knowledge of God, Adam could fashion the world to his liking but within the will of his creator. But after he sinned, he lost the vision and knowledge of God.

God removed Adam from the garden; or rather, God removed the garden from the earth and Adam was left in a barren desert. The eternal spark of life, the spirit of God departed and left Adam. Thus he was unplugged from the source of life and became a mortal soul, a carnal being just like the animals. His body became self-aware and it developed the intellect. He started to perceive his world through this intellect, a level of intelligence that is no higher than that of the animals. In doing so, he left the seat of ruler-ship of the realm empty. Satan quickly took advantage, assume the position of ruler and took over. He trapped the Adam in the animal state to never get out of it. He enslaved him to rule over him. Evil then jumped from its original domain in the tree to the body of Adam, the father of all man.

The body of Adam became the temple of evil. Once evil entered this temple, it subdued Adam flesh, soul and spirit under its dominion. And once the Spirit of God departed from Adam, he became defenseless. He became exactly like the animals. Understand that

God was the source of renewal for Adam. After Adam lost the knowledge of God, he became subservient to his intellect and the darkness of evil. The realm then lost its caretaker and became subject to chaos, decay, and corruption. Thus, creation has been groaning and calling on God to make things right. It calls on God to reinstate the true ruler of the realm. Apostle Paul mentioned that in his letter to the Romans.

In Romans 8: 19-23 KJV, Paul explained. *"For the earnest expectation of the creature waiteth for the manifestation of the sons of God. For the creature was made subject to vanity, not willingly, but by reason of him who hath subjected the same in hope, Because the creature itself also shall be delivered from the bondage of corruption into the glorious liberty of the children of God. For we know that the whole creation groaneth and travaileth in pain together until now. And not only they, but ourselves also, which have the firstfruits of the Spirit, even we ourselves groan within ourselves, waiting for the adoption, to wit, the redemption of our body."*

Until the advent of his Messiah, Jesus the Christ, God dealt with the dead intellect, the mind, and the spirit of the flesh to save Adam. He did it to reanimate the spirit of the man, to bring his intellect up to a point where he can reason better than the animals. God strategized to establish a relationship with the man through the law. He used the law as a mirror to show man his true nature. Then later in time through his Christ, he would reinstate man's spiritual nature through the renewal of his mind and a cleansing of his soul while he is alive on earth in this life. But until then, man's consciousness would remain steeped in evil. He would be lawless and wicked. This is why the prophet Jeremiah made the following statement. *"The heart is deceitful above all things, and desperately wicked: who can know it? (Jeremiah 17: 9 KJV).* In His Messiah, God plans to wipe away the darkness and wickedness.

God sent his Spirit to harvest the sons of God. Man is a spiritual experiment. Ever since the great fall, God monitored all the civilizations born of Adam. God has strategized to fish out the seed of good that would be born in Adam's lineage. God started the process of gathering the good seed from Adam in the garden. After the death of this remnant, he tried again in Abraham. When the sons of Abraham rejected his rules, he sealed the remnant among them and expel the wicked seed to the nations. In this dispensation, he is trying with his Son Jesus, the Christ. Satan also strategize to maintain his world by multiplying the seed of evil.

Every man born of Adam is a subject of the kingdom of evil. However, in his grace, God prepared a way to purchase the sons of Adam, those who wish to be free from the bondage of the prince of evil. God wants to wash the darkness off of the soul of those who are seeking righteousness and justice to restore them to Adam's original state. This is why the prophet Isaiah said, *"Come now, and let us reason together, saith the LORD: though your sins be as scarlet, they shall be as white as snow; though they be red like crimson, they shall be as wool (Isaiah 1:18 KJV)"*.

GOD DIVIDED THE SONS OF ADAM INTO TWO SEEDS

After Eve ate of the fruit and convinced her husband to do the same, God sentenced each of them. He sentenced the woman to experience pain during child birth. He sentenced Adam to hard labor, and he sentenced the serpent to eat dust throughout its existence. However, while sentencing the serpent, God prophesied against it and said, *"Because you have done this, cursed are you above all livestock and every beast of the field! On your belly will you go, and dust you will eat, all the days of your life. And I will put enmity between you and the woman, and between your seed and her seed. He will crush your head, and you will strike his heel" (Genesis 3:15–16 BSB)*.

This was the first prophecy. In the above passage, God divided the sons of Adam into two seeds. One seed he said would belong to the serpent and the other to the woman. The two seeds are not carnal, they are spiritual. The seed of the woman is the spirit God breathe into Adam to animate his soul. The seed of the serpent is the evil spirit Adam ingested from the fruit which turned his body into the vessel of two spirits. Man therefore became a double minded, a two spirited being. Adam carried the two spirits in his body. When Eve conceived twins, the spirit of evil succeeded in possessing both human bodies. He conquered one but the other resisted. This established the trend and pattern of existence of the human race on earth. The two sons of Eve served as prototype. Eve gave birth to two sons, revealing two different types of people. Cain was the physical incarnation of the seed of the serpent, while his twin brother Abel embodied the seed of the woman. These two seeds would populate the world of man. Their offspring would exist at odds with each other until the seed of the woman can vanquish the evil from the world of man. God planned to filter the two seeds in each generation of man. He planned to gather the seeds of the woman on one side and the seeds of the serpent on the other. As Adam's descendants grew in number, God established the seed of the woman but it always existed in a constant struggle with the seed of Satan who has always occupy the majority and hold the wealth, the power and control of the civilizations of man.

With this remnant seed of Good, God built the nation of the righteous, those who are called the saints. This nation is built on holiness, righteousness, and justice. In every generation of man since Adam, God sends his spirit to identify and preserve these saints. As these saints grow in number, their justice and righteousness shined into the world to show the path man should take to reconcile with God. After a man reconciles with God, He seals him with his Holy Spirit and once sealed with the Holy Spirit, this man would have the power to resist and overcome the assaults of evil. Overcoming the assaults of evil cannot happen without reconciliation between man and God. Why reconciliation? This is because after man became a being of the intellect, all of his thoughts became evil and he became a rebel who stands against all of the laws of righteousness and justice. His entire existence evolved around rebelling against God. To the Corinthians apostle Paul said it this way, "The natural man does not accept the things that come from the Spirit of God. For they are foolishness to him, and he cannot understand them, because they are spiritually discerned (1 Corinthians 2:14 KJV)". To the Romans he said, "Because the carnal mind is enmity against God; for it is not subject to the law of God, nor indeed can be. So then, those who are in the flesh cannot please God" (Romans 8:7-9 NKJV).

This is why King Solomon made the following statement: *"But the path of the just is as the shining light, that shineth more and more unto the perfect day. The way of the wicked is as darkness: they know not at what they stumble (Proverbs 4: 18 – 19 KJV)"*. The first two people born of Eve proved the determination of evil to possess all the sons of Adam forever. Satan wants man to suffer the fate of eternal damnation in the lake of fire. For at a fixed time in eternity, God will destroy the damned and everything evil, Satan included. Satan knows that; he knows that his fate is sealed. His goal is to destroy everything good in man. He strategized to corrupt all men, to turn them into pure evil. He wants to bring them with him into the depth of the second death.

Jesus instructed us that Satan is a murderer and he has been since the beginning. Satan succeeded in causing the spiritual death of billions of angels in the great war. He did the same thing to Adam and Eve in the garden. As God predicted, Adam and Eve lost their spiritual lives after eating the fruit. Consequently, they gave birth to Cain and Abel without the spiritual connection they had with God when they were created. Cain and Abel were the first generation of carnal men. Cain and Abel epitomized the two seeds and set the tone for all civilizations of man.

The bible says that both brothers offered sacrifice to the Lord. Abel offered a living sacrifice to the Lord, the first of his harvest. Abel was a shepherd. He offered a lamb as a living sacrifice to the living Lord. Abel offered a life to the living God to thank Him for the life He had given him. He showed his gratitude to God for life. But Cain who was a farmer, offered the fruits of the earth as a sacrifice to the Lord. Instead of going to his brother to exchange his earthly harvest for a lamb to offer to the living God, Cain decided to offer dead fruits with no life to the God of life. It is not that Cain was unaware of what to do. The two learned from Adam, who learn from the Lord, how and what to sacrifice to the Lord. Abel followed the tradition and execute the sacrifice as he learned it from his father. But Cain disobey the sacrificial tradition set by God. His sacrifice did not please God. His offering was rejected and because of that he became angry and jealous because God accepted the offering of his brother and rejected his. This anger and jealousy served as an open door for Satan to enter his heart. Consequently, Cain became the vessel of Satan. Satan used Cain's body to destroy his righteous brother. Cain offered his body as a tool to evil by allowing jealousy and pride to rule his heart. And in a raging fit of anger and pride, Cain killed his brother.

Notice that the body of Cain was the instrument of evil. God warned him and gave him a choice to choose good and flee from evil. God tried to reason with Cain in Genesis 4: 6-7 in these words, *"Why are you angry," said the LORD to Cain, "and why has your countenance fallen? If you do what is right, will you not be accepted? But if you refuse to do what is right, sin is crouching at your door; it desires you, but you must master it"*. Notice what God said to Cain, *"if you refuse to do what is right, sin is crouching at your door; it desires you"*. Cain knew the right thing to do but he followed in the footstep of his father Adam. God advised Cain to master the sin. What was the sin? It was disobedience which fostered anger and jealousy which later became murder. Cain did not hear the warning, or listen to God's advice. He gave into the evil and murdered his twin brother Abel. Because at the time of the murder, jealousy had already conquered all the good in Cain. Cain's heart was closed to the truth because there was no truth in him. God could not reason with him. The murder of Abel was Satan's first move to destroy the seed of Good from the congregation of man. It was his strategy to have only his seed populate the world of man.

After the death of Abel, God immediately supplied another seed. So, he raised Seth in place of Abel to preserve the good seed. The sons of Seth grew up to embrace righteousness to balance the equation. Throughout the generations of Cain and Seth, the two seeds have coexisted. But few men chose the good path of justice and righteousness, few men chose to resist evil.

Many righteous men came from the seeds of Seth and Cain, but the majority veered to the left. Those who followed justice and righteousness were called the saints. When this first generation of saints died out, Satan got his wish. He multiplied the seed of evil and proliferated the Earth with it. Evil multiplied to take over the world of man, but God continued to preserve the seed of good. Yet, wickedness abounded on earth. This proliferation of evil prompted the great restart of the civilizations of man. God repented from creating man and wanted to exterminate the human race. But because of the few saints who remained on Earth, he decided to restart instead. The first great restart took place during the time of Noah.

On Earth, the situation became so bad that God sent the flood to destroy all flesh. We read this in Genesis 6:13. *"Then God said to Noah, "The end of all living creatures has come before Me, because through them the earth is full of violence. Now behold, I will destroy both them and the earth"*. But Noah found favor in the eyes of the Lord. He was a righteous man, blameless in his generation; Noah walked with God (Genesis 6: 8-9 KJV). God hid Noah and his family during the flood and protected them from harm. Noah came out of the boat when the waters receded to continue God's mandate to Adam. Because of Noah, God spared Earth. Noah and his sons restarted civilization and the two seeds saga continued.

The sons of Noah revert to the ways of the previous corrupt generations destroyed by the flood after some time. They walked out of the boat and disregarded the righteous path of Noah. They broke God's laws and revamp the corruption that existed in the land. But several generations after Noah, God found the hidden seed. As the nations started evolving, God sought after this righteous seed and found one man. The spiritual seed of righteousness did not die. It blossomed in Abram. God cultivated a close relationship with him. God saw that Abram's obedience and love were genuine. He changed Abram's name and signed a contract with him.

God promised to bless the entire human race through Abram's lineage. He renamed him Abraham and chose him as the father of many nations. God would bless the whole world through one of these nations. He knew that evil would once again proliferate the world of man and that he would have to perform another great restart. God would need a holy nation to hide his saints. This nation would be a vessel to hide them from the coming destruction. God found this nation in Jacob; he called it Israel.

CHAPTER 2

THE BEGINNING OF THE CONGREGATION OF ISRAEL

The tale of the two seeds continued with Israel. Two seeds sprung from the ancestry of Abraham as well. Abraham had a son from his wife named Isaac, who then had two sons named Esau and Jacob. Thus, the pattern of the two seeds started all over again. In Isaac, two nations were born. In this instance, God even states his choice of the two by telling Rebekah, the wife of Isaac. *"Two nations are in thy womb, and two manner of people shall be separated from thy bowels; and the one people shall be stronger than the other people; and the elder shall serve the younger (Genesis 25: 23 KJV)".*

In Malachi 1: 2-3 (KJV), the Lord told Israel, *"I loved you," says the LORD.* "But you ask, 'How did you love us?' "Wasn't Esau Jacob's brother?" declares the Lord. *"I loved Jacob, but Esau I hated. I turned his mountains into a wasteland and left his inheritance to the jackals in the desert."*

God started the plan to redeem the woman's seed with Abraham. He promised Abraham that he would make him a great nation and bless the whole world through him. In Abraham, God would fulfill his first prophecy that stated: "The seed of the woman will crush the head of the serpent."

God set out to create an obedient nation, a lawful remnant of the good seed. This new nation would be a witness of his justice, love, mercy, and righteousness to all the nations. God chose Jacob, the seed of Isaac, to create this nation. God called it the nation of the saints, Israel.

The theme of the two seeds continued in the sons of Isaac. Jacob, the son of Isaac would have suffered the same fate as Abel without the intervention of the Lord. The Lord God protected Jacob from the murderous quest of his brother Esau. Esau proved that he was the seed of the serpent with his jealous, murderous, and prideful heart. Jacob, because of the blessing of his father, found favor in the eyes of the Lord. God chose him to be the father of the seed of the woman. God planned to reestablish the relationship he had with Adam with the descendants of Jacob if they excel in righteousness and justice. However, Israel followed in the footsteps of the lawless nations of the world. They pursued relationships with idols instead of the God of gods.

The whole world had gone astray to idol worship. God raised the two sons of Isaac, Esau and Jacob, for the righteousness experiment. As Cain dealt with Abel, Esau dealt with Jacob. As mankind evolved from families to civilization, it pursued a relationship with idols. Jacob cried to God to save his life, and God spared him. God separated the two and allowed them to prosper. Jacob found favor in the eyes of God and prospered in developing a relationship with him. His brother Esau prospered materially. Jacob's fathered one nation while Esau fathered many. The sons of Esau chose the ways of Cain and formed alliances with the idolatrous nations of the world. As a result, they got lost in idolatry.

On the other hand, God chose Jacob to form a nation where he could gather all the saints who seek to worship the one true God. He changed Jacob's name to Israel and made him a nation. Moreover, He gave this nation the laws of righteousness. He established them as the second congregation of saints among mankind. However, the descendants of Jacob learned the evil ways of the other nations. The seed of Good among them embarked on the righteous path upon which Abram thread. But the other seed which held the great majority among the people rejected righteousness and Justice. God was not surprised by this behavior.

He allowed the seeds of Good and evil to coexist in Israel but He preserved the good. Because through this remnant of the good seed, He would fulfill the first prophecy. He would usher the coming of his Messiah, *Jesus of Nazareth*. Jesus, born in Nazareth, is the one who would come and separate the two seeds forever. He is the one who would proclaim the acceptable year of the Lord. This acceptable year of the Lord is the time in which an exit would be granted to every man who wishes to escape the chains of sin and the grip of Satan. It started with the birth of Jesus. We are living at the end of this year.

The Lord God heard the cries of the sons of Adam under the weight of sin, and He sent Jesus to proclaim the way to freedom, giving them a way to flee before He exterminates evil from the face of the earth. This is why Jesus proclaim in John 14:6 that, "*I am the way and the truth and the life. No one comes to the Father except through Me*". Yes, God plans to separate the two seeds for eternity. But first, He wanted to gather those who yearn for righteousness and justice under the banner of grace, in the ark of Jesus, the church. He wanted to provide those who seek eternal life a refuge to help them escape the final judgment and the eternal damnation in the lake of fire. He wanted to preserve them for the final great restart.

God revealed the annihilation of the seed of evil from earth to David, King of Israel. David in turn revealed it in psalm 92 advising the saints to stay clear of evil. In psalm 92:6-7, David stated, "A senseless man does not know, and a fool does not understand, that though the wicked sprout like grass, and all evildoers flourish, they will be forever destroyed.

God chose Israel because, from Abraham's descendants, He did promise to bless the race of man. God chose Jacob, signed a contract with him, and prospered him. He blessed him with twelve children. Those twelve and their families ventured into Egypt to hide from the great famine of their time. They later grew to become mighty in number. Egypt used the wisdom of Joseph, the Son of Israel, to profit from the great famine. Hence, it became the dominant nation on Earth. As the most powerful nation on Earth, the Egyptians used their might to gain dominance over the whole world. But they did not thank the Israelites for being a blessing for the country.

Instead, the pharaohs enslaved them. God promised a savior to them. This savior was Moses. Moses was born, adopted by the Pharaoh's daughter, grew up in Pharaoh's palace until he was forty years old. He discovered that he was one of the slaves. He turned sympathetic and murdered an Egyptian for abusing a Hebrew. He then ran away to the wilderness, where he lived as a shepherd for forty years. When he was eighty years old, God sent him back to face the Pharaoh and claim the people of Israel.

Moses did what God commanded, and he retrieved Israel from the grip of the Egyptians. He then ventured into the wilderness with them to reach the promised land. Moses' primary goal after leaving Egypt was to stop with the Israelite nation in the desert to go worship God on the sacred mountain. There they would wait for God's instructions on how to proceed to the promised land from the desert. God would tell them what style of government to adopt as well as instruct them on how to manage the congregation. But, when Israel arrived in the desert, they turned their worship to other gods. For this action alone, God could have exterminated them. Still, He allowed them to continue because of Moses, the righteous among them

Moses went up on the mountain to receive the laws of God to train Israel in righteousness. While he was absent from among them, they forged gods of gold to worship. We read about this event in Exodus 32: 9-14. *"And the LORD said unto Moses, I have seen this people, and, behold, it is a stiffnecked people: Now therefore let me alone, that my wrath may wax hot against them, and that I may consume them: and I will make of thee a great nation. And Moses besought the LORD his God, and said, LORD, why doth thy wrath wax hot against thy people, which thou hast brought forth out of the land of Egypt with great power, and with a mighty hand? Wherefore should the Egyptians speak, and say, for mischief did he bring them out, to slay them in the mountains, and to consume them from the face of the earth? Turn from thy fierce wrath, and repent of this evil against thy people. Remember Abraham, Isaac, and Israel, thy servants, to whom thou swarest by thine own self, and saidst unto them, I will multiply your seed as the stars of heaven, and all this land that I have spoken of will I give unto your seed, and they shall inherit it forever. And the LORD repented of the evil which he thought to do unto his people."*

The Lord forgive the people and let them live to see another day. He gave them time to repent. But Israel proved God right. It was a rebellious people. It failed to repent. They rebelled against God and Moses. And because of their disbelief, they roamed the desert for forty years. They disobeyed the Lord, frustrated Moses, and lost focus during this time. From the entire generation that left Egypt, only two made it to the promised land. The rest refused to obey the commands of the Lord. They chose to continue the adulterous and idolatrous ways they learned in Egypt. The two who entered the promised land had Abraham's characters. Hence, they were the seed of righteousness, and the Spirit of God dwelt with them.

But the seed of Satan among the people fell through the net of holiness and grieved the Holy Spirit. Physical Israel was a congregation of people with similar features, but it was still one nation of two seeds. God sought the righteous seed from the congregation that walked out of Egypt. He only found two. God called all Israel to the new life. He invited them to the promised land. God called the people out of Egypt because of His contract with their fathers and because He had plans for them.

Israel as a whole received the call. An estimated 2.5 million Hebrews left Egypt for the promised land. They walked out of the gates of Egypt on the same day, same hour. Only two entered the promised land. Only Joshua and Caleb received the promise.

Even Moses, the great leader, did not enter the promised land. Their children could enter it but not the original generation that left Egypt. In Numbers 14:24 (BSB), God spoke of Caleb in the following terms. *"But my servant Caleb, because he had another spirit with him, and hath followed me fully, him will I bring into the land where into he went; and his seed shall possess it."*

Notice here that God said that Caleb had a different spirit; a spirit pleasing to him. He was alluding to the Holy Spirit. The only way Caleb could have completed the desert race is by the power of the Holy Spirit. The Holy Spirit gave him focus, faith, and assurance.

Hence, He could see beyond the natural. The Lord was looking for those who had the same spiritual disposition as Caleb. He searched all Israel for those with the same spirit. He did not find many. The seed of evil occupied the overwhelming majority in Israel.

The Holy Spirit wrestled with that majority until he couldn't anymore. He left them in the desert to die out. Now, it's time to deal with their children. Joshua led the children of Israel to the promise land. Once Israel's children made it to that land and became a nation, they went right back to the ways of their fathers.

The Israelites became adherent to this world and his ruler Satan. They repeated the behaviors their forefathers depicted in the desert. As you continue reading, be mindful that the seed of evil has always occupied the majority among men. This situation will continue until Jesus removed the sons of God from among the seeds of Satan.

Fast-forward centuries after Egypt, Israel had lost its identity. They were as disobedient as the other nations. Israel was to be a holy people, a righteous nation among the peoples of the world. But Israel failed to fulfill that purpose. Only a remnant among them understood that purpose and was able to fulfill it. Israel gained the reputation of a rebellious people. It became known throughout the nations as the people who frustrated the God of life. God then expelled them from the promised land he gave to their fathers.

The relationship between God and Israel was conditional as it has always been with every man in the history of humanity. God always told Israel, "If you obey my law, I will raise you among the nations." There is a reason why God ordered them to obey the law. Obeying the law was the only way to become sanctified to walk in justice and righteousness. That was the path to escape the grip of the evil that was in their blood. In the congregation of the sons of Adam, God has always sought and is actively seeking the people who obey his laws to seal them with his Spirit. The prophet Samuel explained it to King Saul saying, "Hath the Lord as great delight in burnt offerings and sacrifices, as in obeying the voice of the Lord? Behold, to obey is better than sacrifice, and to hearken than the fat of rams" (1 Samuel 15:22 KGV).

God's people value holiness, justice and righteousness. They are referred to as the saints or the just throughout the history of humanity. This is a people that purifies itself to achieve holiness. Their holiness then attracts God's Holy Spirit. The Holy Spirit then drafts these holy ones back into the tree of life from where Adam was removed by his own volition. Until the expulsion of Israel to the nations, the Lord searched, found, and maintained this people. He sought after this people in every generation in the civilizations of man. He is still searching for it in the present generations.

Israel also failed to fulfill its purpose. The God of spirits wanted to govern Israel in the Spirit. They would have direct contact with Him through their spirits. Each individual would have a spiritual connection to God, and thus, God would be their spiritual king. They would have access to the knowledge of God again as Adam did. They would then witness the love and power of God to the world and show them the path to freedom from sin. But the majority of Israel failed to see God's intentions.

Thus, Israel lost the promised land twice. The entire generation that left Egypt died in the desert. They never made it to that land. They had Egypt in their blood. Its corrupt customs were their culture. They did not choose the way of the Lord. The second lost occurred after God had secured the land to give it to them. After they breached the contract of righteousness that God had with them several times, God split the nation into two kingdoms, namely Israel and Judah. The kingdom of Israel was exiled to the nations. Judah survived long enough to see the birth of the Messiah, but was destroyed by the Romans. God promised to return them to the land but during perilous time.

The majority in Israel was unjust, proficient in rebelling against all righteousness. They failed to abide by the clear condition stated by Moses. In Deuteronomy 30:15 – 20, Moses told them *"See, I have set before thee this day life and good, and death and evil; In that I command thee this day to love the LORD thy God, to walk in his ways, and to keep his commandments and his statutes and his judgments, that thou mayest live and multiply: and the LORD thy God shall bless thee in the land whither thou goest to possess it. But if thine heart turn away, so that thou wilt not hear, but shalt be drawn away, and worship other gods, and serve them; I denounce unto you this day, that ye shall surely perish, and that ye shall not prolong your days upon the land, whither thou passest over Jordan to go to possess it. I call heaven and earth to record this day against you, that I have set before you, life and death, blessing and cursing: therefore, choose life, that both thou and thy seed may live: That thou mayest love the LORD thy God, and that thou mayest obey his voice, and that thou mayest cleave unto him: for he is thy life, and the length of thy days: that thou mayest dwell in the land which the LORD sware unto thy fathers, to Abraham, to Isaac, and to Jacob, to give them."* The people of Israel was to be just, righteous, and holy. These characteristics transcend time and space, for they are eternal. This is why wise Solomon instructed his son saying: "There is life in the path of righteousness, but another path leads to death" (Proverbs 12:28 BSB). In Deuteronomy 7:6 (BSB), Moses spoke onto the people in these terms, saying, *"You are a people holy to the LORD your God. The LORD your God has chosen you to be a people for His prized possession, above all peoples on the face of the earth."*

God ordered Israel to be a holy nation. He intended for them to separate themselves from the philosophies, pagan cultures and unjust pattern of thinking of the nations. God did not want them to adopt the lawlessness of the other nations. They would embrace the philosophy of heaven. In Exodus 19:5, Moses' writing reiterates God's will. Moses give the people the specific condition to remain within the grace of God in the following message. *"If you will indeed obey My voice and keep my covenant, you will be My treasured possession out of all the nations for the whole earth is mine."* (notice that God gave them a condition to be his people. The condition was to obey his voice and maintain his contract.)

This conditional language echoes throughout the Bible. Physical Israel was the foreshadow of the global nation. It was a prototype of the global nation of the saints. Israel represented a microcosm of the whole human race. After they failed to embrace the grace of God, they lost their identity as the people of God. As a result, the Lord split them into two kingdoms, Judah and Israel. The kingdom of Israel got lost in idolatry, so God expelled it to the nations.

The kingdom of Judah remained in the land. There too, the two seeds coexisted and endured in the land. After they executed the King of the Righteous, God allowed the Romans to end their civilization. The Romans killed the majority and expelled the rest of the people throughout the nations. The Romans then renamed the land Palestine. Israel disobeyed and broke the covenants of the Lord for several centuries. The Lord exiled them all over the world to go where they could mix with their own kind—the seed of Satan. The Holy Spirit let them go; to go do as they pleased.

In his sermon, John the Baptist called them by their breed. In Mathew 3: 7-9, we read, *"But when he saw many of the Pharisees and Sadducees come to his baptism, he said unto them, O generation of vipers, who hath warned you to flee from the wrath to come? Bring forth therefore fruits meet for repentance: And think not to say within yourselves, we have Abraham to our father: for I say unto you, that God is able of these stones to raise up children unto Abraham. And now also the axe is laid unto the root of the trees: therefore, every tree which bringeth not forth good fruit is hewn down, and cast into the fire."* Jesus identified them as the seed of Satan and called them by their nature, brood of vipers. In Mathew 23: 32-33, Jesus stated, *"Fill up, then, the measure of the sin of your fathers. You snakes! You brood of vipers! How will you escape the sentence of hell?"*

He also confronted them again in John 8: 31-47:

> *"Then said Jesus to those Jews which believed on him, if ye continue in my word, then are ye my disciples indeed; And ye shall know the truth, and the truth shall make you free. They answered him, we be Abraham's seed, and were never in bondage to any man: how sayest thou, Ye shall be made free? Jesus answered them, Verily, verily, I say unto you, whosoever committeth sin is the servant of sin. And the servant abideth not in the house for ever: but the Son abideth ever. If the Son therefore shall make you free, ye shall be free indeed. I know that ye are Abraham's seed; but ye seek to kill me, because my*

word hath no place in you. I speak that which I have seen with my father: and ye do that which ye have seen with your father. And because I tell you the truth, ye believe me not. Which of you convinceth me of sin? And if I say the truth, why do ye not believe me? He that is of God heareth God's words: ye therefore hear them not, because ye are not of God.

They answered and said unto him, Abraham is our father. Jesus saith unto them, If ye were Abraham's children, ye would do the works of Abraham. But now ye seek to kill me, a man that hath told you the truth, which I have heard of God: this did not Abraham. Ye do the deeds of your father. Then said they to him, we be not born of fornication; we have one Father, even God.

Jesus said unto them, If God were your Father, ye would love me: for I proceeded forth and came from God; neither came I of myself, but he sent me. Why do ye not understand my speech? even because ye cannot hear my word. Ye are of your father the devil, and the lusts of your father ye will do. He was a murderer from the beginning, and abode not in the truth, because there is no truth in him. When he speaketh a lie, he speaketh of his own: for he is a liar, and the father of it."

Notice that Jesus identified and connected the Jews to Satan. He told them they were the sons of Satan to reject the notion that they were Abraham's children. In them, they did not have the spirit that Abraham had, the Spirit of truth, righteousness, and justice. Jesus was astonished by their inability to understand the truth. He inquired *"Why do ye not understand my speech"*. Then he answered saying, it is because your father is the devil. They were not of God. Those who are of God, hear the voice of God when He calls. In John 10:27-28 (NKJV), Jesus stated, *"My sheep hear My voice, and I know them, and they follow Me. And I give them eternal life, and they shall never perish; neither shall anyone snatch them out of My hand".* Jesus was looking for the seed of righteousness among them, those who love justice and truth. He could only find a remnant in Israel.

God always identifies his sons through holiness and seals them with his spirit. The Holy Spirit is the one who chooses. For instance, The Holy Spirit is the one who chose who could enter the promise land after Israel left Egypt. An estimated 2.5 million souls left Egypt to go to the promised land. Alarmingly, only Joshua and Caleb, the two who were sanctified and holy, entered the promise land out of that generation. The Lord allowed their Children to enter the land. After the children of the Exodus entered the Land, the Holy Spirit was the one who chose their leaders. He chose some to be judges, some to be prophets, some to be wise men, some to be super men, and others to be kings.

The Holy Spirit is the one who seals up the righteous, the people of God. Once an individual is sealed, he/she becomes the son or daughter of God. While the Lord sealed the kings, prophets, and other lay people in Israel, the majority of Israel proved to be of the brood of vipers. After the kings of Israel lost the anointing of the Holy Spirit, they turned their allegiance to idols. They resolved to idol worship. The population ended up making sacrifices to idols. Some even sacrificed their children to Moloch. In fact, they killed all the messengers of God. Israel received the law of God to sanctify them and show them the path of righteousness but they ignored it.

Obeying the law would sanctify them. Their spirit would be in sync with the Spirit of the king of righteousness. Instead, they ran away from the just and righteous path. They became apostates. On their apostate spree, they rejected God's rule for that of a man. Then under the governance of men, they became corrupt over time. Their corruption then repulsed the Holy Spirit.

He was the only one who could have helped them maintain their identity as the people of God. They chose the spirit of the world. Hence, they reversed to a state worse than that of the very nations God destroyed to give them the land. Jesus came and lamented their great loss. He rebuked Jerusalem with these words. *"O Jerusalem,*

Jerusalem, the one who kills the prophets and stones those who are sent to her! How often I wanted to gather your children together, as a hen gathers her chicks under her wings, but you were not willing! See! Your house is left to you desolate; for I say to you, you shall see Me no more till you say, 'Blessed is He who comes in the name of the Lord!" (Matthew 23:37–39 KJV).

Prophet Isaiah foresaw the judgment of Jerusalem and prophesied of it centuries before Jesus walked the earth. Israel failed to recognize the coming of its redeemer. It missed the day of its visitation. They did not have the Spirit of God to help them understand. They did not know that this Jesus, who was among them, was the Holy One of Israel, the very prophet that Moses predicted would come in these words, *"The Lord thy God will raise up unto thee a Prophet from the midst of thee, of thy brethren, like unto me; unto him ye shall hearken* (Deuteronomy 18:15-19 KJV)." And even while professing they believed in Moses, they could not remember his words. They failed to recognize their prophet, their king and their God.

Israel killed the king of the saints. They went from the chosen people to a rejected one. Prophet Isaiah stated that *"Unless the LORD of Hosts had left us a few survivors, we would have become like Sodom, we would have resembled Gomorrah" (Isaiah 1:9 KJV).* God signed a new contract with His Son, Jesus, through which the whole world can benefit. God filtered the righteous seeds among that last generation who lived in the kingdom of Judah and transferred them to Jesus' church before he expelled the rest of Judah to the nations. He then assembled them in one congregation to join with the righteous among the nations. Jesus stated in his prayer, *"I have revealed Your name to those You have given Me out of the world. They were Yours; You gave them to Me, and they have kept Your word" (John 17:6 BSB).* Pay attention to the word gifts in the above verse. God gave his son the charge of all the saints, those who keep God's word.

CHAPTER 3

THE RENAMING OF THE CONGREGATION OF THE SAINTS, THE NEW ISRAEL, THE CHURCH

In the first century of our era, Jesus called a group of disciples in a small corner of the world. He gathered them to introduce the concept of the Church. This church would be a new ark, like that of Noah, except it would be spiritual. It was designed to become the new hiding place for the congregation of the saints. Jesus established it as a fellowship. It would be the fellowship of the Christ. Its halls would be made of the word of God and it would be covered under the banner of the Holy Spirit. Under this banner, Jesus gathered a band of brothers, washed them with his blood, united them in his love, give them the spirit birth by sealing them with his spirit. Jesus ordained that hell and the grave should not prevail against his Church. The version of the Church that Jesus envisioned would weather the storm of time. It would be powerful. His Church would chase away the powers of evil and bring heaven's atmosphere to earth. Jesus achieves that in the upper room during Pentecost and the church lasted under the supervision of the Holy Spirit.

But after the death of the apostles, the church lost its potency and for most the vision of the apostles faded away. In its place rose an individualistic and religious institution and the materialistic spirit of mammon took over. And as the world evolved, this materialistic version of the Church seems to have evolved and grew strong. It splits the congregation into two Churches, the spiritual and the material. In Jesus Christ, the Messiah, God made the provision to retrieve the remnant of the righteous seed. He came to save those who got lost among the nations and those in bondage under the grip of Satan. Jesus came to turn the tide of the war.

Jesus was born of Mary but did not have a human father. Thus, he was born to fulfill God's first prophecy. He is the seed of the woman. Jesus instructed those he ordered to follow him that there are two paths—the broad and the narrow. He further told them that he would build his Church on the narrow path. He instructed them that it would be the gateway for the fountain of living water to flow saying: *"He that believeth on me, as the scripture hath said, out of his belly shall flow rivers of living water* (John 7:38, KJV). Those who embark on the journey to find that fountain would have to walk the narrow path. *"Enter ye in at the strait gate: for wide is the gate, and broad is the way, that leadeth to destruction, and many there be which go in there at: Because strait is the gate, and narrow is the way, which leadeth unto life, and few there be that find it* (Matthew 7:13-14 BSB)"*. The broad way is for the many, and the narrow is for the few! From Adam to John the Baptist, the congregation of saints walked the same narrow way. They entered the fellowship's halls through the narrow gate. The instructions of Jesus mapped the way, the way of the Holy Spirit of life. He confirmed that in Matthew 7:13-14. Jesus came to take over the management of the congregation of the saints as God's Messiah.

Now, let's take a closer look at these two ways. Allow me to translate the broad way into the way of disobedience and the narrow into the way of the righteous. The focus of this writing is to tell the tale of the progress of these two ways in the church. The broad way represents the way of evil and those who walk on that way are the seed of the serpent. The narrow way represents the way of justice and righteousness and those who walk on it are the seed of the woman.

The pattern of these two seeds that started in the garden after evil invaded the world of man is still with us. Jesus instructed us that we will recognize them by their fruits. In the following chapters we will attempt to identify the two seeds in the church by examining the fruits of its congregations.

The two seeds have been riding on the wings of time from generation to generation. They are alive and well, living among us in the Church. The seed of evil is working tirelessly to keep the Christians living in sin. As they become more influential in the congregations, they are systematically replacing the true gospel of repentance with one that attracts a crowd of self-seekers. Jesus' Church is the new Israel. It is a reinvention of the congregation of the saints that God, the Father, established in Canaan. And as Israel was a double-minded people, the Church is also a double-minded people. There are two manners of people in the church congregations. One people is a community of brothers who love one another and fellowship with one another. The other people is an institution of intellectuals, self-seekers who are seeking prestige pride and the love of this world. And in this book, we will refer to them as the two churches.

After the demise of Israel, the Lord set out to revamp the nation of the saints. He's again gathering the righteous seeds expelled throughout the whole world. God assembled the spiritual seed that trickled down from Adam to John the Baptist in their time. As he sent Moses to free Israel out of Egyptian bondage, He sent Jesus to free the captives of the world in our time.

God has a way of giving the sons of Adam a glance at the future using things of the past. He dealt with the descendants of Abraham in their time. Israel was a rehearsal – a foreshadow of the real event. God has not rejected them. He has a plan for them. However, they too will be redeemed by surrendering to the kingship of Jesus who is their Christ. The real event will encompass all the saints in the world. Therefore, the Church of Jesus Christ is the real event. Jesus called this new congregation Church. Jesus' Church evolved to be a great nation and a global refuge for the holy seed. But is the whole church population part of the holy seed? Far from it! Like Israel, the physical population of the Church consists of two seeds—the seed of the woman and the seed of the serpent. The Church and Israel have few differences but many similarities. These two nations resemble each other in behavior, obedience, and habits. Their relations with the world are the same. Like Israel, the majority of the current Church is on the verge of losing the promised land.

THE BEGINNING OF THE CHURCH OF JESUS THE CHRIST

God seeks those among the nations who will be obedient and faithful. He started with Israel because of His promise to Abraham. God gave the real Messiah to Israel in the form of Jesus, the one who would free the descendants of Abraham from sin, the real bondage. Yet, Israel rejected him because worldly ambitions blinded them. As a result, they couldn't see the plan of God.

Jesus came in obedience to the Father and flawlessly executed the plan of salvation. Again, he aimed to revive the congregation of Israel from its slumber. When Israel rejected his call, he gave birth to this new congregation he called the Church. The Church is a new nation built on the rock of the gospel of peace preached by the twelve disciples. Jesus trained them before his death and resurrection. He then left Earth to go sit at the right hand of the Father. His disciples became apostles, and their primary task was to find the lost tribes of the old Israel. Like Noah, they were to gather the lost tribes of Israel into the church, the spiritual ark. They were to preach the gospel of repentance for their salvation.

After he conquered death and the grave and rose victorious, Jesus went back to his Father. He left the Holy Spirit in charge of managing his affairs and the twelve apostles as hired hands. When Israel rejected Jesus as the Messiah, as it was prophesied, he turned his attention to the whole world. He offered his salvation to every man who accepted him and followed his teachings.

Consequently, he entered a covenant with those who believed and signed it with his blood. The Church multiplied through the preaching of the apostles. Peter explained to the Church that Jesus became a stone of offense to those who rejected him. But to those who believe, he is a precious stone. He exclaimed, *"But to those who do not believe, 'The stone the builders rejected has become the cornerstone,' and, 'A stone of stumbling and a rock of offense.'*

They stumble because they disobey the word—and to this they were appointed. But you (the Church) you are a chosen people, a royal priesthood, a holy nation, a people for God's own possession, to proclaim the virtues of Him who called you out of darkness into His marvelous light" (1 Peter 2:7-9 BSB).

The apostle Peter identified the Church as a holy nation, a nation that would proclaim the holiness of God to the world. A holy church is what Jesus has in mind. Jesus' church had the same purpose as Israel. He wants the church to be a holy nation. This holy nation would carry the mission of the saints from the previous generation to the new. Their mission is to preach the gospel of repentance to the world over. Pay attention! The gospel of Christ is of repentance not of tolerance. Repentance leads to peace and help one understand the love of God. When Jesus send the disciples, he instructed them to urge the people to repent for the kingdom of God was near them. He did not instruct them to go invite the crowd to join a gathering.

THE CHURCH UNDER CAPTIVITY

The early Church suffered persecutions under the Romans and the Jews of the synagogue of Satan in Israel, the Gnostics, and other seeds of Satan who infiltrated the Church. And like Israel ventured into Egypt, the Church formed an unholy alliance with Constantine, the Roman emperor at the time. After the Romans and the Jews massacred the apostles, the early Christians had no guidance. They started to seek help from the world. Hence, the Roman Empire seized this opportunity to merge its kingdom with the Church. They steal the momentum of the Church's growth movement. They infiltrate the

Church of Jesus Christ. They killed the apostles and the elders. They combined the church with the dying Roman Empire, and merged their pagan holiday and celebrations on of the idols in the church. They hid their customs and pagan religions and carry them over to the new world, to our era. Roman emperor Constantine, inspired by Satan, faked a conversion and proclaimed himself a Christian.

Immediately after, he named himself the representative of God on Earth (Vicarius-Filii-Dei) and supreme pontiff. He then took control of the Church and linked it to the Roman Empire. Consequently, he established the papacy.

The papacy confiscated all the writings of the apostles and the teachings of the Old Testament. Constantine locked some under the Vatican and burned the rest. The papacy made it a deadly offense to own documents of an apostle's writing. They burned to death everyone they found with such records. As a result, they succeeded in hiding the truth, allowing for their influential sway over the world. The papacy replaced the doctrines of the apostles with fake doctrines. Hence, they plunged the whole world into idolatry for twelve hundred years.

So, under the bondage of the papacy, the true Church became captive. Yet, the Lord continued to filter his seeds from the crowd. The early Church did the same thing that Jacob and his children did. They sought refuge under the protection of the Romans. As a result, they willingly entered under the bondage of the papacy of Constantine. And as the Egyptians used the sons of Israel to grow their kingdom, the papacy system used the Christians. They used the name of God to grow and establish dominion over the kings of Earth. After that, the first category of the harvest of the apostles died. They left the Church of Christ in bondage under the Roman Empire's papacy, disguised as a church. God raised an unlikely liberator in the person of Martin Luther to free the true church from Roman bondage. The Holy Spirit used Luther to remove the veil of idolatrous teaching. As a result, some could see clear, once again. They flee from under the grip of Catholicism and its devilish doctrines.

THE CHURCH LEFT ROMAN CAPTIVITY

Martin Luther split from the Catholic Church in 1517. This year marks the beginning of the end of the twelve hundred years of Babylon's conquering spree over the people. Many people believed that those who saw the light would be strengthened to continue on the way of the apostles. But that did not happen!

Luther gained access to copies of the apostles' manuscripts and learned the truth. He presented his protest against the teachings of Catholicism in the form of the 95 Theses. He took a stand against the false doctrines of the Babylonian Church. However, Luther was still operating on the intellectual training of the catholic philosophy. He did not embrace the spiritual. He did not give way to the Holy Spirit!

When the Holy Spirit inspired Luther to confront Catholicism, the papacy had already succeeded in erasing the customs of the apostles. The books Luther read did not contain all the teachings of the apostles or Jesus Christ. The customs passed down mouth to mouth were no longer remembered. Only the Holy Spirit could revamp these teachings. But Luther was a theologian, a man of the letter. He was only privy to some of the letters written by the apostles.

Luther was successful in separating from Catholicism. But he maintained some of the customs of his former master. He only focused on the letters left by Paul and the other apostles. It doesn't seem that he opened the door to the Holy Spirit for more insight into the matter. Luther never even heard of a Holy Spirit, let alone understood his role in the matter. Thus, he never instructed his congregation to seek the Holy Spirit for the lost teachings. As more documents leaked, others discovered the truth about Catholicism. As a result, they made a choice to stop worshiping idols.

Luther gave birth to a new church, the Protestant Church. He established an institution. The church Jesus started was a community of brothers who were ordered to love one another to the point of dying for one another. But the many who followed Luther in his protest were individuals who were seeking self-interest. But because of the few who sincerely loved God among them, God allowed the movement to prosper. Among the great many who fled to Luther's camp, Satan sent his own. These seeds of Satan strongly opposed Luther. Satan spewed a flood of discord, using them to destabilize the movement quickly. Luther could not distinguish between the seeds of Satan and the seeds of righteousness among them. The many who sought to make names for themselves in Luther's reforms formed denominations of their own. But they were all divided!

The Protestants had no unity among themselves. Most of them had Babylon in their blood, customs, and views of God. They struggled to unify as a congregation. Thus, other reformers stood in fierce opposition to Luther. We don't know whether they were agents of the Catholic Church, such as the Jesuit spies. Whether the Catholic Church sent them to infiltrate the movement, we cannot tell.

One thing we know is that those who infiltrated Luther's organization succeeded. They infiltrated the organization to destabilize and stop Luther's advancement. Jesus ordered his disciples to love one another. This is how the world would know they are his followers. This love of one another would be the sign that they belonged to him. But love and unity did not exist among those who joined Luther's camp. Jesus ordered and I quote, *"A new commandment I give you say Jesus: Love one another. As I have loved you, so also you must love one another. By this all men will know that you are my disciples, if you love one another" (John 13:34–35 BSB).*

However, their doctrines and theologies did not focus on obeying this command. They did not teach it to their disciples. Luther aimed to end the spreading of Catholicism's false doctrines, but the lack of unity among his followers kept the Holy Spirit at bay, creating opportunities for Satan. The papacy formed alliances with most of these denominations formed in the mayhem. They promised to stop prosecuting the protestants to coexist. As a result, the papacy quickly formed schools to create leaders who, in turn, taught the congregations to compromise. This was a ploy of Satan to have the time to inject his false doctrines into their midst.

Luther revived the Church, but he did not finish the job. During Luther's time of reform, the Holy Spirit inspired some to prepare for the third and final age. It is the time in which we are currently living.

Among these protestants, God elected those who were His. Likewise, Satan established his imposters in these denominations as well.

Babylon lost its power over the kings of Earth a couple of hundred years after Luther's reform. But Catholicism transferred its influential customs, doctrines, and dogmas to its daughter churches, these churches sprung from the denominations created by Luther's reform. We are living at the time of the great apostasy. The denominations that are the daughters of Catholicism are still preaching its dogma. The elect, the seed of righteousness, and the people of God are among these daughter churches. The Holy Spirit is calling them out. He wants to prepare them in holiness for the latter-day rain of power. He is calling them to distance themselves from Satan's crowd, for their judgment is coming.

This is the perfect time for the elect to get out of Babylon. The reform carried us to this time – a time when knowledge is abounding exponentially. Ours is the era for the great divide, the time when those who serve God will be recognized.

In our time, a great throng of those who identify themselves as Christians is exiting the Church. This exodus is occurring because these people have never really surrendered to the authority of Jesus. They are their own bosses. They are independent people who do not believe in brotherhood and unity. They gather with the body of Christ but are not part of it. Their love is waxed cold as Jesus instructed us they it would in Mathew 24: 12, *The verse reads, "And because iniquity shall abound, the love of many shall wax cold."* They are currently fulfilling this prophecy.

We will refer to those whose love has waxed cold in this book as the apostates. Whether they are conscious of it or not, they are of the enemy. They are sent to infiltrate the Church. They have infiltrated the Church with the sole purpose of diminishing the gospel of Jesus. They deny the power of God and create a counterfeit Christianity. These apostates preach the ideologies of those who war against holiness, justice, and righteousness. Catholicism is regaining its power over the peoples of the world. It is regaining its strength.

It is about to call back all its daughter churches to take their places in this new age. It is calling them to contribute to the formation of Satan's new world. God's remnant lost the spike of Pentecost. We need it back. Learning the Bible is necessary, but it is not the ultimate goal. Instead, the goal is to be filled with the Holy Spirit. To reestablish the Church of the Pentecost, we need the Holy Spirit. The Holy Spirit is the one charged with the mission to find and gather the sons of God and seal them for the new life.

THE TWO CHURCHES IN THE CHRISTIAN CONGREGATION

We're living in a time when the Christian belief is no longer Jesus Christ crucified. Many have abandon the cross for fame, power and prosperity. As it was in the time of Israel, there are several beliefs and worldly ideologies dividing the church. There are two types of churches on earth currently. On one hand, there is the sanctified, spirit-filled Church which focuses on building the spiritual man. On the other hand, there is the carnal church which focuses on building the self. The spiritual church seeks and attracts the Holy Spirit of God the Father, the power the Lord Jesus Christ promised to give to his disciples before they begin the proclamation of the gospel of repentance. On the other hand, the carnal church seeks the love of the world, prosperity, prestige, fame and great reputation among men. They are the most religious and are controlled by the spirit of Satan, Beelzebub, and the Antichrist.

The carnal ideologies of the world are used by church leaders to maintain control of the people. The doctors of theology tell the people that seeking to be holy is a futile exercise. The doctors of the law, the doctors of theology control the narratives preached on the pulpits of churches. They are members of committees who comfortably sit on the leadership of congregations dictating how the church should conform to the self instead of the spirit. Their mission is to blind and condition the masses to accept the rites of their religion. They go around the world to make proselytes. They instruct these proselytes in their gospels to profit off of them. The carnal church never left Catholicism. Its mind is set on acquiring material gains. It is philosophical and self-reliant. Moreover, it rejects the words of Jesus for those of men. It also contradicts the guidance of the Holy Spirit. It diminishes him and refers to him as a thing – a manifestation.

Some use the Holy Spirit as a servant who is only there for healing. They are mocking the command of God to be holy. They believe that this command to be holy is not relevant to our time. They stopped focusing on holiness. In addition, they stopped seeking heaven and left the narrow path of the cross. They rejected the gospel of the cross to turn back into the camp of the enemy. However, if they don't repent and return to their first love, they will suffer more significant losses than the Israelites. Those who do not meet God's standards will suffer the second death. Those who will escape will be those who become Spirit, those who are born of the Spirit.

God dealt with the flesh of man in the Old Testament. In this new contract, God is seeking spirits. In John 4:24 (BSB), Jesus explained it to the woman in this wise, *"God is Spirit, and His worshipers must worship Him in spirit and in truth."* God wants to deal with the spirit of man, the new man born of the Holy Spirit.

What you will see as you continue reading is a replay of the scenarios that caused the downfall of the Israelites in the church congregations. The Church is repeating these mistakes to prove Solomon's statement. *"All things are wearisome; more than one can describe. The eye is not satisfied with seeing, nor is the ear content with hearing. What has been is what will be, and what has been done will be done again. There is nothing new under the sun" (Ecclesiastes 1:8–9 BSB).*

Until the new Earth and the new heaven come, nature will recycle all materials and ideas. The Lord God called all the world under the new contract, but He only elected a few. Like He was for Israel, the Holy Spirit is the Spirit who identified them as the Church of God.

The Holy Spirit will only work with the true Church. He will refine it in the true doctrine of holiness, righteousness, and justice. Moreover, he will filter the remnant of those who belong to God among the denominations of the Protestants, while the rest will go back to their mother, Babylon.

We will refer to these filtered remnants in this book as the true Church. It is this fellowship that the Holy Spirit of God manages. It stands for righteousness and justice. It is walking in the desert of holiness toward the city God promised to all the righteous. Hence, it is a spiritual church. We will learn more about the two seeds present in the congregation of the Church in the next chapter.

CHAPTER 4

THE ELECTS OF GOD AND SATAN'S CUNNING IMPOSTERS IN THE CONGREGATIONS OF THE CHURCH

Israel failed in its mission and God expelled it to the nations. God reassigned the mission to the church, the church of Jesus Christ. The church are the elects, sealed by the Father's spirit, the Holy Spirit. Jesus started it with the 12 disciples. The purpose of the Church is to call the world to repentance, train those who repent in the path of holiness to receive the Holy Spirit and send them to repeat this process where ever they go to multiply the just and righteous on earth. Jesus came to establish a nation of just and righteous men for God. His mission was to find the lost sheep, redirect them away from the corruption present in this world.

For those who accept Jesus's sacrifice on the cross, who recognize their wrongdoing, confess their sins, and stop sinning, his Father empowered him to wash their iniquities by his blood and draft them in the Spirit. Jesus paid for the sins of humanity on the cross and elected them to be sealed by the Father's Spirit. However, wherever these elects exist on earth, Satan plants his seeds. There are two seeds growing in the Church, dividing it into two entities. The saga of the Church started with the revelation of its foundation, the king of righteousness, and Satan's conning ministers, the unjust and unrighteous seeds.

While having supper with his disciples, Jesus asks them the following question: *"'Who do you say I am?' Simon answered, 'Though art the Christ, the son of the living God.' And Jesus answered and said unto him, 'Blessed art thou, Simon Bar Jona: for flesh and blood hath not revealed it unto thee, but my Father which is in heaven. And I say also unto thee, that thou art Peter, and upon this rock I will build my Church; and the gates of hell shall not prevail against it'"* (Matthew 16:15–18 BSB).

Upon this rock of the revelation that Peter received from heaven, Jesus Christ built his Church. It was built to last for eternity, and no power in hell or on earth should or would prevail against it. However, it would not be for lack of trying on the part of the armies of hell. After Jesus, the King of the saints, founded the Church, Satan quickly infiltrated it. Satan sent millions of his servants to the Church, whose mission is to sow defective seeds and create a counterfeit church. They are now the majority. When Christians failed to discern the wise of the devil as Jesus and his disciples could, they became corrupted. For instance, Jesus chose the twelve disciples. And yet, among them, Satan placed the son of perdition, Judas Iscariot, to spy on him and undermine the entire operation.

Jesus knew who he was and why he was among them because the Holy Spirit pointed him out. Although it was part of the plan, Jesus was made aware of it, for the Father plans nothing in secret from his righteous servants. In John 6:70 (KJV), Jesus acknowledged that fact, saying, *"Did I not choose you, the twelve, and one of you is a devil?"*

When Satan realized that his inside man was revealed, he went so far as to use Peter to veer Jesus away from the path of the cross. Jesus discerned his tactic and rebuked him. Some believe that this was the only time Satan used this tactic to destabilize the men of God and stop them in their tracts. That is wrong! Satan is still using this tactic on a larger scale today. It is especially successful when the agents of Satan find so-called men or women of God who love carnal pleasures, money, power, and fame. Satan will quickly pay their price. And once a person's name lands on Satan's payroll, they cannot preach about Jesus Christ and his cross.

There are many devils among the leaders of the Church, and their number is growing exponentially. We read warnings from Jesus and the apostles throughout the New Testament to stay vigilant to recognize such figures. At the very foundation of the Church, Jesus warned his disciples about the coming of false prophets in these terms, saying: *"Beware of false prophets, which come to you in sheep's clothing, but inwardly they are ravening wolves. Ye shall know them by their fruits. Do men gather grapes of thorns, or figs of thistles? Even so every good tree bringeth forth good fruit; but a corrupt tree bringeth forth evil fruit. A good tree cannot bring forth evil fruit, neither can a corrupt tree bring forth good fruit. Every tree that bringeth not forth good fruit is hewn down, and cast into the fire. Wherefore by their fruits ye shall know them (Mathew 7: 15-20 KJV).*

In his farewell to the Ephesians, elder Paul said, *"I know that after my departure, savage wolves will come in among you and will not spare the flock. Even from your own number, men will rise up and distort the truth to draw away disciples after them. Therefore, be alert and remember that for three years I never stopped warning each of you night and day with tears" (Acts 20:30 BSB).*

During the first age of the Church, the apostle Jude warned the first harvest with these words: *"Beloved, when I gave all diligence to write unto you of the common salvation, it was needful for me to write unto you, and exhort you that ye should earnestly contend for the faith which was once delivered unto the saints. For there are certain men crept in unawares, who were before of old ordained to this condemnation, ungodly men, turning the grace of our God into lasciviousness, and denying the only Lord God, and our Lord Jesus Christ" (Jude 1:4 BSB).*

The apostle Jude wrote these words to the Christians of his time, but they are also relevant for our generation. The men he referred to have the same personality traits as Judas. Hence, they are proud, luxurious, prestigious, and selfish. They love high places, places of preeminence; they also love fame, power, and money. Hell has stationed hundreds of thousands of these Judas in strategic places in our generation. They are present in the societies of men for regrouping and realigning hell's efforts for the final attack on this Church. Hell's goal is to capture as many Christian souls as possible.

The Church needs to know that they are here. They are disguised as lambs but have the nature of voracious wolves. They are currently leading the apostate Church. Satan can feel the vibration of the coming chariots, for the Master is coming in person to harvest the souls of His own. The Redeemer is coming with the chariots of fire to pick up the saints. Thus, today's Church is under a full-blown assault, designed to destroy it from within. It faces this subversive assault which aim is to diminish the importance of the gospel of repentance and even replace the Father, Jesus the Christ, and the Holy Spirit in the Church by replacing the real gospel with a counterfeit one.

In their gospel, most of the saying of Jesus are considered too harsh. It is a counterfeit gospel aiming at corrupting many. This kind of gospel keeps many from being sealed by the Holy Spirit. Thus, it multiplies the seed of Satan in the congregation of the Church. These gospels have resulted in giving birth to a church full with materialists who despise righteousness and justice. The apostle Paul wanted us to stay vigilant to discern when the Church would compromise the true gospel to go and prostitute itself with other gods, adopting doctrines from unclean spirits.

Well, we are living that dreaded time. Satan's agents used to operate in the shadows, but now they are operating in daylight because they have systematically removed the truth in most denominations with their lies. There is no one left who dares to stand for the truth. In fact, it is becoming more and more challenging to distinguish the truth from the lie. If you confess the name of Jesus Christ to obtain salvation from the retribution to come, hold fast to the original gospel of Jesus that was given to you. And this is the gospel as the apostles delivered it:

Jesus is the Christ, the son of God the Father Almighty, who created heaven and earth. He was born on earth with the sole purpose of dying to save humanity from hell and the second death. Jesus was conceived by the power of the Holy Spirit and born of the Virgin Mary. He suffered under Pontius Pilate, was crucified, died, and was buried. He descended to the dead. Having accomplished his mission, on the third day, he rose again. He ascended to heaven and is seated at the right hand of the Father. He will come again to judge the living and the dead. He founded the congregation of the "saints" he called the Church and left it under the management of the Holy Spirit. He commissioned his disciples to go around the world, preach repentance, and announce the forgiveness of sins. Their responsibility is to bring the acceptable year of the Lord to the inhabitants of Earth. Those who believe in the gospel, accept the sacrifice of the cross, repent of their sins, and apply his teaching of righteousness and justice in their lives to become holy, Jesus will wash with his blood and grant forgiveness and everlasting life by the seal of the Holy Spirit.

Jesus Christ of Nazareth is the only way to obtain everlasting life and escape the punishments of hell and the second death. He paid the ultimate price for the souls of man. The doctrine of salvation is rooted in Jesus's sacrifice, the cross he carried, and the blood he shed. All other doctrines are of the devil. As the scoffers grow bolder, they have become these ungodly men ordained to the condemnation Apostle Jude warned us about. They have introduced many variations to this above-mentioned gospel, switching the focus of many to the material world and others to spiritism. The spirit of Satan inspires them, for they are his seeds.

The Influence of the Seed of Evil in the Church

Beloved, beware of the counterfeits! For everything that God creates, Satan tries to create a counterfeit. He tried it with Israel and now the Church of Jesus Christ. The false doctrine saga has not just started. The parasites pedaling these doctrines existed in Israel. First, they attacked the law to render it of no effect. They interpreted the laws of the Old Testament to fit their agenda. Now, they switched their focus to the Church.

Only now, they have become more confident, as they are using a replicated process that worked in Israel and during the first harvest of the Church. They were able to destroy both kingdoms in Israel. Now, they influence everything in the Church to cause countless Christians to deviate from the right path. During his time on earth, Jesus fought against the false doctrines that infiltrated the culture of Israel. For instance, when the teachers taught the Israelites the doctrine of selfishness and parsimony and spread hatred among the brotherhood of the congregation of Israel, Jesus faced this doctrine heads on. In the Gospel of Matthew, Jesus confronted some of them.

Starting in Matthew 5:41–48 (BSB), to quote a few of them, Jesus said, *"And if any man will sue thee at the law, and take away thy coat, let him have thy cloke also. And whosoever shall compel thee to go a mile, go with him twain. Give to him that asketh thee, and from him that would borrow of thee turn not thou away. Ye have heard that it hath been said; Thou shalt love thy neighbor and hate thine enemy. But I say unto you, love your enemies, bless them that curse you, do good to them that hate you, and pray for them which despitefully use you, and persecute you; That ye may be the children of your Father which is in heaven: for He maketh his sun to rise on the evil and on the good, and sendeth rain on the just and on the unjust. For if ye love them which love you, what reward have ye? Do not even the publicans the same? And if ye salute your brethren only, what do ye more than others? Do not even the publicans so? Be ye therefore perfect, even as your Father which is in heaven is perfect."*

In other words, Jesus told them to be like the Father, for the Father is good and does good to all created beings at all times and in all things. Elder Paul had to deal with the day setters—the clan of Jews who had infiltrated the early Church—to tell the people it was the Sabbath that saved them in an attempt to make the cross of none effect. He advised the Church with these words: *"Let no man therefore judge you in meat, or in drink, or in respect of a holyday, or of the new moon, or of the sabbath days: Which is a shadow of things to come; but the body is of Christ. Let no man beguile you of your reward in a voluntary humility and worshipping of angels, intruding into those things which he hath not seen, vainly puffed up by his fleshly mind, and not holding the Head, from which all the body by joints and bands having nourishment ministered, and knit together, increased with the increase of God. Wherefore if ye be dead with Christ from the rudiments of the world, why, as though living in the world, are ye subject to ordinances, (Touch not; taste not; handle not; Which all are to perish with the using;) after the commandments and doctrines of men? Which things have indeed a shew of wisdom in will worship, and humility, and neglecting of the body: not in any honour to the satisfying of the flesh"* (Colossians 2:16–23)

Well, in our time, the peddlers of false doctrines are using other tactics to infiltrate the Church and spread their ideologies. First, they attack the divinity of Jesus. They teach that Jesus is not the only way to God, that he was an angel. Second, they preach that Christians are friends of the world and that Jesus came to unite the whole world. But in reality, Jesus the Savior is not an angel. He is not Michael! He has never been and never will be. Jesus told his disciples that he would go to the Father and send the Holy Spirit to them, who would lead them in all truth. Under the baptism of the Holy Spirit, the apostle John spoke thus about Jesus, saying, He is the Word incarnated, the exact image of the invisible God and the only way to God. John stated that, *"In the beginning was the Word, and the Word was with God, and the Word was God. He was in the beginning with God. All things were made through Him, and without Him nothing was made that was made (John 1: 1-4).*

My question to those who postulate the theory that Jesus is an angel is the following one. How do you explain John's statement that *"All things were made through Him, and without Him nothing was made that was made?"* How is he an angel when he is their creator? John was not the only one who made this statement. Apostle Paul wrote the Colossians on the same subject to instruct them, saying, *"The son (referring to Jesus) (Who) is the image of the invisible God, the firstborn of every creature: For by him were all things created, that are in heaven, and that are in earth, visible and invisible, whether they be thrones, or dominions, or principalities, or powers: all things were created by him, and for him: And he is before all things, and by him all things consist. And he is the head of the body, the Church: who is the beginning, the firstborn from the dead; that in all things he might have the preeminence (Colossians 1: 15-18)".* Jesus said, *"I am the way, the truth, and the life: no man cometh unto the Father, but by me" (John 14:6 BSB).*

He did not come to unite the world either. In Matthew 10:34-36 (KJV), Jesus stated it himself, saying: *"Think not that I am come to send peace on earth: I came not to send peace, but a sword. For I am come to set a man at variance against his father, and the daughter against her mother, and the daughter in law against her mother-in-law. And a man's foes shall be they of his own household."*

Jesus came to call those who belong to his Father. It included the small percentage of humanity who is yearning for righteousness, justice, and order. He came to save those who are obedient to righteousness and justice and long to live under the dominion of God, the Father, the Creator of all things. They portray the Jesus of the Bible as a pacifist, but the Jesus of the Bible was no pacifist. He was a pragmatic who understood the state of humanity. Jesus did not come to unite the world but to put enmity in it, to filter the seed of good and separate it from evil. If you believe Jesus of Nazareth is the Christ and the only one who can save you, you do well. Hold fast to what you have until he returns with the crown, for it is for those who continue in the right doctrine until the end.

THE ANTICHRIST SPIRIT IN CHURCH LEADERSHIP

In every church congregation, all the attendees sing songs referring to Christ. They sincerely believe they are serving Jesus of Nazareth. But have all of them pledged allegiance to Jesus of Nazareth? It is rarely mentioned in the Church, but there are two Christs being preached on the pulpits of the current churches in the world. There is the preaching of Jesus Christ, born of Mary, conceived by the Holy Spirit, and the Antichrist, the demon for whom Satan is working. He has been removing the teachings of Jesus Christ of Nazareth in the churches to replace them with the false doctrines of the liberal mindset. This imposter is already in the world, waiting for his time to appear on the scenes.

Before his carnal revelation to the world, the Antichrist operates in the shadow of ignorance, turning what used to be truth into lies and evil into good. He had his demons infiltrate many sects of Christianity to lay in each of them certain latent doctrines that they mixed with the real gospel to confuse and confound the masses. And now, many of these dormant doctrines are being activated as true doctrines because the presence of he, who restricts (the Holy Spirit), is diminishing in the congregations as they become more religious. Many Christians do not know the difference between Jesus the Christ and the Antichrist. And yet, the time for his revelation to the world is at hand. But before he shows up in the flesh, the Spirit-filled Christian will be able to identify his servants by the doctrines they adopt.

The doctrines of the Antichrist have taken roots, and their influence has grown exponentially in the world during the last two thousand years to create a counterfeit gospel. It is a gospel disguised in a fake love and acceptance movement, telling the masses that if they do not accept sins and corruptions and abominations, they do not love. In truth, if God calls something a sin, no amount of love will change that. And if one accepts its practice, he/she is guilty by association and fall under the same condemnation. Hence, he/she will suffer the same punishment as the person perpetrating the sin.

Satan has anointed many so-called leaders to teach man to believe in the liberality and prosperity of this age, to preach this above-mentioned gospel that accepts abomination and all types of corruption in the name of love. He trains them in his theological institutions to fight for his denominations, causes, and world. He inspires in them the feel-good, do-good gospel. He trained them to ignore the true gospel and adopt the spirit of religion instead of the spirit of Christ.

This religious Christianity is to join the rest of the world's religions to form the Unified Church. This Unified Church is a coalition of religions where all the false religions will join together to create the one-world religion of Satan, having in its head, the Antichrist as bishop and Satan as God. And those he had anointed have grown bold, confident, famous, and rich while they spread this apostasy among the congregations of the saints. The spirit of the anti-Christ anoints them. This spirit is the imposter who's been impersonating the Holy Spirit of God. When he is revealed to the world, he will set himself in the place of the true Christ.

He is Satan's incarnation in the flesh. He can give powers to his followers so that they can operate miracles to deceive even the elect if he could. There are two nations in the Church—God's saints and Satan's materialists. God's saints are sanctified and filled with the Holy Spirit. In contrast, Satan's materialists are philosophical and religious. In this writing, we will continue discussing the two. The Spirit of God inspired this volume to address the people of God and remind them that God still values holiness, righteousness, and justice. He wants them to be holy, for the time of the outpouring of the Holy Spirit is at hand.

THE COUNTERFEIT GOSPELS

The false Christ and his religious followers have their own gospels, and these counterfeit gospels are being preached every day in the churches. They are being preached on pulpits all over the world. For instance, the current teachers preach to some that once one confesses the name of Jesus and attends a church, Jesus will make them prosper because the true blessings of God are great jobs, lots of money, and prosperity.

They preach that there are no conditions to becoming a disciple of Jesus Christ and that the love of God is unconditional. This is not the whole truth. You will see why as you continue reading. They preach that if you are a Christian, everything in your life should go right, and you should be comfortable. You have no enemy, and once you confess the name of Jesus, you are born again. They teach that once you accept Jesus, you are free but never explain what that freedom is. Indeed, accepting Jesus frees you, but you are only free to be holy, to walk the way of righteousness and justice, and to make perfect your sacrifice to God. The blood of Jesus breaks the chain that made it impossible before. Remember, Jesus does not free you to go seek material goods and become a potentate in this world. On the contrary, he freed you to seek heaven.

They teach that as a Christian, you are a citizen of the world. As a result, many Christians, instead of seeking the kingdom of God, go into compromising alliances with the world because they perceive themselves as advocates for equality and social justice in the world. You might have heard that you can love the world and be involved in all kinds of worldly endeavors, practice all kinds of white magic, be members of all kinds of secret societies, enjoy worldly music, idolize athletes and sports, idolize Hollywood stars, idolize music stars, while remaining in the service of Jesus.

Some of these false guides even teach that it is alright to practice yoga, pagan meditations, witchcraft, or even pray to angels and idols as saints to better connect with Christ. Some of you have heard that you never lose your salvation once you are saved. Moreover, some of these institutions teach that there is no condition to serve God. One only need to recite the prayer of confession, these beliefs are not part of the true gospel.

You must know that there is a true gospel and a false one. The true gospel requires abstinence from the world and its pleasures. The false gospel instructs those who accept it to mingle in world affairs. The true gospel demand holiness, while the false gospel diminishes its importance and relevance. Those who subscribe to the false gospel will become more religious, proud, boastful, selfish, and greedy. In contrast, those who subscribe to the true gospel will be humble, wise, and spiritual. The followers of these false gospels are the apostates.

CHAPTER 5

As the Church Evolves to Become a Worldly Institution

As the church evolved to become a worldly institution, Jesus is calling those who are his out of that crowd. The congregation of the church has been overrun by philosophers, intellectuals, businessman, profit seekers, and members of deviant secret societies. They are changing the gospel narrative. They are molding and creating a self-centered, world-pleasing, ego-boasting people. They're preparing their followers to join the world-citizenry. The modern philosophical Sanhedrin is preaching a gospel of tolerance while they avoid the gospel of repentance. The institutional church is tolerant of the corruptions and abominations going on in the world. They call it love. Their followers are offended by the truth and don't see any reason for changing their lives. They generate large crowds and billions of dollars in profit. Still among this selfish crowd, there exists a remnant of the seed of good. Jesus came to identify and recruit these God seekers, these lovers of Justice and righteousness. If you are seeking for God instead of profit, Jesus is looking for you.

In the gospel, Jesus reveals the characteristics of the qualified and the established saints. The saints are righteous and just. As a result, these people love virtue and justice and have a zeal for them.

They sought God, and consequently, God found them. They aren't many, but there are a few in every generation in time. The real gospel instructs us that, to qualify for sainthood, one needs to follow Jesus, and he/she must renounce the world, its riches, its pleasures, and its fame. In addition, he/she should be willing to forfeit his/her own life for the cause of righteousness. For Jesus says, *"If any man will come after me, let him deny himself, take up his cross, and follow me. Whoever wants to save his life will lose it, but whoever loses his life for my sake will find it. What will it profit a man if he gains the whole world yet forfeits his soul? Or what can a man give in exchange for his soul?" (Matthew 16:24–26 BSB).*

Notice what Jesus says in the verse: "One must deny the self" to come to him. One must give up the self to gain his/her soul. While the philosophers are trying to flatter the world with their gospel of tolerance to become one with it, the real Jesus Christ instructed his saints that they are not of the world and that the world will hate them. In John 15:18 (BSB), Jesus told his disciples, *"If the world hates you, understand that it hated me first. If you were of the world, it would love you as its own. Instead, the world hates you, because you are not of the world, but I have chosen you out of the world."*

In Matthew 10:16 (BSB), Jesus said, *"Look, I am sending you out like sheep among wolves; therefore, be as shrewd as snakes and as innocent as doves. But beware of men; for they will hand you over to their councils and flog you in their synagogues."*

Similarly, in verse 34 of the same chapter, Jesus told his disciples, *"Think not that I am come to send peace on earth: I came not to send peace, but a sword, a sword even between brothers born of the same mother."*

To confront the idea that once one confesses, he/she does not need to do anything else to get saved, the apostle Paul told the Philippians, *"Therefore, my beloved, just as you have always obeyed, not only in my presence, but now even more in my absence, continue to work out your salvation with fear and trembling" (Philippians 2:12 BSB).*

In Jude 1:5-7 (BSB), we read, *"But I want to remind you, though you once knew this, that the Lord, having saved the people out of the land of Egypt, afterward destroyed those who did not believe. And the angels who did not keep their proper domain, but left their own abode, He has reserved in everlasting chains under darkness for the judgment of the great day; as Sodom and Gomorrah, and the cities around them in a similar manner to these, having given themselves over to sexual immorality and gone after strange flesh, are set forth as an example, suffering the vengeance of eternal fire."*

These verses are designed to inspire a need for holiness and great controversy among those who read them. They should inspire holiness among those seeking God but will be controversial among those seeking the lusts of the world. They should also remind the scoffers who say that it is not that serious that judgment awaits them. They say, "God would never really act with such decisive judgment against our generation; He is a loving God." They ignored that God holds the scepters of justice, holiness, and righteousness in his hand. And as the Judge, He must give justice, straighten what is crooked, and destroy all corruptions. Justice must be done, and righteousness must be upheld. They are playing the fool thinking that ignorance will save them. Even the human law keepers understand that ignorance of the law is no excuse. God will judge every man and every sin. Facing this unchanging fact, Jesus decided to come take the punishment for man. These scoffers are some of the most loving people you can encounter, but they do not understand love at all. God loves man. Hence, He gave him the law to recognize his condition. He was supposed to obey it and change his ways. He failed miserably.

But the law tactic was simply to prove to man that he was hopeless and helpless and needed a savior. In due time, God then sent his only begotten Son to save us from the righteous justice of His government as he provisioned to do from the foundation of the world. Justice and righteousness are the foundations of creation. Therefore, without them, the very existence of God's creation is at risk. David, the prophet, alluded to this when he said in Psalm 89:14 (BSB*)*, *"Righteousness and justice are the foundation of Your throne; loving devotion and truth go before You."*

To the scoffers, love is all they need, so they ignore righteousness and justice. However, God is serious about maintaining these two pillars intact. The lake of fire is being candled in his anger. It is prepared as the final destination of all those who violate the laws that make up these two pillars. Some of God's finest created angels have been scheduled for destruction in this lake of fire because they have violated these concepts.

As a just God, He will not treat man any differently. Man's predicament is direr than any one of us can fathom, as hell is being overfilled and it is expanding its boundaries to receive the souls who ignore the laws of righteousness and justice. This volume is addressed to several people in this great Christian nation. It is written to encourage Spiritual Christians and urge them to stay the course of holiness, justice, and righteousness. It is written to call the complaisant Christians to sober up and wake up to holiness and righteousness. It also addresses those who embrace a religion instead of the Holy Spirit to warn them that God will separate the wheat from the tares. The instructions therein are also for the new converts who are currently being misled. Let me clarify that when I say the laws of justice and righteousness, I am not referring to the ceremonial laws of the Jews. I am referring to the spiritual laws of Jesus Christ starting with the commandment to love one another.

This book is also designed to enlighten those established in the faith who do not understand the value of righteousness and justice and help them straighten their ways and veer them from the paths that lead to hell. For Jesus said unto his followers, *"Unless your righteousness shall exceed the righteousness of the scribes and Pharisees, ye shall in no case enter into the Kingdom of Heaven" (Matthew 5:20 KJV).*

If you confess to knowing God, you must wake up and stop thinking as a child. Examine where you stand. If you subscribed to any of these false beliefs, repent and come to God. He is loving but equally just and righteous. Jesus came to give you a choice when there was none. Choose Jesus in order to be drafted into the tree of good. Denounce evil and live free.

Have you ever felt that something is missing in your Christian life? If you answer yes to this question, continue reading. Do you feel that God seems to be far from you no matter what you do? Do you feel that God is unapproachable, and yet, you want to serve him? If yes, continue reading.

In this volume, I will show you why your stride toward God has failed and what is stopping you. As the voice crying in the wilderness, I am calling to warn you, to tell you to prepare the way of the Lord, for he is about to gather the saints to make a grand entrance.

I am writing to capture the attention of the chosen generation, the royal priesthood, the holy nation, and the peculiar people. "Come out from among them, my people." Don't let the seeds of evil who infiltrate the church corrupt your ways. This call is for those called of this generation to be the elect, who should show forth the praises of Him who has called them out of darkness and into His marvelous light. It is for those who want to serve God but are told they must follow cultural traditions that render them complacent. These words will sound radical to those who are perishing, but they will enlighten the elect.

Two Manner of People in the Church

If you are a member of a church congregation, among the two manner of people, which one are you? Remember that God told Rebekah, the wife of Isaac, that she would give birth to two-manner of people? Jesus also told us that there would be two-manner of people in the Church.

Jesus said that we would recognize each people by their fruits. His people will be recognized by righteousness and justice generated by their fellowship with God's Spirit and their love for one another. However, the other people will be recognized by their lack of spiritual focus, their love for money, power, and prestige, and their disregard for righteousness and justice and love for their brothers. They will focus on the things of the earth, not the spirit.

These two people are of two different polarities; one is religious, and the other one is spiritual. The majority of today's churches operate on religious grounds. As they become more and more like the catholic religion from which they came, they become popular. As a result, many people flood their assemblies.

In contrast, the church that Jesus founded operates on spiritual grounds. This is the ground upon which the apostles stood. In reality, Jesus came to remove the people of God, out of traditional religion. He did not come to establish his own religion to mix with the pile. Instead, Jesus came to help man establish a relationship with God, the Spirit.

As he told the Samaritan woman, *"But a time is coming and has now come when the true worshipers will worship the Father in spirit and in truth, for the Father is seeking such as these to worship Him" (John 4:24 BSB)*. This time started with the event of Pentecost. God is still seeking for the spiritual seed among the congregations of the church. God is Spirit, and His worshipers must worship Him in spirit and in truth. In this statement, Jesus established a big difference between religious Christianity and spiritual Christianity.

God is Spirit and He is the God of all spirits. Those who worship him must do it in spirit and in truth. The Christians who are not worshiping Him in spirit are simply religious. Hence, the religious church is susceptible to the spirit of apostasy because it has no direct relationship with God. The religious Christians forge relationship with the world to gain their respect and friendship.

In contrast, spiritual Christianity follows a Father and son relationship between man, who should be born again as a spirit to become the son of God the Father of all spirits. In spiritual Christianity, the goal of the Christian is to be one with Jesus as Jesus is with his Father. If you inquire how the spiritual Christian achieves this oneness, the answer is simple. The spiritual Christian surrenders to the Spirit who guided Jesus and his apostles and connected them to the Father.

Jesus is one with his Father because the two have the same Spirit. The Spirit of the Father fully dwells in Jesus. To be a Christian is to be like Jesus; thus, the Christian should be one in whom the Spirit of the Father dwells. The true Christian is not in words, but in action, holiness, Justice, obedience and righteousness. However, in the status quo the religious churches ignore these basics and failed to make that connection with the Holy Spirit to become one with Him and therefore they can't be like Jesus. They are Christians in words, not in substance. The religious church operates on philosophies and cultural traditions, not the traditions of the saints but those of the world. The worldly traditions differ significantly from the traditions of the saints.

Struggling under the weight of the spirit of apostasy, these religious churches cannot see things the way Jesus saw them when he spent time on earth. But there is an overlap as the two churches are mingled together. This is no coincidence, as Jesus predicted it would happen. So, if you call yourself a Christian, how do you know which side you stand on?

The current spiritual church, the remnant, seeks consecration and constant contact with God. It practices the holy culture of righteousness and justice. But religious churches today forgot about these fundamental concepts. They have taken a subjective approach toward the culture of the saints. Therefore, they have developed different cultures within which they operate. These worldly-compliant churches have shifted their focus. They focus on pleasing the world instead of God. All the while, the remnant of the spiritual church is trying to serve God in holiness by the Spirit of truth.

Consequently, religious churches always seek profit. Jesus is seeking the souls of the lost, and he commissioned the Christians to do the same. From Peter to Paul to the countless number of others massacred by fire and the sword throughout the ages, the older generation of spiritual Christians fulfilled this commission in their time. Yet the religious churches avoid this commission. The spiritual Christian plans to be sanctified, be born of the spirit, proclaim the Gospel of God, and wait on God to give them what they need to survive.

In contrast, religious Christians mingle with the world, rely on the world systems, and make plans to live and die on earth comfortably. They think of themselves as citizens of this world and seek favor from its rulers. They store their treasures in this world. However, Jesus warned his disciples against this practice by saying, *"Do not store up for yourselves treasures on earth, where moth and rust destroy, and where thieves break in and steal. But store up for yourselves treasures in heaven, where moth and rust do not destroy, and where thieves do not break in and steal. For where your treasure is, there your heart will be also." Matthew 6:21 (BSB).*

Jesus said, *"Seek ye first the Kingdom of God."* He meant that we must prioritize reaching heaven, and everything else should be secondary. Instead of investing time in consecration, the institutional churches invest their time, energy, and passion in pursuing worldly endeavors. This crowd doesn't focus on investing time in spreading the gospel of salvation and life. Instead, it will spread the word for causes such as environmental preservation, stopping world hunger, standing for political affiliations, or fighting against a particular disease. It is under a strong delusion. It ignores the roots of the problems,—which are sin and Satan. It makes no plans to preach the gospel of Jesus to evangelize its neighbors who are being slaughtered like sheep by Satan and his demons on an hourly basis. In 2 Timothy 4:3-5 BSB, Paul told Timothy to *"Preach the word; be prepared in season and out of season; reprove, rebuke, and encourage with every form of patient instruction. For the time will come when men will not tolerate sound doctrine, but with itching ears they will gather around themselves teachers to suit their own desires. So, they will turn their ears away from the truth and turn aside to myths. But you, be sober in all things, endure hardship, do the work of an evangelist, fulfill your ministry.* Well, that time is now. The current churches have indeed gathered around themselves teachers to suit their own desires. But where are the evangelists? Where are those who were supposed to preach the word; to be prepared in season and out of season; to reprove, to rebuke, and encourage with every form of patient instruction. They are not here. They are absent. They went the way of the Pharisees and Sadducees.

CHAPTER 6

THE REPROBATE IN THE WAR

Are you aware of the War? The Christian nation has always been at war with Satan and his crowd. But now that we are at the end of all things, everyone must ascertain their position on the battlefield. The battles have intensified. The enemy is using brutish force to attack all sides and is invading every territory left unsecured. He has nothing to lose, for he had already lost it all at the cross.

The Christians who understand this fact are putting on the armor of God to face him in these final battles. However, many subscribed to their religious customs and failed to understand the severity of the situation. And as the apostle Paul stated, they become reprobates. Every Christian needs to stand at their battle station to fight this war.

Do you, as a Christian, have a winning tactical strategy to fight this war? If you are relying on the traditional religious practices of this world, you might be playing into the hand of the enemy. He will block your spiritual intuitions and blind you. You will not yield the fruits the Master deems useful. Remember, Jesus said that every tree that does not produce good fruit is hewn down and thrown in the fire. These good fruits are spiritual fruits. One needs to be drafted in the spiritual tree to yield these spiritual fruits. Are you producing good fruits?

The members of the church of old were members of that tree—the tree of good. The Holy Spirit drafted them for a noble purpose. However, today's religious church ignored this holy path and followed the comfortable path of loving this world. Jesus did not call us for the comforts of the world or to become better patriots of a particular earthly nation. Instead, he called us to be patriots of the nation of the saints. Hence, we are to follow the holy and righteous culture.

We are to be beacons of light and hope to speak the truth of the gospel to the world without any compromise. We are called to stir up the status quo. Jesus called us to be a peculiar people in the world, not to look like the world itself. He called us to work and perform the same charitable and spiritual works he was performing when he was on earth.

> *Then he called his twelve disciples together, and gave them power and authority over all devils, and to cure diseases. And he sent them to preach the kingdom of God, and to heal the sick. And he said unto them, take nothing for your journey, neither staves, nor scrip, neither bread, neither money; neither have two coats apiece. And whatsoever house ye enter into, there abide, and thence depart. And whosoever will not receive you, when ye go out of that city, shake off the very dust from your feet for a testimony against them. And they departed, and went through the towns, preaching the gospel, and healing everywhere (Luke 9: 1-6, KJV).*

Yes, the Christian is assigned two types of works to show that the kingdom of God is among us. He/she is commissioned to perform charitable and spiritual works. Charitable works involve feeding the hungry, sheltering the homeless, taking care of the poor, clothing the naked, be a father to the fatherless, a hope for the hopeless, visit the sick and those who are incarcerated to show them the goodness of God and announce to them the gospel of liberty. In James 2:14-26 (KJV), the apostle raised the question of the value of faith without good works. The apostle asked about charitable works in verse 14 saying, *"What does it profit, my brethren, if someone says he has faith but does not have works?"* In verse 20, again, he asked, *"But wilt thou know, O vain man, that faith without works is dead?"* In Matthew 5:42 (KJV), Jesus commanded his disciples to, *"Give to the one who asks you, and do not turn away from the one who wants to borrow from you".* Jesus performed charitable works to be an example among his disciples. Jesus fed the hungry, he was a father to the fatherless, a hope for the hopeless. However, charitable work is simply part of the overall works. Jesus talking to his disciples on practical spiritual works, stated, *"Believe Me that I am in the Father and the Father is in me, or at least believe on account of the works themselves. Truly, truly, I tell you, whoever believes in me will also do the works that I am doing. He will do even greater things than these, because I am going to the Father. And I will do whatever you ask in My name, so that the Father may be glorified in the Son"* (John 14:11–13 BSB).

Again, in Mathew 16:17–18 (BSB), Jesus listed the spiritual works that a believer should perform in the following words, *"Whoever believes and is baptized will be saved, but whoever does not believe will be condemned. And these signs will accompany those who believe: In My name they will drive out demons; they will speak in new tongues; they will pick up snakes with their hands, and if they drink any deadly poison, it will not harm them; they will lay their hands on the sick, and they will be made well."*

Are you among those who believe? Are you Jesus' disciple? When was the last time you healed a sick person or drove out a demon? Have you ever wondered why you, as a believer, cannot do the works that Jesus did while he was on earth? What about his promise? Does it apply to you? If you are a believer, the answers should be yes. However, depending on your spiritual orientation, the answers to these questions could also be a resounding no. If you are a religious Christian, your primary focus remains on showing off to satisfy the ego, but not to do the works of the Father to glorify the Father. And just like the Pharisees of Israel, the religious Christians learned to live without doing any of these works of faith. Instead, they merely theorized about their belief. For them, it is enough to have their names on the roster of the local corporate church. They gather in a group and sing a couple of songs. They think that this is all the work they have to perform.

And because the religious churches are working on dead faith, healing the sick, raising the dead, speaking in tongues, picking up snakes, and the belief that if a believer drinks any deadly poison, he/she will not be harmed, are now placed in the realm of the weird. They are thrown away from normal spiritual duties. It is a common belief that once one accepts Jesus, he/she is saved. However, when it comes to performing the sign that would accompany the believer, they are told that to have that kind of faith is ludicrous.

Somehow, religious Christians believe that Jesus can still save the world but can no longer heal people or raise the dead. Religious Christians believe in medical institutions and leave the work of healing the sick to the hospitals. They say that there are hospitals that heal people. When the demons drive our neighbors to insanity or drug addiction, we say that psychiatrists and drug treatment centers can cater to these suffering people. As Christians, we don't need to worry about that.

Many people believe that performing these miracles is the job of a special elite in the church. However, this belief is a loophole created by Satan through which he is sending his miracle workers to impersonate the real men of God and entrap the masses. This behavior also creates a social class system in the church of Christ. Others believe that healing the sick and casting out demons are not for our time.

Yet, Jesus said that these signs would follow those who believe. In addition to their unconditional love for one another, believers will be recognized by these signs. How do they recognize you as a Christian? Is it by the type of car you drive, the kind of house you have, your demeanor, the neighborhood where you live, your level of sophistication, or your smile? Does the big building called church that you attend, the many times you go to church, the money you give to the church, your friendship with pastors, the number of times you pray a day, the many times you read the Bible, the theology degree you have, or your ability to preach the word define your Christianity? None of these accolades matter. Yet, they are the attributes of today's Christians, especially how they are identified in today's show-business church.

The works of the Christian are defined in what they do in the church, whether or not they can put on a good show. Yet to Jesus, you should be undoing the deeds of darkness by raising the dead, healing the sick, and casting out demons. That's the work he gave you to do. But to do this work you need power from above, not philosophy or theology. Today's religious Christian only performs some charitable works and ignore the other part. Moreover, they don't do charity to the members of their congregations but to strangers of different faiths while the problems of their brothers and sisters in the same congregation are ignored.

Also, casting out demons is considered a myth among the religious Christians. The current theological teaching does not acknowledge demons. The majority of theologians say that demons do not exist. They are just stories told to scare little children or the simple. If you believe they do exist, you must be crazy. They are all in your head.

Instead, we have psychologists to deal with mental illness. Our society is civilized. We do not have demons here. However, some of the same people pedaling this rhetoric are offering sacrifices to these same demons that they claim do not exist to become famous and rich in this world. They know that the demon population outnumbers the human population on earth at a ratio of 10,000 to 1. They know that Satan's demons are all over us. Yet, they seal their mouths. They are rich and famous, and they occupy the high governmental offices in the world. They have preeminence in all things on earth, and they are working with Satan to establish his new world order.

As a result, they have also infiltrated the religious church, controlling how it operates. Many of them are members of Satanic secret societies that have nothing to do with Jesus Christ of Nazareth. Many of them are unbelievers. And yet these groups occupy the leadership roles in most of the influential churches on earth. They are pastors, church members, deacons, world-renowned evangelists who preach the gospel of tolerance instead of repentance. They are also regular members. They are the elite. It does not bother us, but it should. These religious leaders inform us that only special people have the gifts of the Holy Spirit, and that these gifts are not for anyone.

As we will see later, Jesus did not come to establish an elitist group on earth. He came to establish a congregation of equal brotherhood. Jesus promised that all those who believe should receive the Holy Spirit and will be able to perform these miracles. Why can't all believers operate the works of Jesus? Is it because they do not have enough faith, or they don't believe enough?

The modern believer has faith that he/she is saved by Jesus when he/she confesses and accepts his kingship, but his/her faith is followed by no similar actions. Perhaps, the flaw is in the definition of belief. Do you believe with all your heart, spirit, and soul? Did you surrender all to Jesus when you believed, or are you in control? To the current church believers, believing in Jesus means being in a partnership. The Christians are told to come to Jesus, renounce some of the world's habits, and bring their intellect and skills to partner with Jesus. To perform the works of Jesus, they must allow the Holy Spirit to use them for the moment when they want that miracle, serving as a medium.

They believe that their ego and the Holy Spirit will partner together as the witches and fortune-tellers do with their unclean spirits. Hence, they do not need to change much. Moreover, they do not have to surrender it all to be transformed by the Holy Spirit. It is not that serious. They only need to partner with Jesus.

In contrast, for Jesus, believing means surrendering it all. He was dead serious about it. It wasn't a partnership. Between Jesus and his Father, there existed the relationship of a potter and his clay. Jesus' body was the father's tool on earth, and the Father's Spirit was in charge of every fiber of his being. Being filled with the Holy Spirit and letting him manage his life was part of his belief. Jesus let the Holy Spirit take over his will, his abilities, and his reasoning in complete obedience. His obedience to God was serious enough for him to leave his throne of glory, come down to earth, suffer in agony, walk the Via Dolorosa, stretch his arms on the cross, and die as a nobody—as a criminal and a pauper.

Jesus surrendered it all to the service of the Father. He then instructed his followers to follow in his footsteps, surrender it all, and be obedient to the Father and the Holy Spirit onto death. When Jesus called Peter and the others with him, he called them saying, *"Come, follow Me, and I will make you fishers of men." And at once they left their nets and followed Him* (Mark 1: 17-18 BSB). Peter and the others followed him right away. This was not a part time for them. They left everything and followed Jesus. Peter and the others had a choice to make. This was a choice between their careers to remain fishers of fish or to become fishers of man. They chose the latter. In Mathew 19: 27–29 we read how Jesus calmed the worries of the disciples for having left everything for his sake. *"Look," Peter replied, "we have left everything to follow You. What then will there be for us?" Jesus said to them, "Truly I tell you, in the renewal of all things, when the Son of Man sits on His glorious throne, you who have followed Me will also sit on twelve thrones, judging the twelve tribes of Israel. And everyone who has left houses or brothers or sisters or father or mother or wife or children or fields for the sake of My name will receive a hundredfold and will inherit eternal life"*. To explain what kinds of obedience and selflessness Jesus required of his disciples, he told them: *"Let the little children come to me and do not hinder them. For the kingdom of God belongs to such as these. Truly I tell you, if anyone does not receive the kingdom of God like a little child, he will never enter it"* (Luke 18:17 BSB).

Our young ones offer a great example. Children have no will of their own. They do not get offended. They do what their parents ask them to do and go where they ask them to go. Jesus said that Christians should be armed with total obedience just like Isaac was. You know his story. To Jesus, the believer needs to surrender it all—personality, strength, power, and wealth—to the Father, the Son, and the Holy Spirit. That being said, I would urge you to exercise caution. You need to surrender it all to Jesus, not man.

Total surrender can happen only after one renounce the world, repent of all his/her sins and consecrate him/herself to the service of God. Jesus instructed his disciples to give up the self, crucify the ego, and offer the body as a tool of service to the Triune God (the Father, the Son, and the Holy Spirit). He did not tell them to operate as mediums. They were to be a temple, and the Holy Spirit would reside and remain there forever. Yet, a large number of the current religious Christians, operating on half repentance have rejected the Trinity. They reject the Holy Spirit for the self. However, the Trinity operates as one.

If you reject the Father, you also reject the Son and the Spirit. If you reject the Son, you also reject the Father and the Spirit. If you reject the Spirit, you also reject the Father and the Son. When you accept Jesus, you accept the Father and the Holy Spirit; for each has work to do in the perfection of the bride. For it is written, *"This is He that came by water and blood, even Jesus Christ; not by water only, but by water and blood. And it is the Spirit that beareth witness, because the Spirit is truth. For there are three that bear record in Heaven: The Father, the Word (who is the incarnated Jesus), and the Holy Ghost; and these three are one. And there are three that bear witness on earth: The Spirit, and the water, and the blood; and these three agree in one"* (1 John 5:7 BSB).

You are chosen by the Father, saved by the Son, and maintained by the Holy Spirit. Jesus bled to redeem the temple, the water cleanses it, and the Spirit seals it, as we will explain later. The majority of religious congregations, rejected the Holy Spirit just as Israel rejected the rule of the father, thinking they only needed the self. Yet, the Holy Spirit is the Spirit who identifies the elect—those who belong to God. How does the congregation of those who call themselves people of God deny him? Like Israel, the congregation which accepts Jesus as King (or so they say) now practices world culture, operates on Greek philosophies, and has customized beliefs to satisfy people instead of God.

In this writing, we will compare the efficiency of the churches that reject the Holy Spirit for riches, fame, and power with that of the early church of Jesus Christ. This volume is the beginning of a series of teaching intended to revive the spiritual church from among the religions. In the real gospel, the apostle Paul admonished the Corinthians in these words, saying: *"Do not be unequally yoked with unbelievers. For what partnership can righteousness have with wickedness? Or what fellowship does light have with darkness? What harmony is there between Christ and Belial? Or what does a believer have in common with an unbeliever? What agreements can exist between the temple of God and idols? For we are the temple of the living God. As God has said: "I will dwell with them and walk among them, and I will be their God, and they will be My people." "Therefore, come out from among them and be separate, says the Lord. Touch no unclean thing, and I will receive you." And: "I will be a Father to you, and you will be My sons and daughters, says the Lord Almighty (2 Corinthians 6:14-17 BSB).*

Did you catch that? The Lord says that to become his sons and daughters, one needs to separate him/herself. One should abstain from touching unclean things, which means one needs to be holy. We will not focus on growing the intellect in the chapters to come in this book. Instead, we are focusing on the Spiritual aspects. We will speak about the one who gives birth to the spirit of man and grows it to perfection. He is the one who is the power of God—the Holy Spirit. We will show that there is no ministry or serving God without the Holy Spirit. We will challenge the false religious beliefs that are conditioning the church of Jesus to fulfill world visions that are far from the vision of heaven. We will also provide advice for those seeking the truth.

Consequently, we will compare the spiritual Christian dogma with the religious Christian philosophy. We will help our readers make sense of the two and understand where they stand in the race in their lives.

CHAPTER 7

THE CHRISTIAN IN THE WAR

Let's start this section of the book by shedding light on the environment where were thrive. Always remember, we are at war! In Revelation 12:7-9 (KJV) we read, *And there was war in heaven: Michael and his angels fought against the dragon; and the dragon fought and his angels, And prevailed not; neither was their place found any more in heaven. And the great dragon was cast out, that old serpent, called the Devil, and Satan, which deceiveth the whole world: he was cast out into the earth, and his angels were cast out with him."* There are those who believe that this war happened long ago and it doesn't apply to them. This is a mistake. Satan's war was a full-blown assault on everything in God's creation. He is still warring. He failed in Heaven. He can no longer attack there, but earth is fair game. In Revelation 12:11 (BSB) we read, And I heard a loud voice in heaven saying: *"Now have come the salvation and the power and the kingdom of our God, and the authority of His Christ. For the accuser of our brothers has been thrown down—he who accuses them day and night before our God. They have conquered him by the blood of the Lamb and by the word of their testimony. And they did not love their lives so as to shy away from death. Therefore rejoice, O heavens, and you who dwell in them! But woe to the earth and the sea; with great fury the devil has come down to you, knowing he has only a short time."* The Christians are *"They who have conquered him by the blood of the Lamb and by the word of their testimony."* Contrary to popular beliefs, the true believers in Christ are soldiers, not compromisers. However, an untrained soldier cannot fight. Even worst, soldiers who do not know they are at war cannot defend themselves.

While the Christians of old were praying for God to stretch out his arm to show his power to the world, the average Christian today prays for long life and prosperity as blessings. They believe that being a Christian means, you must sit on the bench of a church on a certain day of the week. Hence, they come to hide in the church. They don't know about the war. They do not understand that the church is ground zero of this war. It is the place where Satan will attack. This is where his enemies are stationed. When Satan's demons attack and find Christians without armor, they will become a casualty of war.

Do you know about this war? Are you ready for it? A great majority of churchgoers are not aware of this fact. Their leaders never told them either because they do not know themselves or they are in a compromise with the enemy. They are told that Jesus won on the cross but cannot explain what it means. Yes, Jesus himself is victorious indeed. He has won the legal battles, kicked the accuser out of the throne room, and given the sons of Adam a legal right to approach the throne.

Jesus himself has received his crown and is now the King of kings and Lord of lords. He has crushed the head of Satan as it was prophesied. He is the first and original overcomer. Jesus left the earth, but that does not mean the war is over. Every Christian is at war with Satan. Satan and his minions never stop accusing the Christian in front of the throne of Majesty. As the prince of the kingdom of Persia opposed the angel who was sent to answer Daniel's prayers (Daniel 10:13 KJV), so do Satan and his servants oppose your prayers.

Satan still has servants stationed in the heavens, whose only business is to block the prayers of those unsanctified Christians from reaching the court of heaven. It prevents them from receiving any blessings from God. When you are sanctified and your life is right with God, your prayers go up to the throne like a ball of fire; no one can stop them from reaching the throne of God and being answered according to the will of God. As the Lord was attentive to Daniel's prayer, he is also attentive to the prayers of the saints on earth today.

However, these prayers originated from a sinful soul; unless it is for the repentance of that soul's sin are blocked in the second heaven. Every Christian must be an overcomer in this war to enter heaven's gate. For it is written, *"He who overcomes shall be clothed in white garments, and I will not blot out his name from the Book of Life; but I will confess his name before My Father and before His angels" (Revelation 3:5 KJV).* Jesus forged the way and provided the tools and power for you to obtain your own victory. Because only the victorious, he who overcomes, will tread heaven's streets of gold.

Jesus ordered anyone who wants to follow him to pick up their cross. For the battle has been individualized, and every believer has to fight their own foes and conquer their own cross.

The Christian should overcome the world and the temptations of greed, lust, power, and fame. For, *"From the days of John the Baptist until now, the kingdom of heaven has been subject to violence, and the violent lay claim to it" (Matthew 11:12 BSB).* The violent ones are those who do as Jesus did; like those who give up everything to gain heaven. Abram did it when he was asked to leave the comforts of his father's house for an unknown land. He packed his stuff and set out for the desert when he received the command, chasing only a promise.

Jesus did it. He left his throne to come to die on earth as a criminal—a pauper. And now, as a Christian, it is your turn. If you hear Jesus's voice saying, "Come follow me," that is your call. You need to leave Satan's house, this world, just like Abram left his father's house. You must leave the world and its pleasures for the wilderness of holiness. Be aggressive about it! Otherwise, you don't stand a chance to be a winner in this war. *"He that hath hear let him hear," (Matthew 11:15 KJV).*

To follow Jesus is to enter in a contest, a war, a fight to the death of the self or the soul. In order to be like Jesus-the-Christ and to receive the Christian anointing, one must deny the self and embrace the spirit to revived the soul. Jesus said it this way in Luke 14:26–27 (KJV). *"If any man come to me, and hate not his father, and mother, and wife, and children, and brethren, and sisters, yea, and his own life also, he cannot be my disciple. Whosoever doth not bear his cross, and come after me, cannot be my disciple."* The modern religious Christian isn't even aware of having a cross, let alone knowing how to carry one. The leaders of the current church refrain from teaching that to their followers. In the spirit of this contest, elder Paul told Timothy to, *"Fight the good fight of the faith; Take hold of the eternal life to which you were called when you made the good confession before many witnesses" (1 Timothy 6:12 BSB)*. Elder Paul said to the Corinthians, *"Everyone who competes in the games trains with strict discipline. They do it for a crown that is perishable, but we do it for a crown that is imperishable" (1 Corinthians 9:25 BSB)*. In Acts 20:24 (BSB), Luke says, *"But I consider my life of no value to myself, if only I may finish my course and complete the ministry, I have received from the Lord Jesus, the ministry of testifying to the good news of God's grace."*

You need skills and discipline to get onto the battlefield. Or better yet, you need to arm yourself with power to join the fight! The day you confessed Jesus as the King of your life; you had rejected the kingdom that currently rules the earth. You either fight or surrender! Which one will you do? Stop sitting on the reserve bench. The enemy is attacking, and he is using everything he has. So, pick up the weapons of righteousness and justice. As elder Paul told the church of Ephesus, I am telling you to, *"Put on the whole armor of God that ye may be able to stand against the wiles of the devil. For we wrestle not against flesh and blood, but against principalities, against powers, against the rulers of the darkness of this world, against spiritual wickedness in high places. Girt your loins with truth and put on the breastplate of righteousness; shod your feet with the preparation of the gospel of peace. Above all, taking the shield of faith, wherewith ye shall be able to quench all the fiery darts of the wicked. Put on the helmet of salvation, and the sword of the Spirit, which is the word of God. Praying always with all prayer and supplication in the Spirit and watching thereunto with all perseverance and supplication for all saints" (Ephesians 6:11–18 BSB)*.

As you can read in the above verse, elder Paul instructed that we are fighting in the spiritual. This war has been going on for millenniums and is still happening. We are fighting the falling angels and the demonic spirits born from the union of the daughters of Adam with the fallen watchers. We are also fighting the spirits of the men who are in the service of Satan. If Paul was still alive on earth today and were to walk into one of these mega-churches and speak as such, they would tell him that he is paranoid. They would refuse him audience.

The theologians fail to tell the Christians that they are at war. They are underestimating the enemy. He is just a figment of the imagination they say. To them, Satan is just some bad guy out there that man's goodwill can vanquish. Well, they are wrong. They are quick to say, *"Resist the devil and he will flee from you."* This is only one part of the verse. The full verse says, *"Submit yourselves therefore to God. Resist the devil, and he will flee from you"* (James 4:7 BSB).

If you don't fully submit to God, the devil will not flee from you. In fact, the rebellious nature comes from him, and as long as it is in you, you are his subject. Submitting yourself to God means having nothing in you or on you that belongs to Satan, his world, or his servants. It means being fully obedient to the Word of God at all costs, even the death of the body. The reason why the apostle says to submit yourself to God is because only God can rebuke Satan. It is not because he is equal to God, but because of the anointing he received when he ruled in heaven, when he was part of the government.

We were told that Satan was just a worship leader in heaven. However, this is not the whole truth. Satan was one of the first created of the beings of light, and thus, he was one of their first leaders. He was a dignitary in heaven, sort of like a prime minister, and was responsible for the created angels.

In his rank, Satan was anointed to rule over principalities and powers, supervising administrative activities. He also served as a legal enforcer; what we would call an attorney general on earth. Yes, Satan is a prosecutor, and he is out to prosecute every being in creation who is not righteous and just. While Satan was in his post in heaven, his diplomatic cunning was second to that of no other created being in the realms. This is the anointing that went over his head. Hence, it fooled him into believing he could replace God and puffed him up until he tried a coup and was promptly kicked out by Archangel Michael.

The prophet Ezekiel told us a little about Satan in these words. *"Thou hast been in Eden the garden of God; every precious stone was thy covering, the sardius, topaz, and the diamond, the beryl, the onyx, and the jasper, the sapphire, the emerald, and the carbuncle, and gold: the workmanship of thy tabrets and of thy pipes was prepared in thee in the day that thou wast created. Thou art the anointed cherub that covereth; and I have set thee so: thou wast upon the holy mountain of God; thou hast walked up and down in the midst of the stones of fire. Thou wast perfect in thy ways from the day that thou wast created, till iniquity was found in thee" (Ezekiel 28:13–15 KJV).*

Angels are not allowed to walk upon the holy mountain of God or trample in the midst of the stones of fire in heaven. And so, when you talk about Satan, you aren't referring to an angel. Pay attention to Ezekiel's play of words here. He said, *"Thou art the anointed cherub."* This type of language is not used for other angels. Nowhere in the Bible will you ever read the word anointing applied to a cherub besides Satan. It means that Satan was and is still one of his kind—a decorated cherub who was appointed ruler over heaven's mighty angels.

This anointing was a ruling anointing. Satan was one of the beings who could approach the throne of God whenever he wished. He was placed above some of his fellow cherubs, the seraphs, the archangels, and the angels. He was good at what he did and had great influence among the beings of light and power. The government was upon his shoulder. Only the Godhead was above him. So, only the Godhead had more authority than him.

The scary part is that God did not take the anointing away from Satan when he fell from grace. He still has the same anointing and the same power. Archangel Michael, the general of the army of God, who rules over the powers and principalities of war, he who kicked Satan out of heaven, still respected the authority of Satan when he faced him in the issue of Moses' body. In Jude 1:8–10 (BSB), we read, *"Yet in the same way, these dreamers defile their bodies, reject authority, and slander glorious beings. But even the archangel Michael, when he disputed with the devil over the body of Moses, did not presume to bring a slanderous judgment against him, but said, 'The Lord rebuke you!'*

These men, however, slander what they do not understand, and like irrational animals, they will be destroyed by the things they do instinctively."

When Satan committed treason, the government of heaven split. Satan did not understand what would happen, but when God created Adam, Satan saw the potential of the being. He was the only being that could replace him, the only being who could support the same anointing as him. And when God gave Adam dominion over the physical universe, Satan's fear was realized. He had to defile Adam's temple to subdue the being to maintain his government, thus bringing Adam under his dominion.

Satan believed that by doing this, his government would last forever. If he can render Adam and his offspring unworthy, no other beings would be worthy to open the seals of the scroll of the laws of the universe and rule over both visible and invisible universes. However, Satan did not count on Jesus. For after winning on the cross, Jesus was found worthy. In the book of Revelation, we read, *"And I saw in the right hand of him that sat on the throne a book written within and on the backside, sealed with seven seals. And I saw a strong angel proclaiming with a loud voice, who is worthy to open the book, and to loose the seals thereof? And no man in heaven, nor in earth, neither under the earth, was able to open the book, neither to look thereon. And I wept much, because no man was found worthy to open and to read the book, neither to look thereon. And one of the elders saith unto me, Weep not: behold, the Lion of the tribe of Juda, the Root of David, hath prevailed to open the book, and to loose the seven seals thereof. And I beheld, and, lo, in the midst of the throne and of the four beasts, and in the midst of the elders, stood a Lamb as it had been slain, having seven horns and seven eyes, which are the seven Spirits of God sent forth into all the earth. And he came and took the book out of the right hand of him that sat upon the throne. And when he had taken the book, the four beasts and four and twenty elders fell down before the Lamb, having every one of them harps, and golden vials full of odours, which are the prayers of saints. And they sung a new song, saying, Thou art worthy to take the book, and to open the seals thereof: for thou wast slain, and hast redeemed us to God by thy blood out of every kindred, and tongue, and people, and nation; And hast made us unto our God kings and priests:*

and we shall reign on the earth. And I beheld, and I heard the voice of many angels round about the throne and the beasts and the elders: and the number of them was ten thousand times ten thousand, and thousands of thousands Saying with a loud voice, Worthy is the Lamb that was slain to receive power, and riches, and wisdom, and strength, and honour, and glory, and blessing. Every creature which is in heaven, and on the earth, and under the earth, and such as are in the sea, and all that are in them, heard I saying, Blessing, and honour, and glory, and power, be unto him that sitteth upon the throne, and unto the Lamb for ever and ever. And the four beasts said, Amen. And the four and twenty elders fell down and worshipped him that liveth for ever and ever" (Revelation 5:1–10 BSB). Jesus won and was found worthy to receive the anointing to rule over both spirits and matter, a power the fallen cherub never had. Therefore, he has been made subject to the son of man. Jesus is now the lawful ruler of both visible and invisible universes. They belong to him. This is why he stated that "all power was given to me, in heaven and on earth." It was given to him to rule the worlds with the righteous, the blessed of God, and Satan can no longer annoy them. But until his kingdom is inaugurated on earth, Satan will keep his power over all created beings in the physical universe except for those who receive the anointing of power, the Holy Spirit. He can no longer go to heaven to accuse them. His tactic is to trick them to sin so that they can fall under his power.

CHAPTER 8

IGNORANCE OF SATAN AMONG THE CHRISTIANS

Because of lack of knowledge, I see people trying to face Satan's authority because they believe they're somehow his equal. This is a deadly mistake. In some circles, Satan is referred to as the ruler, which is accurate. Satan is still ruler of the lower realms, ruler of all fallen beings. Until Jesus comes to establish his kingdom on earth and throws the Satan, his angels, his demons, hell, and the grave in the lake of fire, Satan will still be a formidable foe, a foe from whose assaults only the Godhead, the Father, the Son, and the Holy Spirit, can protect the descendants of Adam. Satan knows that. He knows his power; he knows the laws of creation and how the government of God operates. And most importantly, he knows God at a level most created beings will never reach.

Satan was also anointed and appointed to oversee the angels and make sure they followed the rules. He was the prosecutor who knew the laws of God in the whole created universe. When Satan appeared to Jesus in the wilderness, he appeared as this overseer to test Jesus and see how he could make Jesus break the laws and rules of God. Since he could not find any sin in Jesus, and there was no Eve to give him access to Jesus' psyche, he had no power over him, and that bothered him. So, he set out to make Jesus break the law, which is the same tactics he used against the patriarch Adam. He taught it to his demons and his human servants to use against the Christians.

They are still using these tactics today. Satan has not changed. Satan is the tempter of all the created beings of the whole universe, even himself. Satan failed because he broke the first law, which states, *"Though shalt have no other God before me."* Satan failed because of his own temptation. While contemplating his beauty, Satan became his own idol and thus became his own god. As a result, the true God rejected him. However, he fell with his knowledge of the universe, his cunning, and his zeal. Satan never had to learn the laws of creation. They were part of his makeup, and as a sheriff with zeal, he existed to make sure the rest of creation obeyed them. That was part of his job in heaven.

When Satan fell from the heights, He was removed from his position in heaven. After he conquered Adam on earth, he used the laws of creation to build a kingdom. Everyone who fell for his temptation became part of his kingdom. Therefore, he is fully engaged in tempting other beings, making them break the laws of God. Satan brings everyone who falls for his temptation under his power. Satan has never tempted a created being outside of the laws of creation. His approach has always been to make his victim transgress the laws of justice and righteousness. He then uses this transgression to accuse them in front of the throne of God.

This is Satan's tactic to bring the creatures of God under his dominion. He makes them transgress. He has been using this strategy from his time in Heaven. There, he tempted the angels and was successful in making them reject God's rules and flagrantly betray him. Billions of them were found guilty and was expelled from their perfect domain. And once he was kicked out of heaven, he turned his attention to the only other place hospitable for life in the universe, —the earth of man. The same flaw that was found in Satan that warranted his expulsion was also present in Adam. He was a self-centered, self-satisfying being who revolted against the Father of fathers, and God of gods. He went after a knowledge that wasn't his, and lost his inheritance in the process.

Although Adam was created in the image of God and given dominion over the physical realm, the Spirit of the Lord had not entirely inhabited him. In the garden, he was in training and had a lot to learn. Adam had not reached maturity yet. He had to learn obedience! But before he could learn, Satan pushed him through the woman to break the only law given to him by God. By doing that, Adam became a transgressor, just like Satan. Thus, Satan trapped his entire lineage in that transgression. Adam was then numbered among the traitors and ended up on the list for destruction by the lake of fire. The only escapees among his descendants will be those who find grace and accept Jesus Christ and enter a marriage alliance with the Godhead.

No human can be saved without this alliance. Adam himself was redeemed in Christ Jesus and is awaiting the marriage of the Lamb. Therefore, if accepting Jesus Christ as your savior gives you eligibility to be counted among those worthy to escape the wrath of God by grace, don't squander it. In the previous passage, Paul was instructing the church that they were in a fight and needed to put on the gears of soldiers to engage the enemy. In the time of Paul, everyone understood that the Holy Spirit was the one who gave the strength and power to achieve this warrior status. After all, he is the person of the Godhead currently stationed on earth. Paul could have said, *"Dress yourselves with the Holy Spirit."*

Jesus ordered his apostles to do the same, but he used different wordings than elder Paul. Jesus urged them to wait until they are clothed with power. In contrast, in today's theology, the scoffers say it is not that serious; they do not need the Holy Spirit. They do not need power. They believe they are educated and can face Satan with their intellect. Hence, there is no war. The Christians need no power to do the work, as their armor is knowledge and prestige. The world is their friend, and thus, they can befriend and form alliances with the leaders in the world.

This theology is relaxed since there is no conflict. Satan is just a myth or another guy who we can conquer with knowledge and goodwill. The apostate church boasts that they don't need the Holy Spirit. Instead, they only need to love their neighbors. In this teaching, we aim to evaluate the effectiveness of this apostate church that claims that it does not need any power to function and do the works of God—the church that rejects the Holy Spirit.

Satan is not worrying about the church that keeps the Holy Spirit at bay. In fact, he welcomes them. They are his seeds. He will give them all the riches they want to keep them from seeking communion with God. Remember, the enemy is clever. His intelligence is beyond ours. He knows that the congregation of the saints starts with the Holy Spirit and ends with him. Anything else is counterfeit.

Satan fears only the Holy Spirit of God—the Spirit that makes the saints, not the saints or some son of Adam who thinks that he can intimidate Satan by screaming. Remember, Satan tackled some of the greatest saints in heaven and won their souls. These were beings of light and power who occupied high offices in heaven. Maintaining Adam's descendants under his control is a breeze compared to maintaining these angels of power. Yet, he has been doing it for millenniums. These beings of light that Satan subdued were already settled in the place you aspire to go live as a Christian. Satan's goal is to keep you from getting there. He is armed with an unimaginable power.

Satan's power is only surpassed by his hatred for our Father, our Lord Jesus Christ, and the sons of Adam in this world. His wish is that Adam and all his children go to the lake of fire with him. It is time we stop compromising. The only way to overcome Satan is to get drafted into the tree of good to become one of the seed of God through sanctification and be sealed by the Holy Spirit. The scoffers say that Satan has no power over them because of the cross. That is only true if there is no sin in your life, and you are sanctified and sealed by the Holy Spirit. But as long as you are living in this body of flesh, unsanctified and not sealed by the Holy Spirit, Satan has power over you.

THE SWORD OF THE SPIRIT

Every Christian needs to understand the government of heaven. It is the eternal government in charge of all creation. Satan is still part of that government and he will remain until Jesus returns to vanquish him into the depth of hell. The true Christian is protected from the power of Satan by the blood of the lamb and the power of the blood is the Holy Spirit. We have an entire generation of people who truly believe that the Holy Spirit only heals the sick because that is what they see on TV. They see the televangelists on TV healing people, telling them that is the only purpose of the Spirit of God. They diminished the Holy Spirit into some kind of spectator or their own personal assistant and exalt the Bible in his stead. They tell their followers to read the Word. While it is important to train in the tradition of the saints by reading the Word, the belief that only knowing the Bible is enough to lead one to victory is false.

However, don't believe I am bashing the Bible. The Bible, just like the law, is a schoolmaster showing the path of holiness, righteousness, and justice. Its purpose is to bring the repentant man to perfection. I believe someone anointed by the Holy Spirit should teach the Christians the word of God. They should learn to memorize it and know it. Not because it gives them the victory but because it is the sword that the Spirit wields to chase the enemy. The Spirit is he who gives them victory.

Hence, Paul explained to Timothy that the word is the tool used for sanctification and renewal of the mind in these verses, saying, *"But continue thou in the things which thou hast learned and hast been assured of, knowing of whom thou hast learned them; and that from a child thou hast known the holy scriptures, which are able to make thee wise unto salvation through faith which is in Christ Jesus. All scripture is given by inspiration of God, and is profitable for doctrine, for reproof, for correction, for instruction in righteousness: That the man of God may be perfect, thoroughly furnished unto all good works"* (2 Timothy 3:14–17 KJV).

In other words, elder Paul was saying, "Practice what you learned from the holy scriptures to empty yourself to become perfect to make room for the Holy Spirit." Take note of the word perfect here. It is the same word Jesus used for sanctification or holiness when commanding his disciples to be perfect. In the status quo, many teach that the Bible is what gives the Christian the victory over circumstances and battles. When in reality, only the Spirit of the word can wield that sword. When the Jewish leaders tried to elevate the word over the Son of God, Jesus confronted them, saying, *"Search the scriptures; for in them ye think ye have eternal life: and they are they which testify of me" (John 5:39 KJV).*

To confront the belief that one only needs to know the word of God to overcome in this war, I ask, what did the Christians of Acts have that made them so potent as Christians? Certainly, you cannot tell me they had the Bible-quoting system we've adopted today. The Bible was not compiled like what we have today. What did they have? Did Peter have our version of the Bible when he preached to the Jews and brought three-thousands of them to conversion? When seventeen-year-old Stephen faced the Jewish mob and perfectly connected the events of the Old Testament with the coming of Jesus to prove to them that Jesus was indeed the Christ they were waiting for and convicted them of his murder, he did not have a theological degree. Stephen did not have the epistles of the apostles. He only had the words of Moses. But he also had the courage and strength to endure stoning without running or complaining. How did he do that? By what force did he withstand the torture?

Stephen did not rehearse Biblical verses to respond to them. Where did he get the knowledge? The answer, my friend, is the Holy Spirit. The Holy Spirit gave him the precise words to say at that time. Jesus promised, *"On My account, you will be brought before governors and kings as witnesses to them and to the Gentiles. But when they hand you over, do not worry about how to respond or what to say. In that hour you will be given what to say. For it will not be you speaking, but the Spirit of your Father speaking through you" (Mathew 10:18–20 BSB).*

This is what I understood from this passage. Jesus wanted to say: "When you face death and persecution for my name, your Father's Spirit (the Holy Spirit) will activate the stored word in you, and you will simply have to let the words out." In times of such stress, the fear will overwhelm your intellect, and you will not know what to say. The only thing the intellect will do is to doubt and lose faith at such a time. If one goes back to the history of the church persecutions, the records are full of stories of intellectual Christians who gave up their faith at the sight of arms. Yet, the Spirit-filled Christian will be singing glory to God and songs of reassurance while they are being burned to death.

Furthermore, throughout my career, I have witnessed great intellectual Christians, doctors in theology, and men with great biblical knowledge, who, after studying the Bible for thirty years, renounced Jesus Christ. Their knowledge of the Bible did not generate faith or holiness. It proved to me that knowledge of the Bible alone only puffs up the self and puts men in high esteem but does not enlighten them spiritually. Without the anointing of the Holy Spirit to decode the word's spiritual meanings, intellectual knowledge of the word only serves to raise and grow the self. I have witnessed several so-called doctors of theology who quit Christianity and many more who stayed with a congregation but lost all faith in God. Hence, they only stayed and used their Christian knowledge to work as professional speakers to gain a salary and earn retirement benefits, not because they were seeking heaven.

The Holy Spirit is the one who gives meaning to the words of the Bible. He is the power of the Word, as he is the Spirit of the Word. He is the power that acts when you use the Word. He is sharper than the double-edged sword that Paul referred to when he stated, *"The word of God is living and active. Sharper than any double-edged sword, it pierces even to dividing soul and spirit, joints and marrow. It judges the thoughts and intentions of the heart"* (Hebrews 4:12 BSB).

The Holy Spirit is the life of the word. He is the one who activates it. The Holy Spirit is the manager, overseer, and director in the church of Jesus Christ. In other words, He is the boss of all these stewards who call themselves pastors. Hence, he is the true guide. When he is somewhere, he brings heaven with him. There is no going to heaven without him, for he is the seal that the people of God receive for the day of redemption. In Revelation 7:2–3 (BSB), we read, *"And I saw another angel ascending from the east, with the seal of the living God. And he called out in a loud voice to the four angels who had been given power to harm the land and the sea: 'Do not harm the land or sea or trees until we have sealed the foreheads of the servants of our God.'"*

After he sealed the 144,000 people from the tribes of Israel, the revelator states in verse 9, *"After this I looked and saw a multitude too large to count, from every nation and tribe and people and tongue, standing before the throne and before the Lamb. They were wearing white robes and were holding palm branches in their hands."* In Ephesians 4:30–31 (BSB), Paul clarified this when he said, *"And do not grieve the Holy Spirit of God, in whom you were sealed for the day of redemption. Get rid of all bitterness, rage and anger, outcry and slander, along with every form of malice."*

Are you one of these multitudes? You need to be sealed by the Holy Spirit to become part of this club. We will help you answer this question in the sections ahead.

Are You Ready for the Marriage of the Lamb?

As the old song says, "Keep your lamps trim and burning for the time is drawing near." Stand up for the fight! Learn to know your enemies and their disguises. Listen to the voice of the Lord. Trim your lamp, and keep it burning with the oil of the Holy Spirit. Jesus told his disciples to be ever vigilant because Satan, the adversary, is like a roaring lion who sets out to devour the children of God.

Jesus compared the coming of the kingdom of heaven, like the incident of the ten virgins who took their lamps and went forth to meet the bridegroom and explained the separation of the two groups in this wise saying: *"And five of them were wise, and five were foolish. They that were foolish took their lamps and took no oil with them: But the wise took oil in their vessels with their lamps. While the bridegroom tarried, they all slumbered and slept. And at midnight there was a cry made, Behold, the bridegroom cometh; go ye out to meet him. Then all those virgins arose and trimmed their lamps. And the foolish said unto the wise, give us of your oil; for our lamps are gone out. But the wise answered, saying, not so; lest there be not enough for us and you: but go ye rather to them that sell, and buy for yourselves. And while they went to buy, the bridegroom came; and they that were ready went in with him to the marriage: and the door was shut. Afterward came also the other virgins, saying, Lord, Lord, open to us. But he answered and said, verily I say unto you, I know you not. Watch therefore, for ye know neither the day nor the hour wherein the Son of man cometh"* (Matthew 25:1–13 BSB).

It's the time of the great divide! Where do you stand? Are you waiting for the groom's arrival? Are you among the wise virgins? Do you have oil in your lamp? The majority of Christians would ask, "What does Jesus mean by oil here?" I believe the oil he is referring to here is the anointing of the Holy Spirit, not the knowledge and philosophy we are taught to value so much today.

You may disagree with this answer. However, if you continue to read, you will soon come up with the same conclusion. These words are addressed to those who slumber and are asleep. Jesus may tarry, but the fact is that he is on his way. A large portion of the members of the body of Christ is swaying to the left. They have abandoned righteousness and adopted the liberal mindset of the world.

It is a tragedy to see the church losing its vigilance and perseverance. There is a cold chill in the congregations—they are already asleep. They are open and vulnerable to all the defective doctrines of hell. The question is, how did that happen? The answer may lie with the practices of the scribes and the teachers of our day!

CHAPTER 9

THE HIRED HAND AND THE TRUE SHEPHARD

Beware of false prophets, which come to you in sheep's clothing, but inwardly they are ravening wolves. Ye shall know them by their fruits. Do men gather grapes of thorns, or figs of thistles? Even so every good tree bringeth forth good fruit; but a corrupt tree bringeth forth evil fruit. A good tree cannot bring forth evil fruit, neither can a corrupt tree bring forth good fruit. Every tree that bringeth not forth good fruit is hewn down, and cast into the fire. Wherefore by their fruits ye shall know them. Not everyone that saith unto me, Lord, Lord, shall enter into the kingdom of heaven; but he that doeth the will of my Father which is in heaven. Many will say to me in that day, Lord, Lord, have we not prophesied in thy name? and in thy name have cast out devils? and in thy name done many wonderful works? And then will I profess unto them, I never knew you: depart from me, ye that work iniquity (Mathew 7: 15-23).

Notice that Jesus rebuked the miracle workers and told them that he did not know them. In this passage Jesus is trying to tell us that miracle working does not make one a Christian. To know Jesus, one's spirit should fellowship with his spirit. To be the Christian who knows Jesus, one needs to be born of the Spirit, the Holy Spirit. Jesus was well aware that his church would become filled with imposters, and he said that they would persist until the time of the harvest. Jesus said many leaders would be in this category because it is in their training. Their intellect is trained, not their spirit. It is customary for an inspired shepherd to go to a theological or Bible school to receive a degree to become a pastor. This is a well-established custom. In the evangelical world, church members call elders of their churches' pastor. Studying in a school to become a pastor is a tradition in my family as well. However, when applied to us, the word pastor can only be seen once in the Bible. In Ephesians 4:11, Paul told us, *"Now these are the gifts Christ gave to the church: the apostles, the prophets, the evangelists, and the pastors and teachers."*

Pay attention to the word gifts in this verse! It means that being a prophet, an evangelist, a pastor and a teacher are results of anointing gifts from the Holy Spirit. One cannot be made a prophet, an evangelist, a pastor or a teacher by a degree granting institution. They are not personality traits one acquires from genetics or training. They cannot be passed down from father to son. A pastor for instance is one who receives a shepherd's heart from the Holy Spirit to care for the sheep to the extent of even dying for them.

David was a true pastor. As a young boy, he was established as a shepherd to overlook the flock of his father. He fought for those sheep. He faced wild beasts to save those sheep. When this selflessness was needed in real life in Israel, David the boy was ready to face Goliath to defend Israel.

While Saul hid in his palace, the shepherd was willing to risk his life for the honor of his people. It happened because Saul was a king but not a pastor. They use the words shepherd, elder (elder as in older, mature in the faith), or overseer throughout the testaments. But I prefer the word shepherd because it takes a special kind of anointing to do this job.

The graduates of the theological schools want to be called pastor. However, they should ensure their roles as a shepherd or overseer first—because they are simply hired hands. Also, we must have reservations about this custom because not everyone can be a pastor—not everyone has the spiritual characteristics to be called one. A man cannot wake up one morning and decide to be a pastor. This role is assigned not based on intellectual training either. Remember, the intellect is the mind of the flesh, steeped in evil. You can only train the intellect to follow righteousness so it can surrender to the Spirit of light. In Acts 20:28 (BSB), Paul said, *"Take heed therefore unto yourselves, and to all the flock, over which the Holy Ghost hath made you overseers, to feed the church of God, which he hath purchased with his own blood."*

This means that the Holy Spirit is the one who selected the overseers in the churches of Acts and any legitimate church for that matter. In the status quo, however, theological schools train aspired church overseers and qualify them for the role. The question I always ask is, by what authority?

Don't you find it peculiar that a theological or Bible school created for the profit of a corporation owned by unbelievers has the right to make that decision? However, the number of pastors in the world today greatly outnumbers the number of apostles and evangelists combined. This is because the training of pastors is big business. Some theological schools charge $50,000 and up to train one pastor.

Well, having the Holy Spirit do it for free wouldn't be good for business. Also, whoever trains the future leaders can pass down their doctrine to the future congregation these future leaders would influence. For these denominations to pass down their rhetoric to the new generations, they build theological schools. And so, the Baptists train pastors to preach the rhetoric of the Baptists. The Seventh-Day Adventists do the same, and the list goes on.

The theological institutions have removed the Holy Spirit as the appointer of overseers in the church—the only one who can test hearts and assigns gifts to men according to their spiritual capacities. They've replaced him with intellectual men blinded by lust, men who don't believe in the power of God. They pass their intellectual beliefs down to the future leaders, who teach the current church members to be intellectuals, creating a congregation void of all spiritual training.

If you don't believe in the Holy Spirit, who gave you the authority to select those who will be pastors of Jesus Christ's church, and by what wisdom do you know who is fit for the role? Where did you get the authority to ordain pastors? The government? Shouldn't the Holy Spirit appoint those pastors as he did for Jesus, Peter, Paul, and all the others before our time? The theological teaching of today is void of all mentions of the Holy Spirit and his role in the church of Jesus Christ. They have a system. They teach the future leaders about their denomination's philosophy, how to be diplomatic, how to analyze the word, how to prepare great speeches, how to prepare financial budgets, and how to manage a corporation.

Moreover, they teach the students ancient languages, such as Greek and Hebrew, but never about how to be filled with the Holy Spirit and the power he brings with him. Those students then receive a classic philosophical and business training but no training on serving and pleasing the Lord God. The consensus is that the church does not need the Holy Spirit. Hence, the pastor can oversee the church operations. These schools fail to teach their students that Jesus Christ is he who sets the agenda of the true church. They failed to inform them that without the Holy Spirit, who connects the church to the mind of the blessed Jesus, they will not have access to how the master thinks the church should operate. So, these theological students become pastors and business managers.

Consequently, these people are managing the church of Jesus as a corporation, as a pyramid of authority, disregarding the fact that Jesus ordered his disciples never to operate his church as the gentiles operate their institutions. The church of Jesus Christ is a community of brothers equally yoked with one another, not an institution. Jesus called them aside and said, *"You know that the rulers of the Gentiles lord it over them, and their superiors exercise authority over them. It shall not be this way among you. Instead, whoever wants to become great among you must be your servant, and whoever wants to be first among you must be your slave just as the Son of Man did not come to be served, but to serve, and to give His life as a ransom for many" (Mathew 20:25–28 BSB).*

The leaders unconsciously aim to replace Jesus, his teachings, and the Holy Spirit in the church altogether; not that this comes from them. It is Satan's strategy to replace the real Jesus with his counterfeit. In John 15:5 (BSB), Jesus says, *"Apart from me you can do nothing."* Yet, this statement is widely ignored or misunderstood. Jesus simply meant that no one could act independently of him to please the Father. The only direct connection one has with Jesus is the Holy Spirit.

How can a pastor then reject the Holy Spirit and believe he is following the plan of the Father? The answer is that he is receiving directions from someone else. When I was in Bible school, I was taught that a regular church, instead of being governed by Jesus, is governed by the pastor or by the mission with which it is affiliated. However, my research revealed that Jesus is the great and only Pastor of the flock. He is the one who died for humanity. Since he is not present in the body, the Holy Spirit assigns a human body as the steward of the congregation to play the role of a pastor, but there are no two pastors of the church. Jesus stated in John 10:11–18 (BSB): *"I am the good shepherd. The good shepherd lays down his life for the sheep. The hired hand is not the shepherd and does not own the sheep. So, when he sees the wolf coming, he abandons the sheep and runs away. Then the wolf attacks the flock and scatters it. The man runs away because he is a hired hand and cares nothing for the sheep. I am the good shepherd; I know my sheep and my sheep know me. Just as the Father knows me and I know the Father and I lay down my life for the sheep. I have other sheep that are not of this sheep pen. I must bring them also. They too will listen to my voice, and there shall be one flock and one shepherd. The reason my Father loves me is that I lay down my life only to take it up again. No one takes it from me, but I lay it down of my own accord. I have authority to lay it down and authority to take it up again. This command I received from my Father."*

In Bible school, my teachers taught me that in the independent church, the pastors are in charge. They determine which direction the church takes. However, I witnessed that many of these theological graduates are novices with no spiritual maturity. Men with great pride and prestige who want to make a name for themselves, rub shoulders with the influential men of the world and be looked at as community leaders. They direct the church toward pleasing the world instead of pleasing the God of gods.

These men, whose goals are to become important and famous, rejected the supervision of the Holy Spirit to give way to their egos. Thus, they become conceded. Hence, their ego is 100 percent in charge, and it grows bigger with every passing day. Without the Holy Spirit, they operate in the darkness of a spiritually blind man. I have met several pastors who complain that they are important leaders in the community and don't get the recognition they deserve.

It means they are not paid enough—their houses are not big enough, or their cars are not nice enough, etc. Others graduate from a theological school after accumulating great debts they must repay. With that mindset, they create churches. Since they have the government's permission and the okay of the theological institutions where they receive the diploma to do so, they don't need God. They merely need to be well dressed and eloquent.

Once the church entity is formed, which is normally a corporation in the United States, they either operate it independently or join with a mission. Similarly, they aim to have big churches, but they don't want Jesus in charge either way. The more members they have, the more important they become. They believe that gathering many people in one place is what pleases the Lord. In this case, the pastors don't make quality Christians to fill the church. Instead, they go for quantity, the more, the merrier.

Jesus is not seeking a crowd who do not obey his words but those who are sanctified, the doers of the Word. Instead of lifting Jesus as Moses lifted the serpent in the desert, the leaders lift themselves, and people follow. They raise themselves as icons in front of the people and the world. "Everyone looks at me! All eyes on me!" And when they fail, they provide the world with more reasons to give Jesus a bad name.

Moreover, their fall sometimes takes half of the congregation with it. They don't act as stewards; instead, they act like owners. They are not imitating Jesus's behavior with his disciples. Jesus did not aim to be famous during his ministry. He blended perfectly with his disciples. He resembled them such that it took Judas, who was one of them, to identify him to the Roman guards when they came to arrest him in the garden of Gethsemane.

Don't think I am generalizing! Just as in the time of Elijah, there are faithful servants of God who are operating honest churches throughout the world. In these churches, the pastors recognize that they are only stewards of the congregation and if they love Jesus, they need to feed his flock. They need to obey Jesus' command to Peter, after his resurrection. Jesus, standing in front of Simon's boat and the fishes he'd netted, asked Simon Peter, *'Simon son of John, do you love Me more than these?' 'Yes, Lord,' he answered, 'You know I love You.' Jesus replied, 'Feed My lambs.' Jesus asked a second time, 'Simon son of John, do you love Me?' 'Yes, Lord,' he answered, 'You know I love You.' Jesus told him, 'Shepherd My sheep.' Jesus asked a third time, 'Simon son of John, do you love Me?' Peter was deeply hurt that Jesus had asked him a third time, 'Do you love Me?' 'Lord, you know all things,' he replied. 'You know I love You.' Jesus said to him, 'Feed My sheep.'"* (John 21:15–17 BSB).

Jesus asked Peter to make a choice between his material possessions and the ministry. He also asked him to preach the message of the cross to his sheep, teach them to walk the path of holiness to receive the Spirit's baptism, and then send them to duplicate the process. However, for the modern preacher, the message of the cross is too simple. Thus, they dilute it with philosophy. They become philosophers, trying to explain God through the intellect.

They mix the Word of God with all kinds of nationalism, all kinds of doctrines, and all kinds of philosophies. Where have they learned to do that if not from Satan? You can't tell me that they learned it from Elder Paul. There isn't an epistle from the New Testament where Elder Paul tried to philosophize the nature of God to show us God. As was that of all the apostles, his focus was Jesus Christ and his cross.

Jesus had straightened the thinking of his disciples on this issue by teaching them that one did not need to know God—that one only needed to know Jesus the Christ. It pleased God to gather every man in Jesus Christ, and then Jesus Christ would introduce the kind to him at the wedding of the Lamb.

Pay close attention to what Jesus said to Thomas. *"'Lord,' said Thomas, 'we do not know where You are going, so how can we know the way?' Jesus answered, 'I am the way, the truth, and the life. No one comes to the Father except through Me. If you had known Me, you would know My Father as well. From now on you do know Him and have seen Him.' Then Philip said to Him, 'Lord, show us the Father, and that will be enough for us.' Jesus replied, 'Philip, I have been with you all this time, and still, you do not know Me? Anyone who has seen Me has seen the Father. How can you say, "Show us the Father"?'"* (John 14:5 to 9 BSB).

In today's theology, the teachers are trying to bypass Jesus to go to the Father. Then again, this is Satan's tactic. He tries to render the cross of Jesus of no effect. Jesus knows what he is doing, and he is calling his people from this chaos to get ready for the Pentecost. Some churches have already heard the call to give Jesus and the Holy Spirit full charge. In these churches, the shepherds are stewards. The message of the cross is preached, and people are sanctified and filled with the Holy Spirit.

The shepherds don't have the final say in anything, but Jesus does. They love Jesus more than fame, money, power, and prestige. They listen to the Holy Spirit to feed Jesus's sheep the right food. However, they are few. They make up about 10 percent of the global churches. They do not have large and luxurious buildings to attract the masses. They look almost primitive in appearance. But they never bow to Satan and his demons.

If you are one of those who have not conceded to Satan and his system, I urge you to keep up the good fight and continue in the race without looking back. You are not alone! You may not have a big church, but you need to take care of what you have and obey the command of Jesus to feed his sheep. Remember that the battle rages on, and it is a fight to the end.

Be of good courage! Charge to the finish line to meet the Master with the crowns. I am not writing to offend anyone but to instruct the people of God on how to recognize the daughters of Babylon and the true church of Jesus Christ. A church that denies the presence and power of the Holy Spirit, he who is the power of God, the beginner and the finisher of the faith of the people of God, is not serving Jesus. Because to believe in the divine nature of Jesus and that he is indeed the Christ, one must be convinced by the Holy Spirit.

The Holy Spirit is the only one who can reveal the faithful Jesus. Otherwise, the Christian will believe in the counterfeit whose spirit has been at work in the world for two thousand years now. Also, without conviction that Jesus is the Christ and the only way to God, one is susceptible to believe false doctrines introduced by the demons. These doctrines shift the focus of the church onto material comforts and patriotic allegiance to earthly countries, not heaven.

And thus, without the Holy Spirit, we have lukewarm Christians operating carnal churches to accomplish Satan's mission. In this matter, elder Paul instructed Timothy by saying, *"In the last days men will be lovers of themselves, lovers of money, boastful, arrogant, abusive, disobedient to their parents, ungrateful, unholy, unloving, unforgiving, slanderous, without self-control, brutal, without love of good, traitorous, reckless, conceited, lovers of pleasure rather than lovers of God, having a form of godliness but denying its power. Turn away from such as these! They are the kind who worm their way into households and captivate vulnerable women weighed down with sins and led astray by various passions"* (2 Timothy 3:3–5 BSB).

"But denying its power" means they deny the Holy Spirit. The power of godliness is the Holy Spirit. The various passions are derived from lust, sexual lust and lust for money, material things, power, and fame. In this passage, Elder Paul described the prevalent characters within the atmosphere of the current churches. For the judgment of God starts in the churches, these characters must be revealed for the revelation of the wheat and the tares.

The other way the churches are operated involves a mission. When a mission oversees the church, its leaders manage the church's finances and doctrinal views. Nonetheless, the Holy Spirit is not in charge; the mission is! And the controllers are people the church members never met and they determine the spiritual direction of the church based upon the philosophy of their theology. Some missions even choose the subjects of the sermons the church pastor should preach on any given Sunday. They are setting the agenda of these churches. But who is setting the agenda of these missions?

In this setting, the church is operating as a franchise. There is no room for inspiration from the Holy Spirit. They don't pray to be changed by the Holy Spirit so that he can inhabit them. These franchisees believe that their natural leadership skills or what they learned at the theological school can do the trick. They think they are self-sufficient. So, since they are not seeking righteousness, justice, and sanctification themselves, they do not teach the flock to seek it, making it irrelevant.

While their intellectual capacities are growing by leaps and bound, their spiritual state doesn't get better; it gets worse. These missions run as business institutions in a pyramidal spiral and are philosophy-oriented. Therefore, their philosophy determines the spiritual state of the churches of which they are in charge, not the cross. Likewise, in the independent churches, the doctrine of the theological school from which the pastor graduated influences his spiritual state. As a result, it also determines the spiritual state of the congregations. But there is no spirituality, no Holy Spirit in their theology.

This is a perfect formula for worldly-minded churches. If the spiritual head is not focusing on holiness, the churches cannot either. Likewise, if the pastors are not focusing on holiness, the individual church can't either. These churches then become carnal and community institutions and perfect establishments to introduce false doctrines. The preachers preach the prosperity gospel, the "once saved, always saved" gospel, the "independence from the Holy Spirit" doctrine, the "there is no rapture" doctrine, the "no holiness, righteousness, and justice needed to see Jesus" doctrine, the "all roads lead to heaven" doctrine, the "hell does not exist" doctrine, and more.

When the true master, the Holy Spirit is absent, the churches then fall under the complete mercy of the specters of hell, the demons of the letter. The people focus only on learning the verses of the Bible. But Elder Paul, who wrote most of the letters that comprise the New Testament, told the Corinthians the following: *"And we have such trust through Christ toward God. Not that we are sufficient of ourselves to think of anything as being from ourselves, but our sufficiency is from God, who also made us sufficient as ministers of the new covenant, not of the letter but of the Spirit; for the letter kills, but the Spirit gives life" (2 Corinthians 3:4–6 NKJV).*

Pay attention to the words in this verse. The new covenant is of the Spirit! That is why modern churches have become so vulnerable to false doctrines. They are still relying on the letters, not the Spirit. Yet Paul stated that *"the letter kills, and the life come from the Spirit"*. However, they give no thoughts to these words. The Holy Spirit manages the covenant. He is the counselor and manager of the church. Yet, modern teachers are appointed as overseers of the churches by human organizations and consider the overseer of the new covenant as just a visitor among them. Since the Holy Spirit is the only one who can keep the demons at bay and the only one Satan truly fears, the pastors are powerless without him. Unlike elder Paul, they believe in the self, the puppet of Satan, and they operate on feelings, not on the Spirit of life, the counselor, comforter, revealer of mysteries, and the Spirit of power, the Holy Spirit.

In Acts 20:28 (BSB), elder Paul tells us that the Holy Spirit is he who appoints the overseers of the churches of Pentecost. This means he is not a simple spectator. He is the Boss! If one's appointment does not come from him, he is not in his employment. The Holy Spirit is the Boss.

As we will see in later chapters of this teaching, even Jesus knew he was the Boss. However, the modern theological system appoints these men who don't believe in God to teach man's doctrines. They remove the Holy Spirit from the church to clear the way for the Antichrist. The hired hands thus overstep their authority and fail to understand their true purpose as stewards—not pastors. Jesus said it best: *"The hired hand is not the shepherd and does not own the sheep. So, when he sees the wolf coming, he leaves the sheep and runs away."* Or better yet, he makes a deal with the wolf to restrain the presence of the true master. Animated by the spirit of Judas, he sells the sheep to the wolf. The wolf lets the hired hand be, letting him grow rich, fat, and famous, while he infiltrates the flock to devour the sheep one by one.

The Tale of Two Churches

How does this happen, you might ask? The false shepherds stop telling the sheep about the dangers of hell, the snares that Satan put in place to trap them, and the barrage of legions of warrior demons attacking them to gain their souls as trophies to bring them to hell. Instead, they tell them that there is no Satan or hell, that their adversary is poverty, and that they can conquer that just by becoming intellectuals. The wolf is Satan. The sheep is the church.

The hired hands are the pastors who rejected the management of the Holy Spirit. In the culture of the liberal megachurches of today, many pastors reject the Holy Spirit. They fail to acknowledge him as the protector of the integrity and holiness of the church. They embrace the spirit of self and prosperity. Satan makes them an offer they cannot refuse. He offers them heaven on earth, which includes wealth, glory, power, and fame. He offered the same things to Jesus, but Jesus was filled with the Holy Spirit and was from heaven above.

Jesus rejected the spirit of Satan vehemently. But since the current pastors reject the Holy Spirit, don't believe in the resurrection of the dead, can't see heaven, and see the world as their heaven, they gladly accept Satan's offer. Therefore, the hired hand (the steward) proclaims himself to be the real pastor in the absence of the Holy Spirit, replacing Jesus altogether.

CHAPTER 10

THE LUKEWARM WORSHIPER

When the Holy Spirit is not in charge, the Christians do not communicate with Jesus. Jesus does not set the agenda—the wolf does. When the Holy Spirit is absent, the wolf spirit takes over. The church then starts to embrace doctrines that are not of God. They stop seeking the presence of God. They become like the world—unjust, unrighteous, full of vices, and seeking worldly blessings instead of the kingdom of God. They become trending—accepting any new lifestyles the world proposes. They become lukewarm.

I visited a few churches once for the research I was conducting for this book. I interviewed a few members of the churches to find out the level of selfishness in the church. I found that most of the members of the churches I surveyed were egocentric, entangled in a narcissistic web of deception. The spirit of self-anoints them. They go to church to ask God to satisfy their desires. It's all about them. Some revealed that they came to church because they liked the pastor, the music, and the people. They came to have a good time. Some revealed that they came to be blessed. Some others revealed that they were seeking healing. Some others told me that they came to receive a miracle. The fact that they were members was pretty unsettling.

I sampled almost three hundred individuals in a population of nine hundred for the five churches I visited. They all came to receive something, not to know Jesus, to bless Jesus, or to offer their due sacrifice to the Father. They are either there for healing, to ask God for a great job, or to ask God for a blessing of some sort. Even while in church, they are not thinking about God. Their minds are on their gains. They think about the materials they need or what they will do during the day or next week. They are distracted. Their worship is self-centered. They don't worship God out of gratitude, but instead, they go to church to demand something from him as if they are entitled.

They treat God the same way you would treat a servant: "Hey, God, fetch me a new job, fetch me a new husband, fetch me a new wife, etc." God told the prophets, *"These people draw near to Me with their mouths and honor Me with their lips, but their hearts are far from Me. Their worship of Me is but rules taught by men. Therefore, I will again confound these people with wonder upon wonder. The wisdom of the wise will vanish, and the intelligence of the intelligent will be hidden"* (Isaiah 29:13; Ezekiel 33:31; Matthew 15:7 BSB).

Likewise, in our churches, the people worship God with rules taught by man. For instance, many church leaders teach the people that it is important to tithe and give offerings to the church as a form of worship, but they fail to tell them that they need to be sanctified before they draw near the altar. Jesus told his disciples, *"Therefore if you are offering your gift at the altar and there remember that your brother has something against you, leave your gift there before the altar. First go and be reconciled to your brother; then come and offer your gift"* (Matthew 5:23–24 BSB).

However, we do things differently in our churches today. We bring offerings to the altar while we are involved in all types of quarrels with our neighbors. We approach the throne of God without repenting of our sins. We eat the supper of the Lord without confessing our sins. We draw near to God with our lips singing "We Love You Lord" while having some sort of hatred in our hearts for our neighbors. We place demands to God in our songs asking Him to "Open the Eyes of Our Hearts". But we keep the Holy Spirit who can do that at bay. We pray and ask, "We want to get close to you God," but refuse to become sanctified. Yet, sanctification has never been more important in the believer's life in this time of the great divide, for the Lord Jesus is coming. When he comes to call his own in the air, only those who are sanctified and filled with the Holy Spirit will hear the call. But people who do not have the Holy Spirit will be deceived by the man of sin. The one who will be revealed to take leadership of those who depart from the faith. Because apostle Paul warned the Thessalonians, saying, *"Let no man deceive you by any means: for that day shall not come, except there comes a falling away first, and that man of sin be revealed, the son of perdition"* (2 Thessalonians 2:1–3 KJV).

The falling away is currently happening in this generation. As the believers get involved in the race for earthly prosperity, prestige, and wealth, they stop searching for heaven. Their entire focus has shifted to worldly feelings of pride and wealth—those perishable things that will mean nothing in the soon-coming eternity. The teachers teach them how to be influential in business, politics, or other areas in this perishable world. But they refused to teach them how to become intimate with God, the only savior. They are not looking for the world to come or the eternal treasure. They prefer what they see in this world so they focus on the eating, the drinking, and the merriments of the world. Like the Sadducees, they don't believe in the resurrection of the dead.

It is the mindset of a Christian who does not have the Holy Spirit. They can't help it because the Spirit of heaven is far from them. Jesus ordered the apostles to avoid worrying about material things saying, *"Therefore take no thought, saying, what shall we eat? or, what shall we drink? or, wherewithal shall we be clothed? For after all these things the Gentiles seek. For your heavenly Father knows that you need all these things. But seek ye first the kingdom of God, and his righteousness; and all these things shall be added unto you"* (Mathew 6:31–33 BSB).

Jesus himself was seeking the kingdom of God and was teaching his disciples the secret that earned King Solomon more riches than any man who lived before him and who would live after him.

When God visited Solomon on that fateful night after building the temple, He told the king to ask him anything he wanted. The wise king asked for a just heart, righteousness, and understanding. The king answered and said, *"Therefore give Your servant an understanding heart to judge Your people and to discern between good and evil. For who is able to govern this great people of Yours?"* And the Lord God replied, *"Since you have asked for this instead of requesting long life or wealth for yourself or death for your enemies—but you have asked for discernment to administer justice, behold, I will do what you have asked. I will give you a wise and discerning heart, so that there will never have been anyone like you, nor will there ever be. Moreover, I will give you what you did not request, both riches and honor, so that during all your days no man in any kingdom will be your equal. So, if you walk in My ways and keep My statutes and commandments, just as your father David did, I will prolong your days"* (1 Kings 3:9–13 BSB).

Pay attention to the condition here. Solomon's hand of the contract was to walk in God's ways and keep his statutes and commandments. If he did those things, God would give him a long life. Solomon failed to keep his hand of the bargain, he died at 75 while his father David died at 120. Solomon asked for heavenly qualities as a king, and he received greatness and riches in return. Solomon was given unfathomable wealth that would baffle even the greatest billionaire in our day. His wealth could not be counted. Also, in Jeremiah 45:5, the prophet told Israel, *"But as for you, do you seek great things for yourself? Stop seeking! For I will bring disaster on every living creature, declares the LORD, but wherever you go I will grant your life as plunder."*

Solomon received more wealth than he could count, but when death the destroyer came, he had to give it all away and go to his grave alone and poor. Jesus did not want that for his disciples. He wanted his disciples to focus on everlasting wealth. Jesus wanted them to focus on a different land where death, the destroyer could not reach, a different world and system. He told them that wherever their worries were, there also would their focus be.

Jesus did not want his disciples to focus on what would grow the material part of man but on what would grow the spiritual side of him. He wanted the disciples to establish a relationship with the Maker, Giver, and Owner of all things, God the Father. Once they had established a Father-and-son relationship with God just as he (Jesus) did, everything else would naturally flow. They would have access to whatever they wanted in the material universe for the asking. The key to developing this intimacy with God is the Holy Spirit. So, if you want to understand, the Holy Spirit is all the riches a man needs.

Some people are surprised about the recent rise of liberality in the church. However, it did not surprise me. When the Spirit of righteousness and justice is absent, the spirits of uncleanness and injustice take over. In Romans 1:21–32 (BSB), we read, *"Because that, when they knew God, they glorified him not as God, neither were thankful; but became vain in their imaginations, and their foolish heart was darkened. Professing themselves to be wise, they became fools, and changed the glory of the incorruptible God into an image made like to corruptible man, and to birds, and four-footed beasts, and creeping things. Wherefore God also gave them up to uncleanness through the lusts of their own hearts, to dishonor their own bodies between themselves. Who changed the truth of God into a lie and worshipped and served the creature more than the Creator, who is blessed forever Amen. For this cause God gave them up unto vile affections: for even their women did change the natural use into that which is against nature: And likewise, also the men, leaving the natural use of the woman, burned in their lust one toward another; men with men working that which is unseemly, and receiving in themselves that recompense of their error which was meet. "And even as they did not like to retain God in their knowledge, God gave them over to a reprobate mind, to do those things which are not convenient. Being filled with all unrighteousness, fornication, wickedness, covetousness, maliciousness; full of envy, murder, debate, deceit, malignity; whisperers, Backbiters, haters of God, despiteful, proud, boasters, inventors of evil things, disobedient to parents, without understanding, covenant breakers, without natural affection, implacable, unmerciful, who knowing the judgment of God, that they which commit such things are worthy of death, not only do the same, but have pleasure in them that do them."*

I don't think elder Paul was addressing the world here. The world does not know God. Elder Paul addressed those who already know the true God, or should I say those who should have known the truth. He refers to the selfish or reprobate church, the church that denied the Spirit of God. Pay attention to the phrase "when they knew God, they glorified him not as God, neither were thankful." It means that they had a revelation of God but rejected it. It addresses the reprobate Christians who failed to worship him in spirit and truth after learning about God, but instead, they turned their worship to the self and the material world. The religious church is serving the self; it is its current idol.

Thus, the church buildings are full of bodies, but few people born again can be found. The mindset of Christians today is self-sufficiency. Hence, they have a vain mind. As a result, they are seeking material things from God. These Christians are taught to pay God in exchange for material blessings. The philosophy is that if you do not pay God, He will not bless you. They develop formulas on how much to give to God if you want to receive a certain amount. They are trying to force the hand of God for financial blessings while they ignore the true blessing, who is the Holy Spirit.

Don't get me wrong! I am not against seed sowing or tithing. They are principles put into place to give the sons of Adam a way to break the curse of poverty in their lives. When properly used, they can grow the Christian Nation materially, but material things on earth should never be the quest of the Christian nation. So, Jesus ordered, *"But seek ye first the kingdom of God, and his righteousness; and all these things shall be added unto you."*

By all these things, Jesus was referring to material things. Jesus commanded that material things should never be the focus; heaven should be. Whatever material blessing we are seeking should be to benefit the whole. The Holy Spirit inspired the first Christians to bring everything they had to the apostles so that everyone could share them. As we read in Acts 4: 32-34, *"And the multitude of them that believed were of one heart and of one soul: neither said any of them that ought of the things which he possessed was his own; but they had all things common. And with great power gave the apostles witness of the resurrection of the Lord Jesus: and great grace was upon them all. Neither was there any among them that lacked: for as many as were possessors of lands or houses sold them, and brought the prices of the things that were sold."*

In Luke 11:11–13 (BSB), Jesus instructs the crowd on what blessing to ask of the Father, saying: *"What father among you, if his son asks for a fish, will give him a snake instead? Or if he asks for an egg, will give him a scorpion? So, if you who are evil know how to give good gifts to your children, how much more will your Father in heaven give the Holy Spirit to those who ask Him!"*

Notice that Jesus did not say to ask the Father for material things but the Spirit of discernment, humility, Justice, righteousness and life. The true blessing is the Holy Spirit whose presence brings the fragrance of heaven on earth. The great majority of today's church population proclaimed that they have surrender to God, but they refuse to comply with his conditions. They refuse to obey his laws. Most of today's church leaders believe that they are operating in the Spirit, but they cannot tell which. One of the reasons Jesus was successful in his mission on earth was the fact that he was able to distinguish between spirits. For instance, in Luke 9:54-55 KJV, we read, *"And when his disciples James and John saw this, they said, Lord, wilt thou that we command fire to come down from heaven, and consume them, even as Elias did? But he turned, and rebuked them, and said, Ye know not what manner of spirit ye are of."* As we have seen earlier, Jesus rebuked Peter after Satan's spirit used him to advise the Lord to veer from the path to Calvary: "But Jesus turned and said to Peter, "Get behind Me, Satan! You are a stumbling block to Me. For you do not have in mind the things of God, but the things of men (Matthew 16:23 BSB)". Sadly, the carnal Peter thought he was in the will of God at that moment. Little did he know, Satan was whispering in his ears compelling him to advice the Lord Jesus to abandon his mission. The current church leadership have devised plans to gather large quantity of people in their churches but fail to teach them. To avoid falling into the traps of Satan, it is important that the Christian operates in the Spirit of Jesus. Apostle Paul advised the Philippians in these words: "Let this mind be in you, which was also in Christ Jesus (Philippians 2:5 KJV)". Wake up, oh church, and return to the true God! Learn of him! He will teach you how-to discern which spirits are operating in your congregations. Then you will be able to discern the will of God for you. If you want to serve the true God, get out from among those who rejected the Holy Spirit. If a church rejects the Holy Spirit, it also rejects Jesus the Christ and his Father, for they work together. Hence, such a church does not serve Jesus. It is animated by a different spirit.

CHAPTER 11

'Tis not by Might nor by Power

The prophet Zechariah spoke thus unto Zerubbabel. *"Thus saith the word of the LORD to Zerubbabel: Not by might nor by power, but by My Spirit, says the LORD of Hosts" (Zechariah 4:6 BSB).* This is one of the greatest revelations God can give to a man. He revealed the secret of creation to Zerubbabel. Moreover, He revealed the tool He used to create the whole universe and the power behind everything He does. It is all done by the Spirit—the Holy Spirit. The Holy Spirit might be a mystery to the world, but to the sons of God, we know him as a manager, counselor, advocate, and more.

The Holy Spirit has charge of all the multiverses that God created. Therefore, he is the manager of everything in creation. In my first year of Bible college, I met a few elders at a Bible study who sowed a thought in my mind that still reverberates twenty years later. They urged me to remember that the Holy Spirit is the general manager of the church of Jesus Christ. One of them told me, "If your church is not being governed by the Holy Spirit, it is not for Jesus Christ." He said that the Holy Spirit decides who fits into what ministry and that he assigns them to that ministry, as elder Paul illustrates in 1 Corinthians 12:4–11 (BSB).

The Bible passage states that *"There are different kinds of gifts, but the same Spirit distributes them. There are different kinds of service, but the same Lord. There are different kinds of working, but in all of them and in everyone it is the same God at work. Now to each one the manifestation of the Spirit is given for the common good. To one there is given through the Spirit a message of wisdom, to another a message of knowledge by means of the same Spirit, to another faith by the same Spirit, to another gifts of healing by that one Spirit, to another miraculous powers, to another prophecy, to another distinguishing between spirits, to another speaking in different kinds of tongues, and still to another the interpretation of tongues. All these are the work of one and the same Spirit, and He distributes them to each one, just as He determines."*

The Holy Spirit assigns all gifts for the functioning of the church. The men covered several Bible passages that proved the Holy Spirit had a greater role in managing the early church during the Bible study. For instance, the men took Acts 13:2 (BSB) to illustrate that the Holy Spirit is the one who qualified and selected the church ministers. The passage read, *"Set apart for me Barnabas and Paul for the work to which I have called them."* They used this passage to show that the Holy Spirit is the one who assigned ministries and church management positions to people, not the government, the clergy, a theological degree, a school, or a man-made mission.

The Holy Spirit is he who ordains everyone, they said. They also took the example of the passage in Acts 5:3-10 to show how Peter remitted Ananias and Sapphira, his wife, unto the judgment of the Holy Spirit. After Satan had influenced their hearts to lie about the true price of the field they sold to give the proceeds to contribute to funding the church, Peter told them, "It is not to me that you have lied but to the Holy Spirit," before he sentenced both to death.

Afterward, they asked me to explain to them why today's church is so autonomous of the Holy Spirit and why they create their own agenda and kick the Holy Spirit out. While their approach was a bit unorthodox, they succeeded in puzzling me. I couldn't give an educated answer. The discussion shook my foundation, to say the least.

Here I was being trained to be a pastor, but I barely knew anything about the Holy Spirit's function in the church. Indeed, I read that Jesus promised to send him as an advocate, a counselor, and a comforter, but the manager angle was new to me. The elders had planted the seed in my mind, and now it was for me to verify their claims. We never studied the role of the Holy Spirit in the church at my school. We discussed denominational doctrines but not the Holy Spirit. I had heard about the Holy Spirit before but only as a healer. As the elders pointed out, I didn't know about him as the one in charge of the church.

My Quest for the Truth

After this encounter, I realized I did not know enough. I started researching vehemently. In my early research, I heard the testimony of an ex-Satanist (Freemason) who converted into a Christian. In his testimony, he said that 80 percent of the churches in the world belonged to Satan. He knew this because when he was practicing witchcraft as a Freemason, he dealt with Satan, who gave him certain powers. He said that Satan first gave him a large sum of money, so he became rich overnight. He used part of the money to open a big church and a theological school. To fill the church with people, Satan gave him the power to make people prosper. His church grew, and Satan gave him a higher degree of power. His second degree of power was to be able to cast out devils out of people. The third degree was to be able to heal people. The fourth degree was the ability to curse his enemies. However, the miracles were all illusions worked out by demons.

For instance, when he cast out demons, the demons would not leave the body. They would loosen their grip on that person for a while but would come back later and manifest differently. Likewise, when he healed someone, the demons would transfer that disease from one person to another in the congregation. He claimed that there are many unsuspecting churches operating under the same guise and are entirely under the control of Satan.

Satan is the one that these leaders serve through secret societies like Freemasonry, Rosicrucianism, and others. And he sets their

The Tale of Two Churches

agenda; he is their counselor. It was hard for me to accept this claim. But the same testimonies kept on coming from different witch doctors, ex-Satanists, and members of secret societies who got saved from all over the world, Africa, the Americas, Europe, and Asia. They all had the same theme. They all testify that Satan has churches disguised as churches of God all over the world.

They instruct the Christians on how to recognize these churches. This is how you will recognize them, they said. Their focus will be on prosperity, fame, prestige, and power as they seek their place in this world. All their sermons will be about prosperity. They will neglect worship or shorten it. They will sing ambiguous songs that do not worship God. They will be boastful, selfish, and philosophical.

The pastors who run these churches will never mention the blood of Jesus, meditate on his sacrifice, or mention sanctification in their sermons. They will reject the supervision of the Holy Spirit. Their sermons will contain the deep wisdom of man, and they will use the Bible to corroborate their claims as theological secrets to make people better. They won't teach sanctification, but they will always have some eastern philosophy to replace the cross, to make it of no effect. Those ex-witches, magicians, and warlocks whom the Lord snatched out of Satan's camp to reveal the truth to his people testify and say that the leadership of these churches is profit-driven. Their theology does not include the cross, and their congregations' fellowship has nothing to do with strengthening each other's faith.

These people's gathering is a session on public relations and business networking. They are strangers that gather together for a couple of hours per week to fake holiness. They care about the money. They aim to instruct people on how to be better earth citizens. They don't care about the poor, the homeless, the rejected, or the incarcerated. They don't care about the person sitting next to them. They only care about the people who can contribute financially. They don't care about the millions of souls perishing by the minute. They don't visit the prisoners, the sick, and the hungry. In their prejudice and racism, they select who can be saved or rejected based on certain social criteria.

Consequently, those who don't meet societal standards don't matter. They don't preach about sanctification, without which elder Paul, the apostle, said that no one would see the Lord. They operate like regular businesses.

The ex-Satanists' instructions became evident to me as I verified that the philosophies prevailing in most of the churches today are Greek philosophies, and Eastern and humanistic philosophies disguised as the gospel. They are not preaching the cross. I witnessed these prevailing cultures in most of the churches I visited. The attendants are intellectuals who are seeking intellectual food. They fail to attract the Holy Spirit, the counselor, and manager, who builds the spiritual man. It is in worshiping God that one attracts the Holy Spirit, but they spend less time in worshipping and more time building themselves.

In the average church congregation, the services last no more than one hour, and 60% of that time is allotted to the pastor to give his sermon. There is no worship service to bless God—no praise session to glorify him. They have no time for testimonies about what miracles the Lord has done among them to build faith in him. And in some churches, the service would go on without one ever hearing the name of Jesus. Some of these churches only boast of their status. Hence, they have beautiful buildings, are wealthy, and have a great reputation.

These church organizations would talk more about their education, denominations, and the wealth they have amassed on earth than they do of Jesus. They refuse to sing the old songs that glorify the Father, the Son, and the Holy Spirit. They avoid pronouncing the name of Jesus. In most of the new songs they sing, the name of Jesus is omitted. They replace it with a pronoun. The Holy Spirit is not welcome in their affairs. Moreover, they barely call on the Holy Spirit except to ask for healing.

This is first-hand observation, my primary research. If this was the way to recognize Satan's churches, I had been visiting several of them. My whole state was full of them. This situation aroused my curiosity and pushed me to investigate these trends further, which I found in all denominations. I was being trained in the same way to become a pastor and duplicate the process. I started to examine the denominational doctrines, looking for the Holy Spirit, but I couldn't find him. For ten years, I researched and verified that the ex-sorcerers, witches, and elders were telling the truth. But that revelation was just the tip of the iceberg. The more I researched about the involvement of the Holy Spirit in the churches, the less I could find him, and the more convinced I became that something wasn't right in the church of Jesus.

I found that some trends and doctrines were not from Jesus. I tried to distinguish between the church and the world but was unsuccessful. They talked, walked, behaved, and dressed just like the world. They are Christians for two hours on Sundays, and the rest of the time, they mingle with the world. They rejected the Holy Spirit for the spirit of profit. I learned that this phenomenon is worldwide. In other parts of the world, church management doesn't differ much. Only in foreign churches do the Christians stay in church longer. Yet, their demands to the Lord are mainly material, and the majority only seek a miracle. They gather in massive numbers in locations where they think the pastor is a prophet who can heal, cast out demons, and pray to grow their businesses.

As I continued my research, I found myself ostracized, accused of offenses I did not commit, not trusted, and treated as an outcast. Still, Jesus went through worse. I will report what I found in my research for the edification of those willing to be saved. In my study, I found that there is indeed confusion in the church of God. Most churches operate by a different spirit. They replaced the Holy Spirit with the spirits of philosophy and profit. I found that the daughters of Babylon have been using philosophy to complement their theology. Philosophy is being used as a tool to help others understand the Christian faith.

However, the apostles' philosophy and theology were Jesus Christ crucified. The cross! This is the philosophy that the apostles adopted. It is the philosophy of true Christians. Elder Paul confronted this philosophical theology, this-worldly religious mindset in his time, and addressed the Corinthians in this wise, *"For I resolved to know nothing while I was with you except Jesus Christ and Him cruci-*

fied. I came to you in weakness and fear, and with much trembling. My message and my preaching were not with persuasive words of wisdom, but with a demonstration of the Spirit's power, so that your faith would not rest on men's wisdom, but on God's power. Among the mature, however, we speak a message of wisdom but not the wisdom of this age or of the rulers of this age, who are coming to nothing. No, we speak of the mysterious and hidden wisdom of God, which He destined for our glory before time began. None of the rulers of this age understood it. For if they had, they would not have crucified the Lord of glory" (1 Corinthians 2:5–8 BSB). Prior to stating these words, he said in chapter 1 of the same letter, *"For Christ did not send me to baptize, but to preach the gospel, not with words of wisdom, lest the cross of Christ be emptied of its power. For the message of the cross is foolishness to those who are perishing, but to us who are being saved it is the power of God. For it is written: 'I will destroy the wisdom of the wise; the intelligence of the intelligent I will frustrate.' Where is the wise man? Where is the scribe? Where is the philosopher of this age? Has not God made foolish the wisdom of the world? For since in the wisdom of God, the world through its wisdom did not know Him, God was pleased through the foolishness of what was preached to save those who believe" (1 Corinthians 1:17–20 BSB).* What was preached was the cross of Jesus Christ.

From reading the Bible's testaments, I could see that the Holy Spirit was the central character, counselor, revealer, comforter, advocate, and manager of every activity that involved man working for God, especially in the advent of the church. I surveyed the opinions and views of several pastors from several denominations to learn their beliefs about the Holy Spirit's roles in their churches.

My research revealed that the church began with the baptism of the Holy Spirit and that its key identifiers were from him. He is the beginner and finisher of the faith. He is the one who revealed that Jesus was the Christ to Peter and he will be the one who marries the Christ with the Church to present them to the God of Spirits. I was expecting all my interviewees to have this same understanding and knowledge of the importance of the presence of the Holy Spirit in their midst. What I learned troubled me. Although their philosophy varied from denomination to denomination, one theme echoes throughout their beliefs. They did not think they needed the Holy Spirit. Most of them believed that the Holy Spirit does not play a central role in today's church. Some referred to him as an it, some thing, or a spiritual gift given to certain people in the presbyteries.

However, as we will see in the following chapters, the Holy Spirit is the one who gives the gifts. Some believe he is their servant, and he is there to heal them only. So, like some sort of Djinn, they put him in a box to conjure when they need him to heal the sick. Some of them told me that the Holy Spirit was only given to the apostles to verify that the churches were legit and that the church does not need a Holy Spirit, that they only must preach the gospel. Others believe that the Holy Spirit is given to all Christians after baptism. As we will see later in this writing, this is a big lie.

After this research, I was convinced that the elders were right. The church had rejected the Holy Spirit from their midst. They called him if they needed to use him as a servant, but letting him take charge was controversial. He stopped showing up. However, the miracles kept on happening, and the leaders believed they had subdued the Holy Spirit to make him work on their terms. But the Holy Spirit is God and sovereign. He does not take orders from anyone. Also, without him, there is no miracle-working power.

It prompted me to inquire about the origin of the power of those who performed miracles. Where does the power of the self-proclaim powerful man of God comes from, even after they reject the power of God, the Holy Spirit? That was when I remembered the testimony of one of the ex-Satanists turned Christian. He said that Satan is equipping his servants with the Leviathan spirit that resides in the sea so that they can operate miracles and prophesize just like a true Christian. And that's how Satan can infiltrate the churches with his miracle workers.

Could the ex-sorcerers be right? Could Satan be the leader of 80 percent of the churches on earth? Could they somehow be serving Satan instead of Jesus Christ?

We will attempt to answer these questions in this book. After many years of me praying and researching the issue, the Lord Jesus gradually enlightened me on what it means to be governed by the

Holy Spirit. I could understand the distinctions between a spiritual church and a religious institution. When the Holy Spirit manages a church, it is spiritual, a community of brothers bound by love, it is powerful and as one body, it communes with Jesus Christ as he communes with his Father. Its members understand the world and reject its ways of living. They can discern the plans of the enemy.

On the other hand, a religious institution exists to please the world and follow man's traditions in favor of cultural norms. As my eyes opened, I understood that there was a difference between a Christian and a son of God. I understood that we were at war with a very clever and cruel enemy. This revelation opened my eyes to see the subtle differences between the early church and the current.

The early church was a Spirit-filled fellowship of equal brothers. They were on fire for God. They used to exhibit their faith in Jesus by healing the sick and casting out devils. They did not have big buildings where to congregate. Instead, they used to meet underground to escape persecution. However, the Holy Spirit used to give them the utterance of heavenly tongues and power over serpents and poisonous beverages, and nothing on earth could bother them.

As a result, demons fled from their presence. They had the power of heaven with them because they were directly connected to God. They had integrity and high morals. They were faithful to death. Additionally, the early church Christians had separated themselves from the world. They only interacted with the world to witness to the lost. They were looking for our Lord to come to take them to the new city God promised to the saints. They had no attachment to the world. When I compared the two, I finally understood why the current church cannot operate miracles and is nothing but the shell of its former self.

Moreover, the current church avoids the Holy Spirit and denies his power. They use materials to exhibit their faith in Jesus. They show their cars, their houses, and the big buildings they call churches to show that they believe in Christ. The leaders seek friends in high places, in government and prestigious locations in their cities. They live for the world, and to avoid pressure, they are willing to compromise the teachings of Christ.

Consequently, the world dictates what they preach. They are seeking wealth, fame, and connections with the powers of the world. They are seeking ways to become more like the world. As it is, they are ripe for the great falling away. They believe all sorts of apostasy while denying Jesus and the power of God. This weakness comes from the flesh—the intellectual mind.

They are of the world but profess to be of God. They remove the Holy Spirit and give all kinds of excuses as to why he is no longer needed in their churches. They become philosophical, practicing the wisdom of Plato and Socrates, which is directly from the kingdom of Satan. They removed the doctrine of the Holy Spirit from the church and made way for doctrines of devils. Devils now reside in the church and are even professing to be pastors and evangelists. This is the apostasy mystery, which we will explain in the chapters ahead. But first, let me explain the person of the Holy Spirit and the roles he plays in God's affairs.

CHAPTER 12

THE PERSON OF THE HOLY SPIRIT

Who is the Holy Spirit? Many refer to the Holy Spirit as an (it), an essence, or an energy force. I hear people describe him as lightning, but that is a grave mistake. It is blasphemy! I often inquire about these people. These same people will believe that there are spirits that can possess people and that those spirits have their own personalities. Yet, they can't believe that the Spirit of the Lord God is a person.

Jesus himself referred to him as a he, as we will see later in this chapter. The Holy Spirit is a person, but at the same time, a mystery to all creation—for he is the Spirit of the Spirit who is the God of all. His true essence is only known by the Godhead. However, we know some of his attributes. The Holy Spirit is omniscient, omnipresent, and omnipotent. He is the power that birthed all creation. He is power. He is all in all! He maintains existence, and He is a member of the Godhead, equal to the Father and the Son.

Jesus alerted us of this fact in Matthew 28:19 (BSB) when he instructed the disciples to baptize the new converts in the name of the Father and of the Son and of the Holy Spirit. And again, we can see that assumption in the benediction of elder Paul in 2 Corinthians 13:14 (BSB), known as the apostolic benediction. *"The grace of the*

Lord Jesus Christ, and the love of God, and the communion of the Holy Ghost, be with you all."

The Holy Spirit is the one who makes communion with God possible. He is the Spirit of life, the only one who knows the mind of God. He has his own personality, and he can feel, be aggrieved, offended, sinned against, etc. The Holy Spirit is often referred to as the third person of the Trinity. He is probably the most misunderstood entity of the Godhead, yet, he is the very power of God.

The Holy Spirit has been there since the beginning with the Father and the Son. He is the manager of all of God's affairs and has been managing everything in creation from the beginning. Before the contract between God and Abraham, the Holy Spirit worked on creation. He participated in the creation of the earth, as we read in Genesis 1:2 (BSB), *"And the earth was without form, and void; and darkness was upon the face of the deep: and the Spirit of God moved upon the face of the waters."* Continuing with the message, we read in Job 26:13 (BSB), *"By the Holy Spirit God hath garnished the heavens; his hand hath formed the crooked serpent."*

The Holy Spirit gave life to Adam and all other living creatures. He is the breath of life. *"Then the LORD God formed a man from the dust of the ground and breathed into his nostrils the breath of life, and the man became a living being"* (Genesis 2:7 BSB). The word breath here can also be translated as the "spirit." David explained this in Psalm 104:29–30 BSB, *"When you hide your face, they are terrified; when you take away their breath, they die and return to the dust, when you send your Spirit, they are created."* The Holy Spirit strives with people, as the Lord says in Genesis 6:3 (BSB), *"My Spirit will not contend with humans forever, for they are mortal; their days will be a hundred and twenty years."*

As you can see, the closer the Holy Spirit is to a human, the longer he/she lives. Before the flood, people used to live for an average of five hundred years. However, when God restricted the presence of his Holy Spirit, this longevity dropped considerably. As we read in Genesis 6:3 (KJV), *"And the LORD said, "My Spirit shall not strive with man forever, for he is indeed flesh; yet his days shall be one hundred and twenty years.""*

The Holy Spirit is the one who selected the servants of God and put them into ministries in the Old and New Testament. Moreover, he raises commoners for uncommon offices and purposes. He also managed the congregation of Israel and anointed the prophets, the priests, and the kings we read about throughout the bible. In the Old Testament, we can see his trace in every major work, from selecting prophets to selecting kings. These are the attributes of a person.

THE HOLY SPIRIT IN THE OLD CONTRACT

The Holy Spirit ruled the nation of Israel from its inception through its stay in the promised land until its expulsion and exile to the nations. Hence, the Holy Spirit was the manager of Israel's governors from Moses until they rejected God's rule and demanded the rule of a man instead. At the beginning of the first age of the human congregation of saints, God gave Israel a messiah in the person of Moses. The Holy Spirit qualified Joshua to be his successor when Moses's ministry was over.

Thus, in the book of Numbers 27:18 (BSB), we read, *"And the Lord said to Moses: 'Take Joshua the son of Nun with you, a man in whom is the Spirit, lay your hand on him."* Notice the way God referred to Joshua when he talked to Moses about him. He said *"a man in whom is the Spirit"*. He ordered Moses to anoint him to lead. The Holy Spirit gives wisdom and understanding and knowledge in all manner of workmanship. *Then the Lord spoke to Moses, saying: "See, I have called by name Bezaleel the son of Uri, the son of Hur, of the tribe of Judah. And I have filled him with the Spirit of God, in wisdom, in understanding, in knowledge, and in all manner of workmanship" (Exodus 31:1–3 BSB).*

Bezaleel, being a commoner, shows that there is a change in the social standing of any man who receives the anointing of the Holy Spirit. To raise Bezaleel as one of the wise men of Israel, the Lord God gave him the Holy Spirit. Hence, the Holy Spirit selected the judges of Israel. *"The Holy Spirit came upon Othniel, who judged Israel and went out to war: and the LORD delivered Chushanrishathaim* king of Mesopotamia into his hand; and his hand prevailed against Chushanrishathaim" (Judges 3:10 BSB). "Then the Spirit of the Lord came on Gideon, and he blew a trumpet, summoning the Abiezrites to follow him" (Judges 6:34 BSB).

The Holy Spirit also gives superhuman strength to selected priests, just as he gave to Samson. *"And the Spirit of the LORD began to move upon Samson at Mahaneh Dan between Zorah and Eshtaol. And the Spirit of the LORD came mightily upon him, and he tore the lion apart as one would have torn apart a young goat, though he had nothing in his hand" (Judges 13:25 BSB).*

In the second age of the people of Israel, the Lord God ruled the people as their King through the Holy Spirit. The Holy Spirit anointed the judges, and they would pass down the instructions of the Lord unto the people. However, Israel, wanting to be like the other nations, demanded that Samuel anoint a human king over them instead. Therefore, we read in 1 Samuel 8:7–9 (BSB), *"The LORD said to Samuel, 'Listen to the voice of the people regarding all that they say to you, for they have not rejected you, but they have rejected Me from being king over them. Like all the deeds which they have done since the day that I brought them up from Egypt even to this day—in that they have forsaken Me and served other gods—so they are doing to you also. Now then, listen to their voice; however, you shall solemnly warn them and tell them of the procedure of the king who will reign over them.'"*

After Samuel enumerated the burdens that a king would put over them, we see that the Lord did not let them take just anyone as a king. Instead, the Lord selected a king for them, and the Holy Spirit guided the king and managed the kingdom. Thus, the Holy Spirit anointed the kings of Israel. For one to serve as king over Israel, he had to be anointed by the Holy Spirit. In 1 Samuel 10:1 (BSB), we read, *"Then Samuel took a flask of olive oil and poured it on Saul's head and kissed him, saying, 'Has not the Lord anointed you ruler over his inheritance?'* The oil represents the Spirit of empowerment (Isaiah 61:1; 1 Samuel 16:13 BSB).

We all remember the story of David, who replaced Saul as king after he lost the favor of the Lord and that the Spirit later departed from him because of his disobedience (1 Samuel 16:14 BSB). When

God removed the kingship from Saul, the Holy Spirit returned to work to choose David to replace him. Then Samuel took the horn of oil and anointed him amid his brethren, and the Spirit of the Lord came upon David from that day forward (1 Samuel 16:1–13 BSB). The Holy Spirit speaks, as David stated in 2 Samuel 23:2, *"The Spirit of the Lord spoke through me."*

The prophet Ezekiel also confirms this fact in his report, saying, *"The Spirit entered me when He spoke to me" (Ezekiel 2:2 BSB)*. The Holy Spirit teaches humans to do the will of God and inspires holiness, as David asked for in Psalm 143:10 (BSB): *"Teach me to do thy will; for thou art my God: thy spirit is good; lead me into the land of uprightness."* One can sin against the Holy Spirit. In Matthew 12:31–32 (BSB), Jesus warned the disciples, saying, *"Therefore I tell you, people will be forgiven for every sin and blasphemy, but blasphemy against the Spirit will not be forgiven. Whoever speaks a word against the Son of Man will be forgiven, but whoever speaks against the Holy Spirit will not be forgiven, either in this age or in the age to come."* The theologians say that one sins against the Holy Spirit when one rejects the salvation of God through Jesus Christ. This is true to some extent because whoever rejects the salvation of God through the cross of Jesus Christ will never be forgiven, but his/her fate is the fire of hell. But there is more here!

Here, we read that Jesus said whoever *"speaks against the Holy Spirit will not be forgiven."* He warned his disciples to be aware of that. He warned them not to minimize the person of the Holy Spirit and to always hold Him in reverence. Anything they said against him, they will have to give account for and will not be forgiven for it. Can one sin against an essence, an inanimate object, or a wind? Or if the Holy Spirit is an inanimate object or a wind, why did Jesus and all the prophets assign a personal pronoun to him, calling him a he? You be the judge!

THE HOLY SPIRIT BEGINS THE NEW CONTRACT

As a manager of the new covenant, the Holy Spirit started the new contract by anointing John, one of the two pillars. John, the son of Zechariah, right from his mother's womb, was assigned a specific work. He was later referred to as John the Baptist. He anointed John to turn the hearts of the parents to their children and the disobedient to the wisdom of the righteous, to make ready a people prepared for the coming of the Lord Jesus, Son of the Living God. Concerning the birth of John, the Baptist, we read in Luke 1:11–17 (BSB): *"Then an angel of the Lord appeared to him, standing at the right side of the altar of incense. When Zechariah saw him, he was startled and was gripped with fear. But the angel said to him: 'Do not be afraid, Zechariah; your prayer has been heard. Your wife Elizabeth will bear you a son, and you are to call him John. He will be a joy and delight to you, and many will rejoice because of his birth, for he will be great in the sight of the Lord. He is never to take wine or other fermented drink, and he will be filled with the Holy Spirit even before he is born. He will bring back many of the people of Israel to the Lord their God. And he will go on before the Lord, in the spirit and power of Elijah, to turn the hearts of the parents to their children and the disobedient to the wisdom of the righteous to make ready a people prepared for the Lord.'"*

Then the Holy Spirit proceeded to conceive Jesus in the womb of Mary. Yes, Jesus is the first-born son of God through the Holy Spirit. In Luke 1:26–37 (BSB), we read that Gabriel came to announce the birth of Jesus. *"In the sixth month, God sent the angel Gabriel to a town in Galilee called Nazareth, to a virgin pledged in marriage to a man named Joseph, who was of the house of David. And the virgin's name was Mary. The angel appeared to her and said, 'Greetings, you who are highly favored! The Lord is with you.'*

Mary was greatly troubled at his words and wondered what kind of greeting this might be. So, the angel told her, 'Do not be afraid, Mary, for you have found favor with God. Behold, you will conceive and give birth to a son, and you are to give Him the name Jesus. He will be great and will be called the Son of the Most High. The Lord God will give Him the throne of His father David, and He will reign over the house of Jacob forever. His kingdom will never end!' 'How can this be,'

Mary asked the angel, 'since I am a virgin?' The angel replied, 'The Holy Spirit will come upon you, and the power of the Most High will overshadow you. So, the Holy One to be born will be called the Son of God. Look, even Elizabeth your relative has conceived a son in her old age, and she who was called barren is in her sixth month. For nothing will be impossible with God.'"

The Holy Spirit managed the ministries of John and Jesus. He identified Jesus as the Messiah of Israel and Savior of the whole world. John testified that he himself did not know that Jesus was the Christ, but that he who sent him told him, *"He upon whom you see the Spirit descend in bodily form is the one."* In Luke 3:21–22 (BSB), we read, *"And now when all the people were baptized, it came to pass, that Jesus also being baptized and praying, the heaven was opened and the Holy Ghost descended in a bodily shape like a dove upon him, and a voice came from heaven, which said, Thou art my beloved son; in thee I am well pleased."* From that date, the Holy Spirit accompanied Jesus and never left him. Therefore, the Holy Spirit was his counselor, his manager, and his power.

Again, in the next chapter of Luke, in verse 1, we see the same Holy Spirit leading Jesus into the wilderness to be tempted by the devil for forty days. In other words, the Holy Spirit prepared Jesus for his ministry. Notice what Luke said here—the Holy Spirit descended in bodily form. He took the form of a gentle dove to show the gentle Savior of man. After that day, he also took over the Lord's agenda, leading him to his ultimate purpose, which was dying on the cross.

Jesus did not start any ministry until he was filled with the Holy Spirit, and the Holy Spirit became his manager. He was baptized with water, completed the forty-day fast, then baptized with the Holy Spirit of power, and ventured into ministry. Jesus did nothing without the Holy Spirit. Hence, in Luke 4:18–19 (BSB), Jesus announces his ministry, saying, *"The Spirit of the Lord is upon me, because HE hath anointed me to preach the gospel to the poor; HE hath sent me to heal the brokenhearted, to preach deliverance to the captives, and recovering of sight to the blind, to set at liberty them that are bruised, to preach the acceptable year of the Lord."*

Notice what Jesus said here that the Spirit of the Lord had anointed him and sent him to do the miracles he did in his ministry. Jesus called these miracles the work of his Father. Therefore, he clearly showed that he was working for the Holy Spirit and God the Father while he was on the earth and that they all worked together. The Holy Spirit was the manager he answered to. After Jesus rose from the dead, he then gathered his disciples and strictly ordered them not to leave Jerusalem and go and wait for the Holy Spirit. And for forty days, they waited in the upper chamber, in prayer and fasting, and on the fortieth day, they received the Holy Spirit.

After that, Peter, who had denied the Messiah, was encouraged in one day to preach the gospel to the same Jews he was afraid would kill him and brought three-thousand of them to the fold. The moral here is that Jesus does not believe in ministry without the Holy Spirit. If we want to follow Jesus, the leader of the church, and become like him, we need to follow his path and obey his commands. Do you see the format?

Jesus lived for thirty years on earth. After that, he was baptized in water, baptized with the Holy Spirit, and completed the regular fast to become a rabbi or a prophet at the time in Israel. Then he announced and started his ministry.

Jesus then selected twelve disciples, baptized them in water to follow John's baptism, trained them for three years, and then had them fast in the upper room for forty days before they received the Holy Spirit. Shouldn't we follow this same pattern in today's church? Shouldn't the church of Jesus follow the traditions of Jesus instead of following those of men? These are the themes we will elaborate upon in the chapters to come.

CHAPTER 13

THERE IS ONE BAPTISM

Jesus sent the Holy Spirit to give power to his people and manage the church. Just as he selected the kings, priests, and prophets of Israel, his mission is to do the same in the church. That is why it wasn't Peter (pastor of the church in Jerusalem), who selected elders Paul and Silas to bring the gospel to the Gentiles, nor was it the counsel of the apostles, in their wisdom, but the Holy Spirit. The apostles had no say in where they go and who they approached. Jesus chose them, and the Holy Spirit sealed and sent them, just like he did for Jesus and the disciples before elder Paul. In fact, elder Paul is the last person the apostles would think of for this mission. However, the Holy Spirit, who trusts the judgment of Jesus, anointed the fiercest persecutor of the Christians of that time to take the gospel to the Gentiles.

The Holy Spirit can test heart and rein and knows who is qualified for the work. And as he did for the apostles, he put elder Paul to work. If men had to choose Paul for a role in the church, they would probably choose him to go preach to the Pharisees as he was one himself. They would probably say he had experience dealing with them.

But the Holy Spirit chose him and sent him into uncharted territory. Everyone who wants to work for God is in the employment of the Holy Spirit. He can see his/her capacity. He can see people's hearts. Thus, the anointing of the Holy Spirit is paramount for every

Christian to work for God. As you just read above, Jesus was baptized with water and the Holy Spirit. What does that mean? That means that there is one baptism with two facades, one for the flesh and one for the spirit. In Ephesians 4:5-6 (KJV), Apostle Paul stated that there is *"One Lord, one faith, one baptism, one God and Father of all, who is above all, and through all, and in you all"*.

Many believe he was talking about the baptism of water. But Apostle Paul was referring to the baptism of fire. There is indeed one baptism but it has two parts, one for the sanctification of the flesh, which symbolizes the cleansing of the temple. We refer to this as being washed by the blood of the Lamb. John called it the baptism of repentance. It was the precursor of the true baptism—the baptism of the spirit, or the baptism of fire. In the baptism of the Spirit, the Holy Spirit comes to cohabit in the human body with the spirit of the man to fill the empty place present in that man's heart. He brings the spirit of this dead man to life. He wakes him up from the spiritual death that conquered Adam and he imbues him with power.

As he anointed the prophets of old who came before John, the Holy Spirit also anointed John for his purposeful ministry. His ministry was to baptize Israel with water to prepare the way of the Lord, as he explained. Hence, John was anointed to prepare the way for Jesus. John the Baptist came to preach repentance to turn the hearts of fathers to their children and the hearts of children to their fathers because the Lord God the Christ was on his way. If he did not find at least some Israelites washed and ready for his presence, it would not be good for Israel. *"Behold, I will send My messenger, who will prepare the way before Me. Then the Lord whom you seek will suddenly come to His temple the Messenger of the covenant, in whom you delight. See, He is coming,' says the LORD of Hosts"* (Malachi 3:1 BSB). In Malachi 4:5–6 (BSB), the Lord clarified further and told Israel, *"Behold, I will send you Elijah the prophet before the coming of the great and dreadful Day of the LORD. And he will turn the hearts of the fathers to their children, and the hearts of the children to their fathers. Otherwise, I will come and strike the land with a curse."*

Well, Elijah did come, and he turned the hearts of fathers to their children, and vice versa, through the baptism of water. This is how Jesus explained the coming of Elijah to his disciples. *"Then his disciples asked him, 'Why do the teachers of religious law insist that Elijah must return before the Messiah comes?' Jesus replied, 'Elijah does indeed come, and he will restore all things. But I tell you that Elijah has already come, and they did not recognize him, but have done to him whatever they wished. In the same way, the Son of Man will suffer at their hands'" (Matthew 17:10–11 BSB).* "After John's messengers had left, Jesus began to speak to the crowds about John, asking, 'What did you go out into the wilderness to see? A reed swaying in the wind. Otherwise, what did you go out to see? A man dressed in fine clothes. Look, those who wear elegant clothing and live-in luxury are found in palaces. But what did you go out to see? A prophet? Yes, I tell you, and more than a prophet. This is the one about whom it is written: *"Behold, I will send My messenger ahead of You, who will prepare Your way before You."* I tell you, among those born of women, there is no one greater than John, yet even the least in the kingdom of God is greater than he.'"

To explain this further, Jesus stated in Mathew 11:12–14 (BSB): *"From the days of John the Baptist until now, the kingdom of heaven has been subject to violence, and the violent lay claim to it. For all the Prophets and the Law prophesied until John. And if you are willing to accept it, he is the Elijah who was to come."* In Mathew 3 (BSB), John the Baptist explained to the people that his baptism was that of repentance. He told them they should wait for another who will baptize them with the Spirit and fire. John stated, *"I indeed baptize you with water unto repentance; but he that cometh after me is mightier than I, (talking about Jesus), whose shoes I am not worthy to bear; he shall baptize you with the Holy Ghost and with Fire" (Mathew 3:11 BSB).*

The baptism of water continued during the ministry of Jesus. And Jesus, after his crucifixion and resurrection from the dead, commissioned his disciples to go all over the world and preach to the whole world and make disciples of all nations by baptizing them in the name of the Father, the Son, and the Holy Spirit. The baptism in question here is the water baptism, which has become the tradition to this day. Every believer is required to be baptized in water to become a disciple.

But to become a son of God, a second baptism is required. Remember, John promised that he who would come after him would baptize with the Holy Spirit. When did the baptism of the Spirit and fire occur, and is it required for every believer? The baptism of fire started in the upper room on the day of Pentecost with the first disciples, including the 12 apostles. Matthias was the replacement of Judas, for Judas did betray the Lord to go to his own place. These disciples then imparted it onto other disciples by the laying of the hand, as was the tradition. And as we will see later, this anointing is required for every believer because the son of man did not come to make only repentant men but sons of God born of the will of the Spirit. These are people who would be ready to stand the ground of righteousness and stand firm till the end of the war.

TO PRODUCE GOOD FRUITS

In John 15:5 (BSB), Jesus urged his disciples to stay connected to him. He said, *"I am the vine; you are the branches. If you remain in me and I in you, you will bear much fruit; apart from me you can do nothing."* In other words, there is no church without him. The very survival of the church depends on this connection. A connected church will not be barren; it will bring forth much fruit. Jesus is looking for a church that bears fruits. To achieve that end, he told the disciples that they should remain connected to the tree at all times, not sporadically. Then they would be able to bear the fruits of the Spirit. How does one connect to the tree and stay connected? Well, to remain connected to Jesus and the tree of life, one needs to be born of the Holy Spirit, to become a Spirit to commune with the Spirit of Jesus. This flow of Spirit will connect the Christians to the mind of Jesus and reveal his agenda for his/her life in the world.

Without the Holy Spirit, a Christian cannot stay connected to that vine and will not bear fruits. But what are those fruits we're referring to? The modern church believes that those fruits are materials, such as a nice career, a beautiful house, a nice car, lots of money, a good reputation, great connections, and the list goes on. To those things, they ascribe the word success. However, that is a misconception; the fruits that Jesus was referring to are spiritual fruits. They are what Jesus considers success. They have nothing to do with the flesh. According to elder Paul, the fruits of the Spirit are love, joy, peace, patience, kindness, goodness, faithfulness, gentleness, and self-control (Galatians 5:22–23 BSB). These are nine personal characteristics by which a person connected to the tree will be identified. Or rather, these are the nine personality traits of the Spirit. They are not found in the flesh, for the flesh cannot produce them. That is why the Bible says the flesh profits nothing. Without the Holy Spirit, no one can develop these characteristics. One can only act as if they have them. And since people are good actors, they act. I can hear the critics asking, "How do you know that?" The answer is simple! The Holy Spirit is the only one who gives them. When a church rejects him, it cannot produce these fruits. Yet, many are pretending while they believe that the Holy Spirit is needed simply for healing. Jesus dealt with this kind in his time. They are those he constantly referred to as hypocrites, the whole clan of leaders in Israel in his time. In Mathew 23:26–29 (BSB), we read Jesus's opinions of them in these words: *"Blind Pharisee! First clean the inside of the cup and dish, so that the outside may become clean as well. Woe to you, scribes and Pharisees, you hypocrites! You are like whitewashed tombs, which look beautiful on the outside, but on the inside are full of dead men's bones and every impurity. In the same way, on the outside you appear to be righteous, but on the inside, you are full of hypocrisy and wickedness. Woe to you, scribes and Pharisees, you hypocrites! You build tombs for the prophets and decorate the monuments of the righteous and you say, 'If we had lived in the days of our fathers, we would not have been partners with them in shedding the blood of the prophets.' So, you testify against yourselves that you are the sons of those who murdered the prophets. Fill up, then, the measure of the sin of your fathers."*

Likewise, this seed is grown in the church today. I call them the scribes and Pharisees of the twentieth century. They are those in the church who look sanctified and righteous on the outside, but inside, they are full of hypocrisy, hatred, and all kinds of lust. The fruits of the Spirit are the emotional states of the spirit being. When the Holy

Spirit is in perfect communion with your spirit, your being is in harmony. Your emotions are joy, love, and peace; your heart is kind and generous, gentle, meek; and your characteristics are faithfulness, righteousness, and justice. These are the characteristics of God's personality, and the process starts with the baptism of the Holy Spirit, which can only occur after the baptism of water.

The water baptism cleanses and sets us ready for sanctification. Once we are sanctified, we are ready to become acquainted with God or enter Gynosko with God. Then the baptism of the Holy Spirit purifies and seals us to the tree. Without being sealed, one can try to connect but will fail every time. And if you are not connected to the vine, you will never reach this equilibrium of God's characteristics.

THE BAPTISM OF WATER: THE FIRST STEP IN BECOMING A CHRISTIAN

Nothing can be done for God without the Holy Spirit. One does not serve or please God without the anointing of the Holy Spirit. Nicodemus went to see Jesus that fateful night to discuss doctrine (John 3:1–21 BSB). He said, *"Rabbi, we know that you are a teacher who comes from God. For no one could perform the signs you are doing if God was not with him."* In verse 3, Jesus replied, *"Verily, verily, I say unto thee, except a man be born again, he cannot see the kingdom of God."* Perplexed by the statement, Nicodemus asked him in verse 4, *"How can a man be born again when he is already old? Surely, he cannot enter a second time into his mother's womb to be born!"* In verse 5, Jesus answered and said, *"Very truly I tell you, one can't enter the kingdom of God unless they are born of water and spirit. Flesh gives birth to flesh, but the Spirit gives birth to spirits. You should not be surprised at my saying; you must be born again. The wind blows wherever it pleases. You hear it's sound but cannot tell where it comes from or where it is going. So it is with everyone born of the Spirit."*

Jesus was merely telling Nicodemus that the second birth comes from the Spirit and that what he came to ask him in the secret of the night couldn't be revealed to him. He was telling him that he must be able to understand heaven first before he could be told about the affairs of heaven. He could not talk to the flesh because the flesh would not understand. This is the kind of understanding only the Spirit can have. In other words, Jesus told him, "Even if I tell you that I am the Christ, you will not believe me because the flesh cannot perceive it." Neither prayer, intellectual knowledge, theological degrees, or the baptism of water can birth the spiritual man. Are all Christians born again? The answer is no!

A Christian should not be confused with a son of God. What is a Christian? According to Webster's definition, a Christian is a person who has received Christian baptism or is a believer in Christianity. It is a relatively broad and vague definition but is somewhat correct. In terms of human carnal understanding to be precise, a Christian is one who confesses Jesus Christ as King of his life, accepts his sacrifice on the cross, testifies his/her faith in baptism, and trains in the way of holiness to sanctify himself/herself. Such a person proves he/she believes after being baptized. In addition, this belief earns him/her the right and eligibility to become a son/daughter of God. In other words, becoming a Christian is getting on the path to becoming a son/daughter of God. This happens in the flesh. To be born of the Spirit—or born again, as Jesus told Nicodemus,—one needs to be anointed by the Holy Spirit so the human spirit can fuse with the Spirit of eternal life or enters Gynosko with the Spirit of life.

This is the engagement with the Lamb, the first step in every marriage. The engagement happens during that fusion. The two spirits become one, just like in a marriage, and the Holy Spirit will then dwell within that person's spirit forever—first in this current body, and then, he will later transform this body into the glorious eternal body for the wedding of the Lamb. Therefore, Jesus said, *"He will remain with you forever."* In John 1:12–13 (BSB), John explained it in this way, *"But to all who did receive Him, to those who believed in His name, He gave <u>the right to become children of God</u>, children born not of blood, nor of the desire or will of man, but born of God."*

This means God the Holy Spirit, just as Jesus told Nicodemus. I read books from authors talking about the Holy Spirit as if he was some sort of novelty item. None of them ever mention the reality that the whole thing falls apart without him. Without him, no one can serve God, for he is the one who gives faith in God. He is the glue that keeps everything together. He is the reason why Christianity survives till our era. He is the presence of Jesus—the connection with the divine. He is the one preparing the bride for the wedding of the Lamb. He is the oil in the lamp of the virgins about whom we read in the parable. He is the fire that will ignite the soul and purify the body to transform this corruptible into incorruptible. He is the living water that Jesus referred to when he said, *"He who believes in Me, as the Scripture said, 'From his innermost being will flow rivers of living water.' But this He spoke of the Spirit, whom those who believed in Him were to receive"* (John 7:38–39 BSB).

THE BAPTISM THAT MAKES THE SON OF GOD

Some Christians argue that once one is baptized with water, they have the Holy Spirit. I beg to differ. The apostle Paul didn't believe this either. He believed that the baptism of water was strictly for repentance. John the Baptist explained this to the Jews who came to get baptized in these words, *"I came to baptize you with water, but one after me will come and he will baptize you with the Holy Spirit and with Fire."* John made mention of the two baptisms. The apostle Paul reiterates the same belief in Acts 19. *"While Apollos was at Corinth, elder Paul took the road through the interior and arrived at Ephesus. There he found some disciples and asked them, 'Did you receive the Holy Spirit when you believed?' They answered, 'No, we have not even heard that there is a Holy Spirit.' So, elder Paul asked, 'Then what baptism did you receive?' 'John's baptism,' they replied. Elder Paul said, 'John's baptism was a baptism of repentance. He told the people to believe in the one coming after him, that is, in Jesus.' On hearing this, they were baptized in the name of the Lord Jesus. When Elder Paul placed his hands on them, the Holy Spirit came on them, and they spoke in tongues and prophesied. There were about twelve men in all"* (Acts 19:1–7 BSB). Notice that they were baptized in the name of Jesus.

The Bible is not clear as to whose name was used for the baptism of John, but elder Paul was clear about one thing. And that is, they needed to receive the Holy Spirit. These twelve men he prayed for were common Christians baptized in water, showing that elder Paul understood the necessity of the Holy Spirit's anointing for all Christians, not for an elite group as we are being told today.

CHAPTER 14

WRONG SPIRIT, WRONG PRIORITY

How many in your church would answer yes to the question elder Paul asked the 12 men? Would you answer yes if this question was addressed to you? The sign to show that one is Spirit-filled is speaking in tongue and prophesy. One can receive the gift directly from Jesus, as he did for the disciples when he breathed on them and said, "Receive the Holy Spirit," who came upon them in the upper room. The other way is to have one who has already received the gift from Jesus, an elder, lay their hand on you and pray for you, as was done for Elder Paul after he met Jesus in Damascus. Remember I said one who received the gift from Jesus. *"So, Ananias departed and entered the house. And laying his hands on him, he said, 'Brother Saul, the Lord Jesus who appeared to you on the road by which you came has sent me so that you may regain your sight and be filled with the Holy Spirit'" (Acts 9:17 BSB).* The presence of the Holy Spirit is a gift Jesus gave to his disciples. Everyone who were in the gathering in the day of Pentecost received that gift, not only the eleventh. Once a disciple receives the Holy Spirit, he becomes like Jesus. This disciple then passes the knowledge to his own disciples. If his disciples abide in the words of Jesus, obey and apply them, he then receives the Holy Spirit from Jesus. Only Jesus can baptize one with the Holy Spirit. After he left earth to go seat at the right hand of the Father, he sent his Holy Spirit to baptize his disciples in the upper room. Then he sent them to make their own disciples in whom they would breathe the same Spirit that was given to them. The new disciples then receive the Spirit of Jesus the Christ so that they have the same mindset as he. Only Jesus can baptize one with the Holy Spirit. For those who say the Holy Spirit was only given to the apostles, I would like to bring to your attention that Ananias was a simple member of the church. The Lord Jesus did not send Peter, John, or James to pray for Saul. Some people ask, "Why is it that the Christians being baptized today aren't filled with the Holy Spirit?"

The answer to this question is that they are not sanctified. They have the wrong priorities. As a result, they attract the wrong spirit. They never made the transition from the intellectual to the spiritual world. They love the flesh and don't want to let it go. The focus of most of today's churches has shifted to the material world. They are feeding the intellect, the flesh. Instead of crucifying the flesh as the bible prescribe, they grow it into a boastful giant to stifle the spirit.

In Galatians, elder Paul alluded to the fruits of the flesh, which are *"sexual immorality, impurity, and debauchery; idolatry and sorcery; hatred, discord, jealousy, and rage; rivalries, divisions, factions, and envy; drunkenness, orgies, and the like" (Galatians 5:19–21 BSB)*. These are the fruits of the spirit of the fallen, the only fruits that the flesh can produce because it is dead and is heading into the grave. It is firmly tuned to the frequencies of hell, and its spirit can only produce what is being broadcast from there.

Every son or daughter of Adam is born with these traits. These are the fruits of the tree of corruption. Hence, they can't attract holiness. The current church is full of these fruits of the intellect. This is the reason for all the scandals we are witnessing today. Pastors are being accused of all kinds of corruption and affiliations with magical societies, where the members of the church are committing all kinds of acts of debauchery.

To be born again, we need to be holy. Only this holiness will attract the presence of the Holy Spirit for a new birth. Jesus's priority was for the kingdom of God to come to earth. Jesus gave several commands that the churches of today ignore to go seek after worldly treasures. Jesus ordered, saying, *"But seek first the kingdom of God and His righteousness, and all these things will be added unto you."* This was not a proposition; it was a command. In Matthew 6:31–3 (BSB), Jesus stated, *"Therefore, take no thought, saying, what shall we eat? or, what shall we drink? or, Wherewithal shall we be clothed? (For after all these things do the Gentiles seek:) for your heavenly Father knoweth that ye have need of all these things. 'But seek ye first the kingdom of God, and his righteousness'; and all these things shall be added unto you.'"*

This is a mystery, a secret upon which we will elaborate more in this book later but let me quickly explain. When Jesus commanded his disciples to seek the kingdom of heaven, he was simply telling them to seek the anointing of the Holy Spirit. Notice that Jesus did not say to live without these things. He said that the Father knows what you need to survive. Jesus was merely telling them that first, they needed to have a spiritual priority, to set their sights on heaven, like Abraham and the patriarchs. They were looking forward to the city with foundations, whose architect and builder is God. In his prayer, we can see this clearly. His first demand was that The Father's kingdom come on earth as it is in heaven. Instead of seeking a refuge and comfort here on earth, Jesus instructed his disciples to look up for the new earth. This theme carried on down to the ministry of Paul.

Elder Paul instructed the Hebrews to long for a better country, a heavenly one. The prophets were looking for this city as well. *In Isaiah 14:32 BSB, the prophet says "The LORD has founded Zion, where His afflicted people will find refuge".* Talking to the Hebrews about the hope of the prophets Paul said, *"Instead, they were longing for a better country, a heavenly one. Therefore, God is not ashamed to be called their God, for He has prepared a city for them." (Hebrews 11:16 BSB).* He also told them to adopt the same hope saying: *"For here, we do not have a permanent city, but we are looking for the city that is to come (Hebrews 13:14 BSB).* God does give material things, but He gives them to those who know their purpose and won't use them as idols to puff up the flesh but as tools to grow the kingdom of God.

Jesus said to his disciples, *"Lay not up for yourselves treasures upon earth, where moth and rust doth corrupt, and where thieves break through and steal. But lay up for yourselves treasures in heaven, where neither moth nor rust doth corrupt, and where thieves do not break through nor steal for where your treasure is, there will your heart be also"* (Matthew 6:19–21 BSB). Where is your treasure? If you gather treasures in Satan's world, that is where your heart will be. And wherever your heart is, there also is your allegiance. God gave us his kingdom in the person of Jesus, but we did not recognize him. He then gave us the Holy Spirit, who manages the kingdom, but still, we are rejecting him for world philosophies that lead to death. When asked by the Pharisees when the kingdom of God would come, Jesus replied, *'The kingdom of God will not come with observable signs. Nor will people say, "Look, here it is," or "There it is." For you see, the kingdom of God is in your midst"* (Luke 17:20–21 BSB). What is the kingdom of God then? The answer is, wherever the Father, the Son, and the Holy Spirit are present, there also is the kingdom of God. Jesus was the kingdom of God present among them. After revealing it to the Pharisees in a parable, he also clarified it for his disciples.

In Luke 17:22 (BSB), we read, *"Then He said to the disciples, 'The time is coming when you will long to see one of the days of the Son of Man, but you will not see it.'"* He merely meant that you are beholding the kingdom of God today, but one day, you will not see it again. However, Luke transcribed it differently, saying, *"Neither shall they say, 'Lo here!' or 'Lo there!' For, behold, the kingdom of God is within you."* Most people don't understand this saying, but let me explain. When Jesus says that the kingdom of God is within you, he means that the Holy Spirit is within you. Many disciples went astray to spiritism because they thought Jesus was talking about the Kabalistic wisdom—the deep wisdom of Satan about the energy gates of the human body. He explained it to his disciples when he told them, *"And I will ask the Father, and He will give you another Advocate to be with you forever, the Spirit of truth. The world cannot receive Him, because it neither sees Him nor knows Him. But you do know Him, for He abides with you and will be in you. I will not leave you as orphans; I will come to you"* (John 14:16–18).

He was saying that the Holy Spirit will be within you. He is the kingdom of God. All good things come from God, and He rewards those who diligently seek him. However, instead of seeking Him, the Christians of today seek the things of this world. The focus of all Christians should be to seek Jesus—the kingdom of God.

In John 3:5 (BSB), Jesus told Nicodemus that *"Except a man be born of water and of the Spirit, he cannot enter the kingdom of God."* When you are born of the Holy Spirit, you are a citizen of heaven. Then you can be invited for a tour to view the things of heaven. Or the Father can reveal his plans to you as he did for Abraham and the prophets. God will invite you to see angels and experience the realms. You cannot be invited in the intellect. It belongs to the flesh, and the flesh is dead or dying.

Don't you get it? Without the birth of the Spirit, you are dead—for you have in you the spirit of a dead man, Adam. In Luke 9:59–60, Jesus asked a man to follow him, saying, *"'Follow Me.' The man replied, 'Lord, first let me go and bury my father.' But Jesus told him, 'Let the dead bury their own dead. You, however, go and proclaim the kingdom of God.'"* Or haven't you heard? God is not the God of the dead but the living. The living is he/she who is born of the Spirit. Therefore, choose the Holy Spirit. Hence, He can bring you to life. Most of the teaching leaders of the church have stopped teaching this fundamental truth.

CHAPTER 15

"THE ONCE SAVED ALWAYS SAVED DOCTRINE"

The Once Saved Always Saved Doctrine" is a Dangerous Doctrine. It gives the modern Christian a wrong sense of security. Does confessing the name of Jesus alone takes one to heaven? In John 3:13 KJV, Jesus makes the following statement and told Nicodemus, *"And no man hath ascended up to heaven, but he that came down from heaven, even the Son of man which is in heaven."* But he also made a promise to his disciples in chapter 14, verse 3 of the same book, saying, *"In My Father's house are many rooms. If it were not so, would I have told you that I am going there to prepare a place for you?"* And if I go and prepare a place for you, I will come back and welcome you into My presence so that you also may be where I am. The theological philosophers propagate that Jesus is coming to take everyone who calls Him 'Lord, Lord to heaven. This is not accurate and Jesus confirmed it in Mathew 7:21-23.

In Mathew 7:21-23 (KJV), Jesus stated, *"Not every one that saith unto me, Lord, Lord, shall enter into the kingdom of heaven; but he that doeth the will of my Father which is in heaven. Many will say to me in that day, Lord, Lord, have we not prophesied in thy name? and in thy name have cast out devils? and in thy name done many wonderful works? And then will I profess unto them, I never knew you: depart from me, ye that work iniquity'"*

Some use John 14:3 to justify the 'once saved, always saved doctrine'. Many of today's Christians believe in it. This doctrine instructs them that no matter what they do after confessing the name of Jesus, they cannot lose their salvation. However, this doctrine is far from the truth. It is one of the most dangerous doctrines for a Christian to believe. Jesus' promise was for the just, the righteous, and the holy, those who are repentant. His promise was for those who overcome the world as he did—those who do the will of his father and who are without sin. In Revelation 21: 26-27 (BSB) we read, *"And into the city will be brought the glory and honor of the nations. But nothing unclean will ever enter it, nor anyone who practices an abomination or a lie, but only those whose names are written in the Lamb's Book of Life"*.

This passage tells us that if there is iniquity in your life, you cannot enter God's heaven. Then why are some telling the Christians that they can continue sinning after the confession and still expect to be saved?

The proponents of the 'once saved, always saved doctrine,' quote Paul in Romans 10:9 (KJV). In the passage, Paul told the Romans: *"That if thou shalt confess with thy mouth the Lord Jesus, and shalt believe in thine heart that God hath raised him from the dead, thou shalt be saved."* Apostle Paul quoted these words from the Prophet Joel. In Joel 2:32 (BSB), the Prophet stated: *"And everyone who calls on the name of the LORD will be saved; for on Mount Zion and in Jerusalem there will be deliverance, as the LORD has promised, among the remnant called by the LORD."*

In the previous chapters, we explained the type of salvation the prophets referred to. We explained that the apostle Paul and the prophet were referring to salvation from the snares of this life, the evil of this time. This salvation referred to Jesus pulling one out of the mires of sin. Once pulled out of this pit of mud, one has to be cleansed by the word to reshape he/her mind, to learn how to gradually remove him/herself from the world and consecrate him/herself to the priesthood of Christ. For this reason, apostle Paul exhorted the Philippians in this wise saying, *"Wherefore, my beloved, as ye have always obeyed, not as in my presence only, but now much more in my absence, work out your own salvation with fear and trembling*

(Philippians 2:12 KJV)". In translation, the apostle was saying that one has to work his/her salvation as body-builders works out to grow and strengthen their muscles.

NO SALVATION WITHOUT REPENTANCE

You must know that if you die with unconfessed sins in your life, they are not forgiven. You will have to pay for those sins. In 1 John 1: 7–10 (KJV) we read, *"But if we walk in the light, as he is in the light, we have fellowship with one another, and the blood of Jesus, his Son, purifies us from all sin. If we claim to be without sin, we deceive ourselves and the truth is not in us. If we confess our sins, he is faithful and just and will forgive us our sins and purify us from all unrighteousness. If we claim we have not sinned, we make him out to be a liar and his word is not in us"*. To walk in the light, a Christian should repent every day, preferably every night before going to sleep. Moreover, we should repent every time our conscience convicts us of sin. We should never let it linger in our consciousness. Because we sin all the time. We sin by words, thoughts, actions and even without knowing. Until the Holy Spirit seal our bodies and mind to the vine, sin will remain natural to us.

God will keep his hand of the bargain to forgive us to allow us to maintain our sanctification. But it is our duty to confess our sins daily. If we repent, we are walking in the light. If we do not repent, we are not walking in the light. It is not a matter of if we sin, it is a matter of what sin we commit. We are living in a sinful world and we interact with sinful people all the time. We have to be constantly examining our hearts, and thoughts. If we live with unconfessed sin, we are opening doors for Satan and his demons to manipulate us and enslave us by turning the sin into a habit and then it becomes an iniquity in the eyes of God. And you know what Jesus think about the workers of iniquity. Confessing our sins keep us sanctified and help us maintain our eligibility to become sons of God.

WORK OUT YOUR OWN SALVATION

The apostle advised us to work out our salvation. This means that apostle Paul understood that the salvation that takes one to heaven is a process. Elder Paul stated in Romans Chapter 10:13 (KJV), "For whosoever shall call upon the name of the Lord shall be saved." Here, the apostle referred to the same Lord Prophet Joel prophesied about in Joel 2:32 (KJV), the Lord Jesus, the Christ. Indeed, the Bible says that whoever calls on the name of the Lord, the Lord being Jesus the Christ, shall be saved. This verse talks about the salvation from the self, from the snares of this world. We are being saved every hour of every day while we exist on earth. Hourly and daily, God protects and saves us from the destructive and fiery darts of the devils and Satan's men servants. God saves us from the daily physical slaughter happening in the world. Hourly and daily, God saves us from the thinking patterns of this world. Our minds are renewed to become like that of Jesus Christ. Our souls are kept safe from the judgement of this world, from the spiritual slaughter. We are given a chance to sanctify ourselves and become sons and daughters of God. This salvation will culminate in our removal from the world at the time of the great destruction.

Contrary to popular opinion, being saved does not mean you are already in heaven. It simply means that whoever calls on the name of the Lord will receive the favor to repent and change course in life. Hence, repentance does not take you to heaven right away. It is the first step on the journey there. This is why Jesus praying to the Father asked him the following, "I pray not that thou shouldest take them out of the world, but that thou shouldest keep them from the evil. They are not of the world, even as I am not of the world (John 17:15 KJV)". Jesus did not ask the Father to take them away from the world but keep them away or save them from the evil of their respective generations.

This means that those who follow Jesus are bound to live on earth but would be kept away from the spirit of evil. In the Lord's prayer, Jesus asked the same thing to the Father, saying, "deliver us from evil," which means save us from evil. When you call on the name of Jesus, he saves you from the grip of hell and the original evil that subdued Adam and his Eve. He sends his Holy Spirit to convince you of sins and to guide you in the path of holiness to help you uproot the spirit of evil that dominates you from birth. He places you on the path of justice and righteousness to walk toward the promised land (the new Jerusalem) through the desert of life. If you remain in his words, he will give you glances of heaven. The populace of the nation of the church was told that heaven is someplace far away. That could not be farther from the truth. For in Luke 17:21(KJV), Jesus stated behold, the kingdom of God is within you.

Jesus advised us that heaven is right here with us. It is a dimension out of the reach of the intellect. Jesus also gave us conditions to enter this spiritual dimension, just as Moses gave the conditions of God to Israel when they were going to the promise land. God delights in those who obey and execute his commands. If you do not accept the sacrifice and obey the words of his son Jesus, you are still in enmity with him not in obedience and his wrath will remain on you. Throughout his teachings, Jesus made it clear that those who will be saved are those who believe and obey to thread on the path of righteousness. Jesus clearly told us that whoever don't believe will be condemned. But he also said that rebellion is the same as unbelief. To obey is to apply the word in every aspect of your life. In Matthew 21:28-32 (NIV), Jesus Addressed the religious cloud in these words saying: What do you think? There was a man who had two sons. He went to the first and said, 'Son, go and work today in the vineyard.' "'I will not,' he answered, but later he changed his mind and went. "Then the father went to the other son and said the same thing. He answered, 'I will, sir,' but he did not go. "Which of the two did what his father wanted?" "The first," they answered. Jesus said to them, "Truly I tell you, the tax collectors and the prostitutes are entering the kingdom of God ahead of you. For John came to you to show you the way of righteousness, and you did not believe him, but the tax collectors and the prostitutes did. And even after you saw this, you did not repent and believe him". You cannot enter heaven if you are living in disobedience, the act that caused Adam's demise. God loves you but he hates the rebellious self.

THE CONDITIONS TO STAY WITHIN GOD'S GRACE

In the early chapters, we talked about the belief that says (the repentance prayer alone can save one and once one says this prayer, he/she automatically have the unconditional love of God). We said that this belief is false. Let me explain this statement in more details here. God does not work with his creation without conditions. As Moses gave God's conditions to the Israelites before they could enter the earthly Jerusalem, so did Jesus Christ advised us that to enter the Jerusalem of Heaven there are conditions. When you read the words of Jesus, pay attention to the *ifs*. After each if, Jesus puts out the conditions to obtain the promise. For example, he stated, *(If) ye continue in my word, then are ye my disciples indeed; And ye shall know the truth, and the truth shall make you free (2 John 1:31-32, BSB)"*. Set you free from what you may ask? Set you free from the snares of this life, the greed, the envy, the pride, the lusts, etc.! In other words, Jesus sets you free to fly on the wings of the Spirit, free to walk the path onward to heaven, and freed you from the (self), which serves as a tool for your enemies. But if you do not abide in his word, you cannot be set free. You cannot enter heaven either in such a case.

THIS IS A BATTLE FOR THE MIND

Therefore, abiding in Jesus' word will keep you sanctified. It will set you apart from the world systems, their thinking patterns and all of their crooked. The further away you are from them, the stronger your salvation. Remember, you can only receive the birth of the spirit while you are sanctified. Then, you can enter heaven. Also, remember, when Jesus comes to take his own, he will bring them to heaven to live there for a thousand years. In Revelation 20:4 (KJV), we read, *"Then I saw the thrones, and those seated on them had been given authority to judge. And I saw the souls of those who had been beheaded for their testimony of Jesus and for the word of God, and those who had not worshiped the beast or its image, and had not received its mark on their foreheads or hands. And they came to life and reigned with Christ for a thousand years."*

This is the eternal salvation. It takes place right before the renewal of all things; after the demise of Satan and his throngs. This is the time when those who are like Christ or those who died for his sake rise up to reign. However, those who are born of the Spirit can enter heaven in dreams and visions while they are still on earth. Heaven is a spiritual place; only spirits go there. And thus, when you become a spirit, the Holy Spirit can take you there, as he did for Paul, John the Revelator, and a list of countless others. The belief that once you confess the name of Jesus, you are automatically ready to enter heaven was not supported by the apostles. Apostles John told us in 2 John 1:9 (BSB) to *"Watch yourselves, so that you do not lose what we have worked for, that you may be fully rewarded. Anyone who runs ahead without remaining in the teaching of Christ does not have God. Whoever remains in His teaching has both the Father and the Son."* In 2 Peter 2:20-22 (BSB), apostle Peter stated, *"If indeed they have escaped the corruption of the world through the knowledge of our Lord and Savior Jesus Christ, only to be entangled and overcome by it again, their final condition is worse than it was at first. It would have been better for them not to have known the way of righteousness than to have known it and turned away from the holy commandment passed on to them. Of them the proverbs are true: 'A dog returns to its vomit,' and, 'A sow that is washed goes back to her wallowing in the mud.'"* As you just read above, both apostles John and Peter believed that one can lose his/her salvation if he/she does not continue in the path.

The condition is to hear the word, accept it, and apply it to your life. It is the tool that will sanctify you. Only when you are sanctified, will you be on the right road to go to heaven. There are those who believe that they will be sanctified when they see Jesus. However, Elder Paul told the Hebrews that you must be sanctified to see Jesus. If you are not, you will not see him. To the Hebrews, Elder Paul said, *"Pursue peace with all men, as well as holiness (which is sanctification), without which no one will see the Lord, or no one will enter heaven, or no one can be born again" (Hebrews 12:14 BSB).* Notice what he told the Hebrews here, pursue peace and holiness. He said to the Romans

(Romans 12:1 BSB), *"I beseech you therefore, brethren, by the mercies of God, that you present your bodies a living sacrifice, holy, acceptable to God, which is your reasonable service."*

Notice that Paul advised the Romans to offer themselves to God as a living, holy sacrifice. This is a reasonable service he said. To be holy is a reasonable service to God. What do you offer to God as a service? To develop the eyes to see Jesus, one needs to walk on the highway of sanctification, better known as the path of holiness. However, many church leaders tell their followers that we are only human—that we cannot be holy—so they lead followers to believe that becoming holy is impossible. Then, the question is, why would Jesus command them to be holy, saying, *"Be ye therefore perfect, even as your Father which is in heaven is perfect,' if it is impossible?"* These two positions generate great confusion among the people. Some theologians reason that a person cannot lose his/her salvation. He/she can only lose his/her rewards. However, Jesus himself told us that many, many who were regular church attendees, miracle workers and so called prophets will be rejected at the gate of heaven (Matthew 7:22-24 KJV). I would trust Jesus over a theologian.

COME AS YOU ARE AND STAY AS YOU ARE

A large percentage of modern Christians don't believe in sanctification. They don't see the need for spiritual maturity. So, since Jesus says, "Come as you are," they decide that they will stay as they are, which is a grave mistake, as we will see later.

This doctrine of 'come as you are and stay as you are' is false since it conflicts with the true doctrine. The true doctrine asks the Christians to repent and renew their minds by learning the word of God which will sanctify them. Moreover, Jesus's view of being born again is entirely different from the evangelical's views. In most churches in the world, a person is born again after performing a confession. The churches subscribe to the belief that once one walks to the podium and says a prayer, one is born again. Jesus believes differently. He said to Nicodemus that he had to be born of water and of spirit to be born again.

Jesus believes that the act of confessing one's sin is the beginning of repentance, followed by the baptism of water to complete the repentance. It is then followed by the teaching of the Word of God for the renewal of the mind. This process results in producing sanctification and empties one of all the vices of the flesh. It helps him/her remove the fruits of the flesh to replace them with the fruits of the spirit until he/she is fully drafted in the vine as a branch. Some would object, asking, "What about the thief on the cross next to Jesus?" The answer is simple! The thief died after the confession. He was a special case, just as there have been many. The thief was indeed saved or snatched from the mouth of hell right before he breathed his last.

SAVE FROM THE MOUTH OF HELL

What most of humanity doesn't understand is that every human being who reaches the age of accountability is assigned a place in hell. Since the sin of Adam courses through his/her blood, he/she is a sinner. That sin is the chain that binds him/her to that fate, but the blood of Jesus can change that. As sons and daughters of Adam, every human soul and spirit has the nature of sin. After Adam sinned, he corrupted the human bloodline. He condemned the whole human race to eternal damnation in hell. Jesus referred to it as Hades or Gehenna. Hell is the abode of falling spirits. And because of sin, every human is among the fallen.

Hell is the destination of the soul of every human being because it does not die. The body is the only thing that dies. I hear people say that so or so is going to hell. This is not true! The sons of Adam are not going to hell, they are born in hell. The only way out is to accept Jesus Christ, follow his teachings, and become born again to go to heaven. Once you accept Jesus, he saves you from that fate. He removes you from the path to hell and puts you onto a different path. If you fail to walk that path and return to the path of hell voluntarily, it is on you, but you will regret it for eternity. Some scoffers preach that there is no hell, that the spirit/soul of man dies with the body. This too, is a false, demonic doctrine.

If this was the case, the cross would have been an exercise in futility. After the death of the body, there would be nothing left to save. Jesus came to save the soul of man because the spirit and soul of man are eternal. I agree with those who say that a loving God would never send anyone to hell. God never sent any man to that place. Man, however, chose to go there by rejecting the gift of God, Jesus Christ, because of their pride and prejudice.

Please, don't let prejudice cause your demise. Man is so divided that he bought into the illusion of nations and cultures. And so, every nation would like to have its own savior. For instance, the Buddhists claimed Buddha as the savior, Islam claimed Mohammed, and the Hindus have Brahma. However, none of these characters could conquer death and the grave.

In reality, we are all descendants of Adam. If a person claims a different lineage, he/she is not a human but an abomination. And since because of Adam's original disobedience, all man sin, God judged it good to place the redemption of man under the obedience of the one righteous man, Jesus the Christ. It is written, *"Neither is there salvation in any other: for there is none other name under heaven given among men, whereby we must be saved" (Acts 4:12 BSB).*

Now, regarding the concept of hell, let me explain further. Hell is a place of great torments, the abode of every sinful man, and there, the demons never stop tormenting the soul of man. They will do it forever. When one is saved, Jesus breaks the chains of sin around his/her spirit and soul. However, the contaminated flesh is hardwired in it. Sin is like a virus in every man's DNA.

Once its original power is broken over the spirit and the soul, it still remains in the flesh in the forms of feelings, habits, culture, taste, allegiance, pride, religion, and other elements. It can only be eradicated by making a complete turnaround, which is repentance. Repentance means a complete change in habits, culture, tastes, preferences, and religion. Those who are living in sin have one destination—hell. When they renounce sin, ask for forgiveness, and accept the lordship of Jesus, he then reroutes them to the way of the kingdom of light.

They are set onto a new path, the path of heaven. Now, the task is to stop sinning and follow Jesus onto the new path—the path of life. The act of confession snatches one from the path to hell and puts him/her on the path of life; we call that *saved*. But once you confess, you now need to learn about the path of life, which means stop sinning.

Jesus addressed the man he healed in John 5:8, saying, *"Get up, pick up your mat, and walk."* Immediately, the man was made well, and he picked up his mat and began to walk. After the Jews harassed the man, Jesus found him at the temple and said to him, *"See, you have been made well. Stop sinning, or something worse may happen to you." (John 5:14 BSB).*

Jesus saved him from this sickness but warned him not to continue down the path of sin. Otherwise, he could find himself back in a predicament that was worse or catch another illness causing his body to die quicker, hastening his spirit's fall to hell. Again, we witness Jesus saying the same thing to the woman prostitute in John 8:10-11 (BSB), *"Then Jesus straightened up and asked her, 'Woman, where are your accusers? Has no one condemned you?' 'No one, Lord,' she answered. 'Then neither do I condemn you,' Jesus declared. 'Now go and sin no more.'"* Jesus saved her from sudden death but asked her to sin no more. He said it because sin is the gateway to hell. It is the chain that bounds every person born from the lineage of Adam.

CHAPTER 16

CHRISTIANS, THE ONLY RESISTANCE TO SATAN'S POWER IN THE WORLD

The Christians are the resistance. They are the ones in the way of the man of perdition—the saints in the present time who carry the tradition of resisting the devil. It is because of the Christians that the world of man has not imploded yet. The invasion had been completed for thousands of years now. We have been born in it, and we are living under the occupation, the bondage of the fallen armies and their dark emperor. That is why sin feels natural; we are conceived in it. We know nothing else.

The morals and spiritual lights that infiltrate this darkness to cause us to question the status quo are from heaven. They originate from the light of Jesus Christ. Some of us have been holding this certain moral standard for years. However, now is the time for the conditioning, when man is rejecting truth, righteousness, justice, and holiness to conform to the emperor's world system.

The armies of Satan are on standby at their battle stations. They are ready to come on earth to inflict pain on the sons of Adam. They are ready to turn the world of man into hell, to spread wars, plagues, and destructions in every corner of the earth. The world is already feeling the heat. These little economic crises, epidemic scares, little wars, and pestilences are only the tip of the iceberg, or, as the Bible puts it, the beginning of sorrows. But there is something holding this change back.

The only reason why there is still a sense of peace and comfort on earth is because the Christians stand in the way of the demons. Because of the sanctified Christians, the presence of the Holy Spirit is still here. The Holy Spirit is the one who is keeping Satan and his minions at bay. He is the only one they are afraid of, as stated previously.

HUMAN POLITIC IS SATAN'S DIPLOMATIC AFFAIR

Why should we join the camp of the enemy? Some may argue that having Christians in government is good for the church. However, I strongly disagree with this statement. I see this action as joining the camp of the enemy. The following reasons explains why I came to that conclusion. God created the heavens and the earth and established Adam as the ruler and prince of it all. But after Adam fell, something strange happened. Satan—the fallen, the ancient serpent, the father of lies, the sworn enemy of all man—took the rulership of the earth during the first invasion and started reigning as the prince of earth.

THE ESOTERIC SATAN AND THE GENUINE SAINT ON EARTH

Satan then created a world for himself. Notice that I say a world, not the earth; he did not and cannot create the earth. So, in this world (system), he poured his corruption, hatred for God, malice, and will to dominate all flesh. He undid the system that God had established and authored another in his image that resembles his will and ego. The sons of man in the whole world gave in to Satan, thinking that they would have peace if they let him have his way.

But the fallen cherub knows no peace. Therefore, as long as Satan is influential on earth, there will be no peace for man.

However, not all the sons of Adam followed Satan. He did not influence all of them. A few of them created the resistance. They resisted Satan by obeying the will of God and fulfilling it at all cost. Starting with Abel, the resistance grew. It made a connection with the great God—blessed be his name! Because of the resistance Satan received from righteous servants like Enoch, Job, Abraham, Jacob, the sons of Israel, and the other prophets, the fragrance of the kingdom of God was maintained on earth through the presence of the Holy Spirit.

Satan could not remain on the surface of the earth for two reasons. The first reason is that Satan works in an esoteric manner. He hides behind the shadow to corrupt all of man and prepares the world for his governance. The second reason is that Satan is afraid of the Holy Spirit, who is upon those who truly love God, obey his words, and do his will at all cost, even unto death. He can't stand those who worship God in spirit and truth. He knows that these don't come to God's presence for material benefits but for spiritual intimacy.

Satan cannot stand to face a servant of God who does not have sin in his/her life. He has no weapons against those who are holy. They are like a high-intensity flame of fire. That is why before he comes close to the servants of God, he tempts them to make them sin first. Also, God puts a hedge of protection around those that Satan cannot penetrate.

For instance, in the case of Job, the whole bet was to see if he served God out of genuine love or if it was because of the blessings that God gave him. *"When Satan presented himself before the throne, God asked him, 'Have you considered My servant Job? For there is no one on earth like him, a man who is blameless and upright, who fears God and shuns evil.' Satan answered the LORD, 'Does Job fear God for nothing? Have You not placed a hedge on every side around him and his household and all that he owns? You have blessed the work of his hands, and his possessions have increased in the land. But stretch out Your hand and strike all that he has, and he will surely curse You to Your face.' 'Very* well,' said the LORD to Satan. 'Everything he has is in your hands, but you must not lay a hand on the man himself'" (Job 1:8–12 BSB).

In a coordinated onslaught, Satan went and destroyed every material thing Job possessed, killed all his ten children, and rendered him a pauper in one day. Still, Job remained faithful. *"On another day, the sons of God came to present themselves before the LORD; and Satan also came with them to present himself before Him. 'Where have you come from?' said the LORD to Satan. 'From roaming through the earth,' he replied, 'and walking back and forth in it.' Then the LORD said to Satan, 'Have you considered My servant Job? For there is no one on earth like him, blameless and upright, fearing God and shunning evil. He still retains his integrity, even though you incited Me against him to ruin him without cause.' Again, the Lord wagered on Job. Then Satan says, 'Skin for skin!' Satan replied. 'A man will give up all he owns in exchange for his life. But stretch out Your hand and strike his flesh and bones, and he will surely curse You to Your face.' 'Very well,' said the LORD to Satan. 'He is in your hands, but you must spare his life'"* (Job 2:1–6 BSB).

Notice what God said here. Satan incited Him against Job. Glory be to God he can no longer go into heaven to accused and incite God wrath against the saints. However, Satan use a different tactic. He inspires man to sin to bring the wrath of God on themselves as he did for the angels he caused to fell from heaven and for the patriarch Adam. He did not succeed in the case of Job. Satan pronounced the secret, but he did not understand it. He said that a man would give everything he owns for his life. That is true, but Satan did not understand how saints think. Job's life was not in the breath of his flesh but in the attachment of his spirit. Satan thought that Job's life was in the breathing of his flesh and the material things he possessed. However, his life went deeper and higher than that. Job's life was his love for God and his unwavering desire to please his Creator.

Job proved that when he stated the following during his trials, *"Even if he slays me, I will trust him."* Job had in him the same spirit that was in Jesus Christ. It is the spirit of obedience to death. We saw a glance of that spirit in Isaac, the son of Abram. Isaac entrusted his life at the hands of his father so much that he was willing to go with the sacrifice. He trusted his father even to the point of lying on an altar blindfolded, not knowing what would happen next.

Similarly, Satan took Job's health, but Job still did not deny the Lord. We know how the story ended. God won the wager and restored Job's riches and family tenfold. This hedge of protection around Job was the Holy Spirit. Satan knows that if this hedge is around a servant of God, and he tries to attack, the Holy Spirit will consume him with unquenchable fires. The Holy Spirit is a consuming fire, and every being in the creation who knows better fears him. It is only man who plays with the Holy Spirit—only man who does not understand the seriousness of their predicament. The angels know him and fear him, and so does all of creation.

Since the prophets and other righteous men were filled with the Spirit, Satan went and hid underground to continue the war and rule the earth in secret. He built his kingdoms underground, under the sea, and in the second heaven. However, Satan rules our world through his representatives, the kings, the princes, the presidents, the governments, the popes, the magicians, the sorcerers, and the members of the secret societies.

The prince of this earth has power over every government on earth; he governs all politics, cultures, economies, and religions. Therefore, anyone who does not have the Spirit of God is subject to Satan's rule.

SATAN TEMPTED JESUS TO CHOOSE THE SELF OVER THE FATHER

That is why he said to Jesus when tempting him, *"All this I will give you if you will bow down and worship me."* But Jesus did not intermingle within Satan's kingdom. He did not sell his kingship for a perishable kingdom. He vehemently rejected the offer of the fallen and maintained his allegiance to the good Father by reminding the devil that all worship, service, and allegiance belong to God, the Father. Therefore, Jesus said to him, *"Away from me, Satan! For it is written: 'Worship the Lord your God and serve him only.'"* Jesus refused to serve Satan by satisfying his flesh, and so he passed the test and was victorious. He later affirmed this victory to his disciples, saying, *"Hereafter I will not talk much with you: for the prince of this world cometh, and hath nothing in me" (John 14:30).*

By "hath nothing in me," Jesus meant that Satan has no authority over his flesh. Satan tempted Jesus to extend the original sin to him, to make him disobey the father to satisfy his flesh like Adam did in Eden but he failed. After that test, Jesus was sanctified to offer himself to the Father as a perfect sacrifice. Satan could not subdue him in the sin of disobedience as he did for Adam. The son of man was victorious. Jesus knew who Satan was and understood his devilish tactics and authority. Jesus knew that Satan only has power over the flesh, in other words, the self. The more emphasis one place on satisfying the flesh, the more power he/she gives Satan over his/her spirit.

As we explained earlier, Satan tested Jesus within the laws of God. Satan tried to make Jesus doubt his essence, but he failed. He then tested Jesus with bread while Jesus was hungry as he did for Adam, but Jesus rebuked him, saying, *"Man shall not live on bread alone but on every word that comes from the mouth of God."* He tried to make Jesus tempt God, but he failed in this endeavor. He said to Jesus, *"It is written: 'He will command his angels concerning you, and they will lift you up in their hands, so that you will not strike your foot against a stone.'"* Jesus answered him, *"It is also written: 'Do not put the Lord your God to the test.'"*

Satan then tempted Jesus with power, for he thought that every man wanted power. Yet, Jesus had the greater power and reminded Satan of that fact. Notice that all the temptations are about satisfying the self. The second temptation can from his surroundings. Satan used Peter to tempt Jesus. When Jesus told his disciples that he had to die, *"Peter took Him aside and began to rebuke Him. "Far be it from You, Lord!" he said. "This shall never happen to You!"* But Jesus turned and said to Peter, *"Get behind Me, Satan! You are a stumbling block to Me. For you do not have in mind the things of God, but the things of men."* Then Jesus told His disciples, *"If anyone wants to come after Me, he must deny himself and take up his cross and follow Me.*

Satan then used Jesus' emotions and feelings to make him sin. On the Mount of Olives, Jesus prayed to the Father asking for an alternative to the cup of suffering he had to drink. In Luke 22:42–43 BSB we read, *"And He withdrew about a stone's throw beyond them, where He knelt down and prayed, "Father, if You are willing, take this cup from Me. Yet not My will, but Yours be done. "Then an angel from heaven appeared to Him and strengthened Him.* Notice that he relinquished himself; either good and evil, if it's the will of the Father, he will do it. He was a perfect sacrifice. The Holy spirit helped him understand that doing the will of the father is the most important thing in existence. Job had this same mind set when stated that even if he slays me, yet, I will still trust him.

THE KINGDOM OF SATAN, PLATFORM OF UNRIGHTEOUSNESS

Don't you know that whoever works under a governor is at his/her mercy and must follow his/her wisdom and direction? Whoever is in Satan's government, he has authority over. Suppose he tried to gain authority over Jesus by offering him power, and Jesus rejected him. Why do some Christians think it is okay to enter Satan's domain and serve him in earth's politics and still think they are doing service to God? Does God approve of corruption, greed, lies, and pride?

God forbids! Politicians are unrighteous hypocrites who lie to people to get elected into office. They are of their father, the devil, the liar. But Jesus said to his disciples, *"For I tell you that unless your righteousness exceeds that of the scribes and Pharisees* (who were the politicians at that time), *you will never enter the kingdom of heaven"* (Matthew 5:20 BSB). And again, to the scribes and Pharisees, Jesus said, *"Ye are of your father the devil, and the lusts of your father ye will do. He was a murderer from the beginning, and abode not in the truth, because there is no truth in him. When he speaketh a lie, he speaketh of his own: for he is a liar, and the father of it"* (John 8:44–45 BSB).

One cannot grow more righteous under the dominion of Satan. There is no righteousness in his kingdom. You might see a form of it, but it is only an act to deceive you. Satan has no justice and truth in him, and those in his kingdom identify with him. A Christian should identify with Jesus, the King of righteousness and justice. True Christians don't mingle with the world and don't venture into world politics. A Christian who ventures into world politics only condemns his/her soul. He/he cannot do anything for the church of God, for this church does not answer to the powers of this world.

The Holy Spirit sets the agenda of the true church of Jesus. If you think that some politician who has claimed the title of Christian—just to get elected—will help you when persecution comes, you have been deceived. If you are in a church that answers to the powers of this world, you are not serving Jesus. So, examine where you stand and whom you serve. The Christians are the resistance. Therefore, we must oppose injustice, lasciviousness, greed, pride, envy, sexual perversion, rebellion against God and unrighteousness.

You too can be part of this resistance. But to join the resistance, you must walk in the way of the Lord Jesus Christ—the way of obedience. Be holy, and be filled with the Holy Spirit! I mean you need to follow his command to be holy, a command given to all Christians. It is an ancient command, as it was decreed in the Old Testament to the Hebrews by Moses. In Leviticus 19:2 (BSB), the Lord told Moses, *"Speak to the entire congregation of the Israelites and tell them: 'Be holy because I, the LORD your God, am holy.'"* The order echoes in the New Testament, in Mathew 5:48, when Jesus said, *"Be ye therefore perfect, even as your Father which is in heaven is perfect."*

This is the same as saying, "be holy or be sanctified!" Notice that Jesus ordered the disciples as Moses ordered the Hebrews. He ordered them to be perfect. Why would both leaders give the same command to their peoples if it is impossible? They wouldn't ask it if it was impossible. Why do they want them to be perfect, and what does it mean to be perfect or holy? Because without holiness, they can't serve God!

Most theologians would say that Israel could not serve God because they could not obey the law. However, the Holy Spirit revealed to me that Israel had the power to obey the law. Many in Israel kept the law every day of their lives. They were not any more special than their counterparts. For instance, the prophets obeyed the law of God. We can see that in 1 Kings 19:14–18 (BSB). In verse 14, we read that when Elijah was depressed about the killing of the prophets, Elijah entered a cave and spent the night. *"And the word of the LORD came to him, saying, 'What are you doing here, Elijah?' 'I have been very zealous for the LORD, the God of Hosts,' he replied, 'but the Israelites have forsaken Your covenant, torn down Your altars, and killed Your prophets with the sword. I am the only one left, and they are seeking my life as well.'"*

After the Lord ordered Elijah to anoint those who would replace the corrupt government, as well as Elisha, who was to succeed him as lead prophet, the Lord God told him in verse 18, *"Nevertheless, I have reserved seven thousand in Israel all whose knees have not bowed to Baal and whose mouths have not kissed him."* The Holy Spirit anointed those who obeyed the law. To be perfect in the eyes of God is to be humble, blameless, impartial, righteous; to be without prejudice or racism; to maintain one's sexual purity; to be free of greed, envy, pride, lust, and vices—in other words, to be free of every ego-centric tendency and guiles.

These themes echo throughout the Bible. To make his people holy, Master Jesus—after baptizing those he called into the apostolic ministry—removed them from the general population. He stayed with them day and night, teaching them the Word and will of God, cleansing their mind to think differently, and teaching them humility. And for three years, he taught them. In John 13:4 (BSB), Jesus gave us a great example of humility. The passage said that he got up from the meal during the last supper, took off his outer clothing, and wrapped a towel around his waist. *"He poured water into a basin and began to wash his disciples' feet, drying them with the towel that was wrapped around him. When he came to Simon Peter, Peter said to him, 'Lord, are you going to wash my feet?' Jesus replied, 'You do not realize now what I am doing, but later you will understand.' Peter protested it and said, 'You shall never wash my feet.' Jesus answered, 'Unless I wash you, you have no part with me.' 'Then, Lord,' Simon Peter replied, 'not just my feet but my hands and my head as well!' Jesus answered, 'Those who have had a bath need only to wash their feet; their whole body is clean. And you are clean, though not every one of you.' For he knew who was going to betray him, and that was why he said not everyone was clean. When he had finished washing their feet, he put on his clothes and returned to his place. 'Do you understand what I have done for you?' he asked them. 'You call me "Teacher" and "Lord," and rightly so, for that is what I am. Now that I, your Lord and Teacher, have washed your feet, you also should wash one another's feet. I have set you an example that you should do as I have done for you. Very truly I tell you, no servant is greater than his master, nor is a messenger greater than the one who sent him. Now that you know these things, you will be blessed if you do them"* (John 13:4–17 BSB).

CHAPTER 17

RESTRICTING THE HOLY SPIRIT

Unless Jesus washes you, you have no part with him. He did not wash his disciples only to cleanse them but also to establish humility and equality among them. This cleansing was to complete and establish the bond of brotherhood and ground all of them to avoid division of rank so that everyone would work in unison.

Elder Peter was baptized with water; he had the bath that cleansed his body. Now to be ready for the baptism of the Holy Spirit and of fire, he had to be washed by the master. The master washed the disciples to reach a level of sanctification that would free them of all human vices, including pride and greed, which had conquered Judas. This last wash helped them to empty their temples of pride to make room to receive a greater portion of the Holy Spirit.

The Holy Spirit will not inhabit a body full of pride, which is one of the fruits of the flesh. To be filled with the Holy Spirit, they needed to free their bodies of fruits of the flesh. And in the case of his disciples, pride was the last one. Once they reached a level of consciousness free of pride, they were ready to be filled with the new personality of the spirit by having their spirit fused with the same Spirit that was in Jesus Christ, thus becoming one with the vine.

In the practice of most churches, you will find a form of holiness but a denial of the power of God. Many leaders restrict the Holy Spirit by diminishing its importance in the church. They think they know better than him because they received a theological degree. They tell the new converts that they have the Holy Spirit because they came to the altar. Telling the new converts that they have the Holy Spirit keeps the leaders from being bothered.

When you ask them, "What is the sign that indicates their churches have the Holy Spirit?" They explain that they have the Holy Spirit because they wouldn't have repented or wanted to go to church if they did not have it. Or better yet, the leaders will stop talking about the Holy Spirit altogether.

They only refer to him when they need healing. Somehow, they believe that everyone has the Holy Spirit. However, we read above how elder Paul did not see the twelve he encountered in Corinth as having the Holy Spirit. He told them that they needed to receive the Holy Spirit. He prayed for them until they were baptized.

Jesus commands the new converts to come to him as they are, but he never tells them to stay as they are. Jesus told Nicodemus that he had to be born again, and he specified that he had to be born of water and spirit. However, the populist theologians tell them differently. They are telling them that they're born again after saying the prayer when the prayer is simply the acknowledgment of one's sins and the acceptance that Jesus is king and that he died to wash away those sins.

Moreover, there is a lack of spirit-filled elders to lay hands on the newly baptized Christians. I found that the elders aren't filled with the Holy Spirit in most churches I have visited. They don't believe in him. They are operating by the book. They are not sanctified, and most don't see it as possible. Or they understand the Word differently than did elder Paul, the apostle of Jesus Christ, who preached the cross of Jesus Christ and the Holy Spirit to the gentiles. The leaders of the church believe that they own the church. They make no room for the Holy Spirit because if he is appropriately acknowledged, he will tell them what to do as he did in the time of the apostles.

The Tale of Two Churches

They don't like having someone telling them what to do. They have a vision, and they want to stick to it. The vision of God does not matter. Also, with the advent of the evangelical movement, having the Holy Spirit now is big business. Elder Paul and the other disciples, after the Pentecost, went around laying a hand on new converts to transfer the gift of the Holy Spirit. But today, this is rarely done.

The elders are not praying for people to receive the Holy Spirit as elder Paul did. You will sooner see them praying for people to be healed than to be filled with the Spirit. They care for the body of flesh to heal it but ignore the body of spirit. This is contrary to what God is seeking. God is seeking spirits. But instead of catering to the spirit man, they cater to the flesh, the enemy of the spiritual man.

Consequently, people come by the thousand to be healed but not filled with the Holy Spirit or to become one with Christ or know Jesus. This also raises suspicions as to what spirit animate them. For if it was the Spirit of Jesus, the Holy Spirit, they would have been used by Jesus to anoint the new converts as he used Ananias to anoint Saul. We read that the Holy Spirit manifested different gifts to different people throughout the Bible. However, at the beginning of the movement and until today, the new converts had a sign. The sign that a new convert is filled with the Holy Spirit is the speaking of new tongues and prophesying.

One can stop speaking in tongues after and receive other gifts, but that is the sign. And so, I am asking you who are reading this book the same questions Elder Paul asked the other twelve Christians in Corinth: *"Did you receive the Holy Spirit when you became believers?"* The gift of the Holy Spirit is an essential element in a Christian's life. It is the power you need to be victorious. Without him, a Christian doesn't stand a chance in this fight.

Hence, the Holy Spirit came to convict the world of sin. The whole world is convicted of sin, but that does not mean the whole world has the Holy Spirit. Only the sons of God can receive the Holy Spirit. In John 14:16-17, we read, *"And I will ask the Father, and He will give you another Advocate to be with you forever, the Spirit of truth. The world cannot receive Him, because it neither sees Him nor knows Him. But you do know Him, for He abides with you and will be in you."*

Becoming a son of God is a three-step process. Getting convicted and repenting of your sins is the first step. Being baptized of water is the confession of faith, which is the second step. The next step is getting baptized with the Holy Spirit. Most Christians stop at step two. But without step three, you are only an infant. Your being will be pulled by the two sides, spiritual or material. Whichever side grows stronger and becomes more mature will win out of the two. In every son or daughter of Adam, the spirit of the flesh is the most dominant force. It will do what will satisfy its desires, such as those we just saw in Galatians 5:19–21 (BSB). In a son of God, the Spirit of God has dominion and he leads the son to be obedient to the father at all cost. Under the dominion of the Father's Spirit, the son will do whatever the father wills, just as Jesus did. Jesus lived his life to please the Father. In Matthew 6:24 (BSB), Jesus said, *"No man can serve two masters: for either he will hate the one and love the other; or else he will hold to the one, and despise the other, Ye cannot serve God and mammon."*

You cannot serve flesh and spirit together. One must decrease for the other to increase. Without the Holy Spirit, the spirit man is who will decrease. To attract the Spirit of God, we need the unity of mind. Another way we restrict the spirit is in our disagreements. To be one body, we must be in one accord and become of one spirit. However, in the status quo, the Christians are ever divided.

Each part of the body has a will of its own. Thus, the body is divided, and the Holy Spirit cannot stay in such division. The churches are fighting, and in this fight, it is every pastor and every member fighting for their church congregation and denomination. In this endless denominational war, the Baptists, the Seventh-Day Adventists, and the Pentecostals, among others, fight for their ideas. Hence, they use Jesus as bait to fill up their temple buildings but ignore his message of brotherhood and unity. In 1 Corinthians 1:12–13, we read Paul's rebukes of their sectorial divisionary tendencies, saying, *"Now this I say, that every one of you saith, I am of Paul; and I of Apollos; and I of Cephas; and I of Christ. Is Christ divided? was Paul crucified for you? or were ye baptized in the name of Paul?"*

Paul wanted them to remain under one banner, Jesus Christ. Similarly, the Christians of today form denominations through which they identify themselves. Each group claims a denomination that would identify with its rhetoric. Many people claim to be Baptist, Seventh-Day Adventist, Methodist, or Pentecostal, but few claim to be followers of Jesus Christ like Paul and the apostles were. They focus on growing their sect but not the spirit. They are continuing the divisions the Corinthians started. In the same spirit of division, church members are divided within their own congregation. The rich don't associate with the poor. They are divided by ethnic descent, skin color, political affiliations, and economic classes. They judge each other based on appearance, educational levels, and other social constructs.

Elder Paul rebuked the Corinthians for the same behavior. He spoke against this division by exhorting the Corinthians in these words, *"Now I exhort you, brethren, by the name of our Lord Jesus Christ, that you all agree and that there be no divisions among you, but that you be made complete in the same mind and in the same judgment"* (1 Corinthians 1:10 BSB). He was so adamant in talking against division among the Christians because he did not want the church to be divided over any ideas. Because a divided church cannot stand! This division is among the many reasons why the Christians of this epoch are not being baptized of the Holy Spirit. In the Acts of the Apostles, we read, *"And when they had prayed, the place was shaken where they were assembled together; and they were all filled with the Holy Ghost, and they spoke the word of God with boldness. And the multitude of them that believed were of one heart and of one soul: neither said any of them that ought of the things which he possessed was his own; but they had all things common"* (Acts 4:31–32 KJV).

They had all things common because they had the same Spirit, the same sentiment. In contrast, when the current church congregations of today pray, everyone is asking for something different in total disagreement, or everyone has their own ideology that they want to hold on to. They do not come in front of the throne with one heart. As they are divided in their denominations, so are they in the congregations, and they individualize Jesus. They pray for the goals of the individuals, not for the goals of the community. But the early Christians prayed in unison, in communion with each other, to ask for the same thing, to seek the same goals, just as Jesus told them to do when he spoke in these words, *"Again, I tell you truly that if two of you on the earth agree about anything you ask for, it will be done for you by My Father in heaven. For where two or three gathers together in My name, there am I with them"* (Matthew 18:19 BSB).

Notice that Jesus did not referrer to the individual prayer. Jesus instructs the individual to pray differently. Instead, he said, two of you. Jesus simply said that the blessing would come to the community and then be distributed to the individual. For instance, in the upper room, the disciples gathered to ask God to stretch his hand to show his power to the world. The Holy Spirit came and bestowed power upon the community, and everyone shared that power. In Matthew 6:6 (KJV), Jesus asked the individual to go pray in his/her closet to conversate with the father. But to the crowd, he said they should gather in the (amen) to pray for the things they need, and they will receive them. Amen is the Hebrew word for "certainty," "truth," and "faith."

When Christians pronounced amen at the end of each community prayer, they merely meant they agreed on one faith, one God, and one Spirit. Today, our customs tell us that we can do it alone. We do not need one another. In today's congregations, no one can agree on anything. The ego is in charge. Although the fight is an individual fight, Jesus asked his soldiers to fight in a group of at least two.

This is why Jesus sent the disciples to evangelize in groups of at least two. The strength of the group is stronger than that of the one. In the same spirit, the apostle Paul dictated to the Hebrews not to abandon their congregations (Hebrews 10:25) because the power of the Holy Spirit is manifested in the gathering of the saints who have one heart and one soul. *"For where two or three gather together in My name, there am I with them said Jesus"* (Matthew 18:19 BSB).

When I raised my concern about the current church ignoring this technique when they pray to a current pastor while I was researching, he told me that they do pray in unison because they have a speaker pray for them. But it is said here that they all raise their voices in unison. Not one person prays while the minds of the others wander. The religious congregations meet, but they are all estranged from one another. The division between them is very strong. Some of them can't stand each other. They can't stand to be in each other's presence. It is every man for himself! They meet to listen to a speech, and then everyone heads to their own occupation and goals. The meetings do not last long. These Christians barely know one another.

They aren't their brother's keepers. They don't have time to pray for one another's problems. The destitute, the unemployed, the widows, the rejected by the world, finds no place in their midst. The poor in their midst go to sleep hungry. If a brother or sister is hungry and go to them to ask for food, they tell him/her that they will pray for him/her and send him/her back with an empty hand. Jesus frowned upon this behavior. He called it a sin. He said that it will be one of the reproaches for those he will deny entrance in heaven when he come in his glory (Matthew 25:42-46). Jesus prohibited his followers to treat even strangers that way. Yet this behavior is the norm in the current church. This is how they treat their fellow Christian brothers. Their fellowship is broken. Even worst, fellowship with one another after church gatherings is not advise by the leaders anymore.

Therefore, when Satan and his demons corner one of them to devour him/her, the others do not know and do not care to know. The faster Satan can divide them, the quicker he destroys or corrupt them. Once, I heard a pastor say, "People get offended when we do not end the church on time." I wanted him to tell me who determines when to end the service at his church. He answered that it was the people and the committee. The answer did not surprise me. This is the norm in the churches. People get offended if the service runs longer than they've decided. For instance, if they decide to only give God one hour, the pastor cannot go over that allotted time because they must go home on time to watch the game.

However, in the Pentecostal Church, the Holy Spirit decided when the service should end because he needed time to give gifts, to give prophecies, to renew and strengthen the soldiers for the fight. In today's churches, the meetings are run like business meetings. It is a do-it-yourself society, and everyone is sent home after a fixed hour of lecture to go home to read the bible. When in their gatherings, they do not have time to pray or worship. They do not have time to glorify the God of Glory. They do not have time to wait for God to talk to them. The services are short because people have better things to do. Some of them must watch the game or go to the country club to meet their friends. Their idols are more important than passing the time with Jesus. Still, they profess to know and understand Jesus.

How do you know someone you barely have time for? Well, they can answer this as well. Their answer is, "We read the Bible." Some of them will tell you that they've read the entire Bible several times. This is a great danger! One can read the whole Bible and learn all that a human can about Jesus. But that does not mean he/she knows Jesus. Say, for instance, you read all that was written about a certain person, we all can agree that until you spend time with that person, you never really know him/her. The Christian needs to be like Jesus. And to be like Jesus, one needs to know him.

Yet, church members are convinced they know Jesus because they read about him. They put their faith in the Word so much that they forgot that reading the Word does not enlighten a man—it is the Holy Spirit who does. We can see that in the interactions of Jesus with the disciples. In John 14, we can see how the disciples doubted him after meeting with him in the flesh daily for three years. In verse 5, *"Thomas said, 'Lord, we do not know where You are going, so how can we know the way?' Jesus answered, 'I am the way, the truth, and the life. <u>No one comes to the Father except through Me</u>. If you had known Me, you would know My Father as well. From now on you do know Him and have seen Him.'"*

To show how far the confusion went, in verse 8, *"Philip said to Him, 'Lord, show us the Father, and that will be enough for us.' Jesus replied, 'Philip, I have been with you all this time, and still you do not know Me? Anyone who has seen Me has seen the Father. How can you say, "Show us the Father"? Do you not believe that I am in the Father and the Father is in Me? The words I say to you, I do not speak on My own. Instead, it is the Father dwelling in Me, performing His works'"* (John 14:5–10 BSB). Keep in mind that Jesus taught them for three years, and yet, they needed the Holy Spirit to fully understand what

Jesus taught them and who Jesus really was. However, today's church is more interested in theology, long monologues, and pontification. They don't want to develop intimacy with Jesus to grow their spirits.

Feeding their intellect is what is important to them. These Christians are all victims of the letter demons, the specters of hell. Heaven is a spiritual place; therefore, the path to it is spiritual. One does not find this path; instead, it finds you. The Holy Spirit is he who chooses and puts one on that path. The Holy Spirit is at work to create a new nation of priests for the Lord of Host, and he is seeking those who are holy to recruit. Would you be one of them? It is time you put away childish things to embrace what is mature.

To appear before the throne of God, one needs to be either a king, a prophet, an intercessor, a true worshiper, or a priest. That is why the apostle Peter said, *"But you are a chosen people, a royal priesthood, a holy nation, a people for God's own possession, to proclaim the virtues of Him who called you out of darkness into His marvelous light"* (1 Peter 2:9 BSB). Are you exercising your office of priest in the kingdom of God, or are you only a spectator in the outer courts of the temple? To find your place in the kingdom, you need to first see the kingdom. But that will not happen if you are not born of the Holy Spirit, just like what Jesus told Nicodemus.

Once you are born of the Holy Spirit, you become a true worshipper. Therefore, you are not a true worshipper without the Holy Spirit. In John 4:23 (BSB), we read what Jesus said to the Samaritan woman: *"But a time is coming and has now come when the true worshipers will worship the Father in spirit and in truth, for the Father is seeking such as these to worship Him."* In Philippians 3:3 (BSB), elder Paul stated, *"For it is we who are the circumcision, we who worship by the Spirit of God, who glory in Christ Jesus, and who put no confidence in the flesh."* In John 6:63 (NIB), Jesus said, *"The Spirit gives life; the flesh counts for nothing. The words I have spoken to you—they are full of the Spirit and life. The flesh profits nothing."*

Do you notice what elder Paul says here? *"We who worship by the Spirit of God…"* What does that mean? It means that the Holy Spirit is he who inspires worship in the heart of the Christians. All you can do without the Spirit is sing a couple of songs while your mind wanders aimlessly. We can't focus on God with flesh because the flesh likes worldly things. However, when the Spirit worships God, we get fully involved. We forget about the earth and join the choir of heaven. This is the type of worship that God deserves. But unless one is born of the Spirit, he/she cannot render true worship to God, which is his/her true service.

CHAPTER 18

KEEP THE MASS IN THE DARK

Somehow, the establishment of religious leaders of our time has revived the old religious system of Israel. They have formed a club of preachers of the gospel of Christ and require those who wants to serve God by preaching the gospel to be part of the club. If you don't belong to the club, they won't even give you the time of day, just like the Sanhedrin club of Jerusalem. If they do not appoint you to preach, you can't do it. Like the catholic hierarchy appoints those who lord over their congregations, so do the protestant institutions in our day. Jesus dealt with that kind when he began his ministry.

The Sanhedrin tried to discredit him at all cost. And when they failed, they resorted to killing him because they could not control what he preached. When Jesus started to teach, they were surprised, wondering where he learned letters—for he was not one of them, and they did not teach him. In John 7:15–18 (BSB), we read, *"About halfway through the feast, Jesus went up to the temple courts and began to teach. The Jews were amazed and asked, 'How did this man attain such learning without having studied?' 'My teaching is not My own,' Jesus replied. 'It comes from Him who sent me. If anyone desires to do his will, he will know whether My teaching is from God or whether I speak on my own. He who speaks on his own authority seeks his own glory, but*

He who seeks the glory of the One who sent him is a man of truth; in Him there is no falsehood."

Likewise in the status quo the new Sanhedrin is filtering the gospel narrative. They say that they are trying to keep people from preaching the wrong things. But they only do that for those who did not go to their theological schools. They do not check on the graduates of their schools who are spreading heresy through the world in order to profit.

The consensus of today's religious leaders in the Christian church is that one has to be a theologian to fulfill the commission. Therefore, one needs to be among the philosophers. As a result, the preachers should go to their schools to learn their theology of God. Many of the religious leaders of today believe that one needs to be a theologian to preach, the same belief held by the Sanhedrin of the time of Jesus. This is a well-protected, well-guarded custom, which becomes a business. It is a rite of passage. They hold the key to success on this front. This system goes so far as to convince the gentiles that if a man is not a theologian, he cannot preach to them. So, everyone who tries to preach without a theology degree is not welcome.

Jesus commissioned every convert to be trained and to be mature in the faith. Once they are mature in the faith, they should set out to go preach the gospel. But in the status quo, one has to go study philosophical theology in a theological school from a body of non-believers to get approval to preach. However, Jesus did not deal with philosophers. He called the twelve and made a fisherman the lead disciple among them, as opposed to Luke and Matthew, who, if one was looking for philosophers among them, would be the best qualified.

The Holy Spirit qualified Peter by revelation and for his zeal and bravura, but not for his intellect. For the intellect of man is at war with God. It is the progenitor of religion and its theology. Webster defines theology as the study of the nature of God and religious belief and theory when systematically developed. But which man can know the nature of God? Even the angels, who are in His presence day and night, cannot boast that they know His nature or know Him fully. How does someone study his nature without ever seeing God or even talking to Him? Every man can see the attributes of God as reflected in nature. They might ignore them, but they are there, displayed everywhere. The Psalmist says in Psalm 19, *"The heavens declare the glory of God; the skies proclaim the work of his hands. Day after day they pour forth speech; night after night they reveal knowledge. Without speech or language, without a sound to be heard, their voice has gone out into all the earth, their words to the ends of the world. In the heavens He has pitched a tent for the sun like a bridegroom emerging from his chamber, like a champion rejoicing to run his course. It rises at one end of the heavens and runs its circuit to the other; nothing is deprived of its warmth" (Psalm 19:2–4 BSB).*

One does not need theology to know about God. Theology only feeds man's intellect but cannot save his soul. What does it serve a man to know all about God and have all the knowledge of the universe and lose his soul? Intimacy with God is what saves man. Jesus knew that, and that is why he came not to teach people about God or theology, but to teach them how to develop a relationship with his father. Although if there was one who could teach about theology, he would be the most qualified. Instead, Jesus came so that man could develop an intimate relationship with God, the one true God. As he stated in his prayer, *"For You granted Him authority over all humanity, so that He may give eternal life to all those You have given Him. Now this is eternal life, that they may know You, the only TRUE God, and Jesus Christ, whom You have sent. I have glorified You on earth by accomplishing the work You gave Me to do" (John 17:2–4 BSB).*

Theology is the study of religions, the enemies of man. All religions are established to drive wedges between God and man. They are not designed to help man know God. For which of the sons of Adam knows the mind of God to know God? Only the Holy Spirit knows God, and only he can teach God to a man. However, since man belittled and rejected the Holy Spirit, they developed their own way to reach God, calling it religion.

These religions claim to teach man how to reach God when no religion knows the path to God. No systematic steps can be developed to reach God. The true God is very close to man yet very far. God is out of the reach of man! Only Jesus is the way to God.

Without Jesus, the way is shut. Hence, only God can reach man in his infinite power. Only He can show man the way to reach and touch him. Only when man is willing to develop a relationship with God, to know him intimately, and place a request for him to come fellowship with him. Only when a man pays the price, pays for his sins, and sanctifies himself, can he know God.

Man has fallen so far that he doesn't even know what sin is, what bondage he is in—let alone how to free himself. Yet, because of his prejudices and ignorance, he thinks he is something he is not and thinks he can reach God on his own. And so, he sets out to create religions with systematic steps to reach God. Man has never succeeded but instead runs in circles. You must understand that any man who tries to reach God without Jesus will experience God's wrath. Because reconciliations between God and Man have already taken place in Jesus Christ. In His love for man, God did open a gateway for man to know Him in the person of Jesus Christ and is maintaining that gateway open through the Holy Spirit.

The Holy Spirit convinces men of sin. Hence, he convinces them to repent, and once they do, he inspires holiness and seals them to Jesus, the Christ. No philosophies or systematic steps can do that. As the Lord said to Zerubbabel, it is all done by the Spirit, the Holy Spirit.

Have you ever wondered why Jesus never called any of the Pharisees or Sadducees to follow him? That is because their philosophies would prevent them from accepting the new teaching on how to receive the Holy Spirit of God—the only way to develop a relationship with him. As elder Paul said, for them, the gospel was foolishness. They were vessels that were already filled with old philosophies and pride. Their status in Israel would not allow them to humble themselves. Even those who believed in Jesus, such as Nicodemus, were ashamed to be seen in public with him. Nicodemus came to Jesus by night to inquire of him and testify his belief, but he was not called into ministry. Apostle Paul was the only Pharisee whom Jesus directly called to ministry.

The Bible does not talk much about the other Jewish leaders who came to believe in Jesus. Why elder Paul, you may ask? Elder

Paul was a Pharisee; indeed, he was persecuting the Christians with great zeal and love for God. But he was ignorant and going by what he was taught. Therefore, he relentlessly persecuted the Christians to bring them to the submission of God. He was oblivious to the plan of God and did not know about his Christ. But when he met the Master, he turned that zeal to work for God, and elder Paul,—just elder Paul—evangelized his world at the time. Or I should say where the Holy Spirit would lead him to go.

The whole world is benefiting from his works today. Jesus called the simple, the unlearned, and the rejected people without status. Jesus called the twelve, and most were considered unlearned except for Luke and Matthew. Elder Paul explained this to the Corinthians, saying: *"Brothers, consider the time of your calling: Not many of you were wise by human standards; not many were powerful; not many were of noble birth. But God chose the foolish things of the world to shame the wise; God chose the weak things of the world to shame the strong"* (1 Corinthians 1:26 BSB).

Many read this passage but fail to understand it. If the apostles lived in our time, their message would have been rejected, because they were no theologians, doctors of the law, or philosophers. Jesus is seeking those who can boast of his strength in their weaknesses. He was looking for those who are humble and who can remain humble after he bestowed the power of the Holy Spirit on them. Elder Paul was one of those. He said, *"Or with these surpassingly great revelations. So, to keep me from becoming conceited, I was given a thorn in my flesh, a messenger of Satan, to torment me. Three times I pleaded with the Lord to take it away from me. But He said to me, 'My grace is sufficient for you, for my power is perfected in weakness.' Therefore, I will boast all the more gladly in my weaknesses, so that the power of Christ may rest on me"* (Corinthians 12:7–9 BSB).

The fact that the disciples proclaiming the wisdom of the knowledge of God were unlearned is among the reasons why they hated, haunted, and slaughtered them like sheep. Their teaching was unknown to them. So, before the religious leaders created these schools that reject the Holy Spirit of God, how was one trained for the service of God in the new contract? They were trained through the apostles and the Holy Spirit!

Following the pattern that Jesus left them, the apostles would train the new converts to sanctify them and let the Holy Spirit finish the rest. As noted in the previous chapter, no one goes into ministry without the approval of the Holy Spirit, not even Jesus, the great Pastor of the flock. Jesus was trained by the Father of fathers. His mind was fused to that of the Father by the power of the Holy Spirit, who became his guide, counselor, and manager. Then the Spirit anointed him to go duplicate the process. He called the twelve, made them his disciples, and taught them the Word that the Father gave him as well as the Father's will. After accomplishing his mission and work, he returned to the Father. He ordered his disciples to go wait for the Holy Spirit in Jerusalem.

On the day of Pentecost, the Holy Spirit showed up and sealed them to Jesus and the Father. They were then enabled with power to fulfill the commissions as they were ordered to go around the world and make disciples out of all nations to repeat the process. In John 20:21 (BSB), Jesus said to his disciples, *"As the Father sent me, I now send you."* After the Holy Spirit anointed them, they came to know the Father, and he came to know them and entered into a covenant with each of them. On that day, the prophecy of Jeremiah was fulfilled. *"'But this is the covenant I will make with the house of Israel after those days,' declares the LORD. 'I will put My law in their minds and inscribe it on their hearts. And I will be their God, and they will be My people. No longer will each man teach his neighbor or his brother, saying, "Know the LORD," because they will all know Me, from the least of them to the greatest,' declares the LORD. 'For I will forgive their iniquity and will remember their sins no more.' Thus, says the LORD, who gives the sun for light by day, who orders the moon and stars for light by night, who stirs up the sea so that its category's roar; the LORD of Hosts is His name"* (Jeremiah 31:33–35 BSB).

God entered a covenant with each of those who were washed by the blood of Jesus, and seal that one with the Holy Spirit. That would remain so for eternity unless that one violates the contract. Notice that the prophecy said that no longer would a man teach his brother, saying, "Know the Lord." That was not needed. There is nowhere in the Bible where you see John sitting with Peter for a lesson. Why it is then that a new convert in today's church—unless he/she goes to a theological institution—must be taught for twenty years?

The disciples of Jesus had to be trained for only three years, and they never needed to be taught again. Once the Holy Spirit had sealed them, they were no longer disciples; they were now a duplicate of Jesus. They were masters ready to develop their own network of disciples. And hence, the Holy Spirit sent them throughout the earth to fulfill the commission they were charged with, and he stayed with them to constantly remind them of the Master's teachings. Knowing what would have happened if they stayed alive to do this properly, Satan killed them quickly and systematically.

It created a void and lack of understanding in the camp of the saints. Instead of going to the source of knowledge and drinking from the fountain, the new Christians relied heavily on the short letters that these apostles had written. I would admit that it is helpful to read the Bible, but it is a book that is coded spiritually. Without the Holy Spirit, an intellectual man doesn't stand a chance to understand the full spiritual scope of the messages encoded in the Bible. It is like a software tool. One can use it every day, but one can never crack the code behind it without spiritual insight and a password.

That is why Jesus sent the Holy Spirit, the same Spirit that helped him understand and know the Father's will. But since the churches evolved from relying on the apostles' letters, they rejected the one who could make sense of the letters and taught philosophy to fill the intellect. So, every week, they learn, and some do it for twenty years. Yet, no matter how much time they spend in the church, they are not being taught what they need to know to go preach the gospel boldly. While the other religions of darkness conquer the world again, the millions who claim to be Christians hide within their comfort zones. Why can't the current church duplicate the process that Jesus taught the disciples to create new apostles?

CHAPTER 19

DEVIATING FROM THE GREAT COMMISSION

And Jesus came and spake unto them, saying, All power is given unto me in heaven and in earth. Go ye therefore, and teach all nations, baptizing them in the name of the Father, and of the Son, and of the Holy Ghost: Teaching them to observe all things whatsoever I have commanded you: and, lo, I am with you alway, even unto the end of the world. Amen." (Matthew 28:18-20 KJV). This message is known as the great commission; the direct command Jesus gave the disciples before he was raptured up in the air to his throne. The command to preach the gospel was not giving to pastors alone. Every Christian is commission to go around the world to preach. For instance, before he sent his disciples to the world, Jesus sent out seventy-two disciples to preach the gospel in certain cities in Israel. He paired them and sent them out after teaching them and explain to them the cost of discipleship. In Luke 10:1-12 (BSB) we read, *"After this, the Lord appointed seventy-two others and sent them two by two ahead of Him to every town and place He was about to visit. And He told them, "The harvest is plentiful, but the workers are few. Ask the Lord of the harvest, therefore, to send out workers into His harvest. Go! I am sending you out like lambs among wolves. Carry no purse or bag or sandals. Do not greet anyone along the road. Whatever house you enter, begin by saying, 'Peace to this house.' If a man of peace is there, your peace will rest on him; if not, it will return to you. Stay at the same house, eating and drinking whatever you are offered. For the worker is worthy of his wages. Do not move around from house to house. If you enter a town and they welcome you, eat whatever is set before you. Heal the sick who are there and tell them, 'The kingdom of God is near you.' But if you enter a town and they do not welcome you, go into the streets and declare, 'Even the dust of your town that clings to our feet, we wipe off as a testimony against you. Yet be sure of this: The kingdom of God is near.' I tell you; it will be more bearable on that day for Sodom than for that town.*

Disciples and Church goers

After his resurrection, Jesus gave his disciples the same commission he received from his father to go around the world to preach the gospel. The twelve and the others who joined the fold went throughout the whole world to fulfill this commission, to make disciples. They died fulfilling it. However, we deviate from this charge in the status quo, meaning we do not make disciples to go preach the gospel. Instead, we make churchgoers.

The two are not the same, but somehow, the Christians believe they are. What is a disciple? Is a churchgoer the same as a disciple? The answer is no! Discipleship is the state or condition of being a follower of another in doctrines and spiritual precepts. It mostly refers to one-on-one training, where teacher and student become like father and son. In the discipleship setting, the teacher spends time with the disciple. He is responsible for the disciple's success or failure in learning the disciplines of the craft. The disciple depends entirely on him.

This type of training was designed to transfer ancient survival arts, survival techniques, religion, sentiment, and character to the next generation. In ancient Israel, the elders were responsible for passing down the history, language, and traditions of the forefathers to the new generation, using disciples. That is why the prophets and the rabbis had disciples and why Jesus used this technique to pass down the ancient teachings. A churchgoer, on the other hand, only learns intellectual concepts. There is no transfer of traditions or spiritual dogma. It is a more impersonal setting, where the teacher knows nothing about the churchgoer 90 percent of the time.

In the churchgoing setting, the churchgoer is more like a customer who comes to the church to purchase something,—namely the lecture. Once the teacher delivers the lecture, the two go on their ways until the next transaction. There are those who say that the church is too crowded, and that pastors cannot take one-on-one students. To answer this concern, let me remind you of Jeremiah's prophecy. Do you remember that the Lord told him that *"No longer will each man teach his neighbor or his brother, saying, "Know the LORD," because they will all know Me, from the least of them to the greatest,' declares the LORD. 'For I will forgive their iniquity and will remember their sins no more.'.*

THE HOLY SPIRIT IS THE TEACHER

Elder Paul was never in the discipleship of Peter or any of the other apostles who walked with Jesus. Yet, within the span of a few years after his encounter with the great Master Jesus, he learned enough to become an apostle. Jesus clearly rejected the idea of calling men teachers. Jesus warned his disciples to refrain from acting like the Scribes and the Pharisees who like to have people honor them in public places. In verses 6 to 8 of Matthew chapter 23 Jesus stated: "Woe to the Scribes and Pharisees, they love the places of honor at banquets, the chief seats in the synagogues, the greetings in the marketplaces, and the title of 'Rabbi' by which they are addressed. But you are not to be called 'Rabbi,' for you have one Teacher, and you are all brothers (Matthew 23: 6-8). Jesus meant that they would be taught by the same teacher, they will have the same doctrine, and operate under one banner. And thus, they should be equal brothers. He was telling them that the Spirit of the Christ, the Holy Spirit, was their teacher and that he would be for everyone who join the fold. Elder Paul never had a one-on-one session with the other apostles to teach him. However, when the Holy Spirit singled him out as an apostle, he taught him the way, and Paul was then able to teach the way to several others. He was able to teach them the best human conducts that pleased the Lord. Some will say that he did see Jesus and learned from him, but I disagree. He saw Jesus once in Damascus when he heard the call. Elder Paul was able to instruct his disciples because the Holy Spirit taught him the characters of God, and he learned directly through the spirit.

To make disciples, one needs to follow Jesus' example. He doesn't need a big church. Like Jesus, a leader needs to select a group of followers, teach them the discipline of Justice, righteousness, the importance of sanctification and the art of worship to attract the Holy Spirit. The Holy Spirit will then seal them and connect them to the universal knowledge of the Christ. Just as Jesus did. Jesus taught his disciples the basics and left them the Holy Spirit to teach them in all truth. God the Holy Spirit is omnipresent, and He can work with everyone on a one-on-one basis as he did for the disciples and elder Paul. The institutions of religious teaching cannot duplicate what Jesus did because they somehow believe that elder Paul taught them everything there is to know about how to please the Lord. They want to be called teachers.

In reality, Paul was still learning from the Holy Spirit when he died. The only one upon whom the Holy Spirit bestowed full knowledge was Jesus Christ. We do not have access to that library. However, the Holy Spirit, the teacher who taught Jesus, still has this information. And has Jesus promised, he sent him to teach us in all truth. I believe that under the right conditions, the Holy Spirit is willing to train new Pauls, Peters, and James in this generation but not through theological schools' settings, where we feed the intellect. Instead, he will teach the knowledge of Christ in places that foster holiness, where the kingdom is welcomed.

THEOLOGIAN DOES NOT MEAN CHRISTIAN

In the status quo, most church leaders are theologians. They believe that the knowledge is the power of God. It is this belief that they spread among the unsuspected congregations. Theological schools charge their students a fee to become theologians. The theologians, once graduated, decide to charge a fee to teach their theology. They give that knowledge to their followers in little measure because it is the trading commodity by which they gain influence, money, power and prestige. However, in order to keep his disciples from this behavior, Jesus order them saying the following: *"And proclaim as you go, saying, 'The kingdom of heaven is at hand. Heal the sick, raise the dead, cleanse lepers, cast out demons. You received without paying; give without pay. Acquire no gold or silver or copper for your belts, no bag for your journey, or two tunics or sandals or a staff, for the laborer deserves his food* (Matthew 10: 7-9, ESV).

Are these words being taught at the theological schools? Far from it. The theological schools teach divinity and theology, the attributes of God. But they do not teach their students how to become one with his Spirit and to develop an intimacy with him. They are teaching the intellect to grow the self. Satan's Theology is self-centered. It is intellectual pride inducing and is bound to worldly desires. It establishes no relationship between God and man. In contrast, Paul introduced a relationship between God and man. Paul spoke of the knowledge of the Christ, a relationship between father and son. He never talked about theology.

To the Corinthians Paul said: *But we preach Christ crucified, unto the Jews a stumbling block, and unto the Greeks foolishness* (1 Corinthian 1: 23 BSB). The knowledge of the Christ is a stumbling block to the Jews because they rejected the king of life. It is foolishness to the Greeks because it has nothing to do with Philosophy which they invented. It has nothing to do with the intellect either. It is a different wisdom to which the created beings weren't privy before the advent of Jesus Christ. It is strictly spiritual. The knowledge of Christ is not observed, it is imbued. This knowledge is transferred from the mind of God to the mind of those who believe. It is the true knowledge of God. It is the knowledge that can help one develop a father and son relationship with God. It is the knowledge Jesus said would lead the disciples in all truth. It is the knowledge of the Holy Spirit.

To the Romans Paul said: *For as many as are led by the Spirit of God, they are the sons of God. For ye have not received the spirit of bondage again to fear; but ye have received the Spirit of adoption, whereby we cry, Abba, Father. The Spirit itself beareth witness with our spirit, that we are the children of God* (Roman 18: 14-16). Earlier, I said Satan theology because many of the theologies being taught in the seminaries are inspired and taught by him or his demons.

Remember, Satan lived with God for a while. He knows him. Before iniquity was found in Satan, he was one of God's favorites. Satan can tell one enough about God to fill a few million books, hence the theology. But none of his teaching is about developing an intimate relationship with God because Satan lost God's favor and God cut all intimate relationship with him. He does not have a relationship with God as the teacher.

However, Satan can teach one enough to fill the intellect and pump one up. He teaches of a God who is far out of humanity's reach. He teaches the importance of the self. His teachings build the ego. He teaches that the flesh is self-sufficient and only needs the knowledge of the bible to please God. Being pumped up, his students of theology graduate from his schools. They become pastors and leaders of churches. They in turn teach their followers the philosophy of secular humanism instead of the Christian dogma of denying the self, holiness, justice, and righteousness, which prepares the temple for God the Holy Spirit to inhabit.

These leaders teach a materialistic gospel and inspire the people to serve the self and humanity instead of the God of spirits. They instruct the members about the societal classes, citizenry, and their duties to the church and country. They lecture them on how it is important to pay their tithe and give offerings. Some churches teach more on tiding than anything else.

The modern religious leaders avoid teachings on sanctification to the church at all costs. Their followers meet once a week, every Sunday, to learn about citizenry. And since the Holy Spirit is not welcome to remind them of what Jesus thought and they cannot meditate on heaven, they conform to the ways of the world to compete for riches. Every week, they learn good manners, listen to great speeches, and learn more techniques to grow their intellect, the self and please the world, but they learn little or nothing about spiritual Christianity and humility. They are constantly learning but never able to come to a knowledge of the truth (2 Timothy 3:7 BSB). In their gatherings, they learn philosophy mixed with a form of secular humanism. The little they heard about Jesus in the last Sunday's sermon is quickly forgotten because the worries of this world and their worldly world involvements take the teaching away.

Jesus knew that there was a possibility this would happen with his disciples, so he gave them a condition to qualify them to receive the Holy Spirit. He told them, *"If you love Me, you will keep My commandments. And I will ask the Father, and He will give you another Advocate to be with you forever,—the Spirit of truth"* (John 14: 16-17). Because they kept Jesus' commandments, the Holy Spirit descended on them and permanently inhabited their bodies. When the Holy Spirit came to them on the day of Pentecost, he chiseled the teachings of the Master in their brain and he stayed with them until their body of flesh died. He is still with them in the grave. He will resurrect them on that great day like he did for Jesus and he will present them to the Father and will be with them forever.

PREACHING INSTEAD OF TEACHING

Today, the one to remind the Christians of the teaching of Jesus Christ, the promised one, is not welcome. So, the church meetings are run like business meetings. In their preaching, the pastors focus on worldly topics. Their sermons are lectures, having a one-way communication. I'm not saying there is no place for a sermon in the work of God, far from it. Jesus himself gave sermons. But I am saying that you should at least be open to answer questions about it when you finish the sermon. Also, a sermon is not a teaching session. A sermon is preaching in nature. It is a call to repentance.

One usually preaches to nonbelievers to convince them of their sins and get them to repent. However, once they repent, they no longer need a sermon. They must be taught. You never see Jesus gathering the disciples to give them a sermon. He always did that with the crowd. The unrepentant crowd needed preaching but not the disciples. In today's Christianity, the leadership takes responsibility for teaching the flock how to seek material riches but never teaches them to seek heaven.

Because most theological schools never teach their graduates, who later become pastors, to seek heaven themselves. They leave the flock to fend for themselves spiritually. They don't teach their church members how to fulfill the great commission either. If a member has to reach a nonbeliever, they tell him or her to bring the nonbeliever to the church. And once the none believer gets to the church, they place him/her in the same audience with the members and preach the same sermon to both. So, the none believer learn something about the gospel, most often some philosophical analysis of a bible passage, not the gospel of repentance. However, the member returns home learning nothing new from that gathering. Then next Sunday when he/she returns, the pastor repeats the process. They don't teach the members anything new. I once asked a few pastors why they adopted this method. One responded saying he does not want the members to tell the nonbelievers the wrong things. Another gave me the following answer. "I don't see the necessity to separate them. The member needs the sermon just as much as the nonbeliever. Another pastor told me that they have bible studies. Neither the first or second answer made sense to me. Although the second answer has some truths in it. Of course the none believer needs the same sermon as the member. This is because the members are spiritual infants with the same mind set they had when they made their confession to leave the world. If the member is not being train in the path, how then does he/she matures in the faith to make his/her own disciple? The third answer sounds good. However, when you take into consideration that in these bible study gatherings, the studies are to analyze prophecies to determine the time for Jesus return or to discuss other topics to showcase the pastor's theological intelligence, it only makes sense to conclude that the members are not being taught what they need to go forth to proclaim the gospel. They don't equip that member to reach nonbelievers. Therefore, their church members cannot go around the world to make disciples of their own as Jesus ordered. They were never someone's disciple themselves.

Jesus did no such thing. He had his disciples with him, traveling, eating, and interacting with him every day. He would then go evangelize with them. They would see what he did, and then later, when they understand the process, he would send them to do the same. He walked the surrounding cities with them: casting out demons, healing, and preaching. They witnessed his deeds and his process.

After he trained them, he sent them out two by two to duplicate the process. He told them what to say and what to do. The disciples then learned hands-on because Jesus walked the walk. Today's philosophical church keeps clear of walking the walk. They send the aspirant leaders to a theological school to study or tell them to read the Bible. However, there is a danger in this. Without the Holy Spirit present to help one understand what he/she read, the Bible reads just like a novel, a history book, and whatever is read is quickly forgotten. For instance, the Jews were always reading the books of Moses, and yet they missed the plan that God had for them in Jesus Christ altogether.

Likewise, a person can read the Bible hundreds of times but can still fail to understand the spiritual messages it contains. Again, we can see the truth of that example with the Ethiopian eunuch reading the book of Isaiah while crossing the desert. No matter how many times he read it, he could not understand what he read. Because it takes the Holy Spirit to make one understand the spiritual lessons found in the book! To teach the true gospel, one needs to be inspired by the Holy Spirit, just as he inspired the prophets and apostles. But when one rejects the Holy Spirit, he/she is guaranteed to teach things that are irrelevant when it comes to doing God's work. So unplugged from the tree, they can't make disciples. They can't perceive the plans of the Lord. They rely on their own plans. The church should know the agenda of the Lord and be trained to contribute. The agenda of the Lord is to save the world.

The Christians should be holy and righteous and just. Then they will become the tool the Lord uses to fulfill this agenda of winning souls as Jesus commanded them to do before he left the earth.

This is a noble cause and has always been. It is a wise practice. As it is stated in Proverbs 11:30 (BSB), *"The fruit of the righteous is a tree of life; and he that winneth souls is wise."*

Furthermore, I think if a Christian sits in a congregation for twenty years and never does anything to show his love for the Lord, that institution has failed him or her. Jesus proved that he loves you by leaving his majestic throne. He came to earth, lived like a pauper, walked the via dolorosa and died for you. How do you prove your love for him? What would you bring to Jesus when you meet him? Would you go to him empty-handed? Will you meet Jesus alone without even one soul that your preaching helped going to heaven?

Remember the parable Jesus gave about the servant who would not use his talent wisely. He was rebuked and sent into the outer darkness for not investing his talent well. Consider salvation as a talent and invest it so that it can be multiplied. Then, you will not be ashamed when you meet the Lord. The harvest is great; you are the workers. Learn to win souls for the Lord.

CHAPTER 20

TO PREACH THE TRUE GOSPEL

A church operating without the Holy Spirit cannot preach the gospel of Jesus Christ. The Holy Spirit is the Spirit of salvation, and to offer salvation, one needs to be animated with that Spirit. If not, one will invite others to join a religion, a denomination, or take a seat in a building. A church operating without the Holy Spirit would not know where to preach or to whom to preach.

To justify this, I can take elder Paul as an example. Elder Paul was not allowed to preach the gospel everywhere he wanted. He wanted to go to Asia to preach, but the Holy Spirit prevented him, as we read in Acts 16:5–6 (BSB): *"So the churches were strengthened in the faith and grew daily in numbers. After the Holy Spirit prevented them from speaking the word in the province of Asia, they traveled through the region of Phrygia and Galatia."* The Holy Spirit was the one who told the apostles whom to preach to. We can see that with Phillip. *"Now an angel of the Lord said to Philip, 'Rise and go toward the south to the road that goes down from Jerusalem to Gaza.' This is a desert place. And he rose and went. And there was an Ethiopian, a eunuch, a court official of Candace, queen of the Ethiopians, who was in charge of all her treasure. He had come to Jerusalem to worship and was returning, seated in his chariot, and he was reading the prophet Isaiah. And the Spirit said to Philip, 'Go over and join this chariot'"* (Acts 8:26–29 BSB).

The Holy Spirit told the disciples where to go. So why would some stay in the church for fifty years and never really preach the gospel? The answer is simple. They never completed the process; they did not receive a second baptism so that the Holy Spirit could direct them. The Holy Spirit cannot send them because he does not know them. They are not his children. He does not have them in his employ. God sent the Holy Spirit to execute the plan of salvation. As Jesus stated at the beginning of his ministry, *"The Spirit of the LORD is upon Me, Because He has anointed Me to preach the gospel to the poor; He has sent Me to heal the brokenhearted, to proclaim liberty to the captives and recovery of sight to the blind, to set at liberty those who are oppressed; To proclaim the acceptable year of the LORD"* (Luke 4:18 BSB).

Did you catch that? The Holy Spirit anointed Jesus to preach the gospel and to do all the good deeds he did during his pilgrimage on earth. This sounds like Jesus had a purpose. He was the instrument the spirit uses to execute the Father's plan. He knew exactly what the Father wanted him to do. The Holy Spirit instructed him. Jesus trained his disciples to become vessels of the Holy Spirit as he was. Peter, James, Jude, and the rest of the apostles were vessels and when the Holy Spirit fills these vessels in the upper room, their purpose changed to become the same as that of Jesus Christ. They now had the same Spirit. Only when one can make that statement with the same sense of purpose can he/she walk the right path. Only the Holy Spirit knows the blueprint of the Father's will and can implant it into one's soul.

Today's fly-by-night ministers believe that they only must preach the wealth gospel to gain church members to fill a building. They disregard the other parts of the great commission and the work that comes with the office. This is because the Holy Spirit did not anoint them. At the beginning of his ministry, Jesus stated, *"The Spirit of the Lord has anointed me to preach."* So, as the Father sent him in the anointing of the Holy Spirit, he also sent his disciples. In the spirit of Love, he sent them saying: *As the Father hath loved me, so have I loved you: continue ye in my love. If ye keep my commandments, ye shall abide in my love; even as I have kept my Father's commandments, and abide in his love. These things have I spoken unto you, that my joy might remain in you, and that your joy might be full. This is my commandment, That ye love one another, as I have loved you (John 15:9-17 KJV),* On the day of his ascension, he commissioned them to go preach the gospel. In the upper room, Jesus anointed them with the power of the Holy Spirit. When he found elder Paul, he sent Ananias to anoint him before he sent him. This was because he wanted every one of them to be able to boast of the claim, "The Spirit of the Lord is upon me, and he has anointed me," when they began their ministry. So, until you can say, "The Spirit of the Lord is upon me, and he has anointed me," you can't go anywhere or do anything for God.

For those who say that Jesus sent the apostles before the event of Pentecost, I say, even then, they weren't alone. The Holy Spirit was around them because Jesus was still here. They were sharing in the oil that was in the lamp of Jesus. But once Jesus was no longer on earth, they needed their own oil, which they received in the upper room. Before the Pentecost, they hid in the upper room because they were afraid. However, after the event of the Pentecost, the twelve did not go to join the bishop of Jerusalem so that they could be part of the committee of the church of Jerusalem. They went every which way to where the Holy Spirit sent them. We are seeing the opposite here these days.

The Holy Spirit is no longer in charge. The pastors are not being anointed; instead, they are given a diploma. They cannot go in the power of the Holy Spirit; instead, they go in the power of the earth's government. They disobey the commandment to abide in the love of Jesus. Therefore, their congregations are loveless. Without love for one another, they can't attract the Holy Spirit; they don't know him. Hence, they can't claim the Holy Spirit sent them. And since he is the hiring manager, the one giving the tools for the job, one must come to him to be equipped for the works of the Father. When they rejected him, they also rejected the power to do the same works Jesus did. They preach a different gospel that appeals to the masses' desires. They are different from elders Paul, Peter, or John, not because they are in a different time, but because they have a different spirit. And so, they tell their followers that healing the sick, raising the dead, and casting out demons was for an elite group.

Jesus never established an elite group in his church. Jesus said that the believers should be able to do the same thing he did and more. He sent his apostles to duplicate what he did, meaning raising the dead, healing the sick, and casting out demons. Moreover, Jesus gave his disciples the same Spirit who trained him for them to be able to train disciples of their own and send them to replicate the process.

On average, today's Christian can discuss their denominations in length. But they are ill informed about the doctrines of holiness, love, brotherhood, righteousness and justice that Jesus commanded his disciples to hold as their core beliefs. Because the majority of Christians today belongs to an organization, not to Jesus Christ. You will find that the Seventh-Day Adventist, the Baptist, the Pentecostal, the Methodist, the Calvinist, and all the rest are well-endowed in the philosophy of their denominations. Therefore, they can discuss it at length to convince whoever would listen that their religion is the best. However, no one trained them to talk about the doctrine of justice, righteousness, love, sanctification, and brotherhood, the only way they can attract the anointing of the Holy Spirit.

A large portion of those professing to be Christian in the status quo are not taught that genuine brotherly love is what proves that one is a Christian. The leader-ship of their churches fail to teach them the four basic pillars they need to establish in their lives to be successful Christians. Justice, love, righteousness and sanctification ride in the same cart. Without justice and righteousness, one cannot be sanctified, and love is a product of sanctification. Paul commanded the Romans to "Owe no man anything, but to love one another, for he that loveth another hath fulfilled the law (Roman 10:8). However, the popular narrative in vast majority of churches is prosperity, selfishness, pride and prestige. The Christians are being taught to be fanatics of a denomination. The denominations put Jesus up front to gain proselytes and once they secure these proselytes, they teach them their doctrines.

Preachers of Men's Religions and Traditions

Jesus encountered this kind in his time and denounced the tactic and told them, *"But woe unto you, scribes and Pharisees, hypocrites! for ye shut up the kingdom of heaven against men: for ye neither go in yourselves, neither suffer ye them that are entering to go in" (Matthew 23:13 BSB)*. He said that because the Pharisees were teaching those proselytes their doctrines, not the way to God. To confirm he was talking about false doctrine and religions of man here, Jesus further stated, *"Woe unto you, scribes and Pharisees, hypocrites! for ye compass sea and land to make one proselyte, and when he is made, ye make him twofold more the child of hell than yourselves" (Matthew 23:15 KJV)*.

In Matthew 5:20–22 KJV, Jesus spent the majority of his sermon on the mount, rectifying false doctrines. The Pharisees taught that one was in danger of judgment after committing murder, but Jesus told the crowd that it was the intent of committing murder that put one in danger of the judgment. This means that once you think about mistreating your brother, you are already in danger of the judgment.

You are judged and condemned after you act on the thought and bring it to fruition. For instance, Jesus said, *"For I say unto you, that except your righteousness shall exceed the righteousness of the scribes and Pharisees, ye shall in no case enter into the kingdom of heaven. Ye have heard that it was said of them of old time, thou shalt not kill; and whosoever shall kill shall be in danger of the judgment: But I say unto you, that whosoever is angry with his brother without a cause shall be in danger of the judgment: and whosoever shall say to his brother, Raca, shall be in danger of the council: but whosoever shall say, thou fool, shall be in danger of hell fire" (Matthew 5:20–22)*.

Jesus went even further to say that for certain matters, the intent is the sin. The Pharisees taught that the act of adultery occurs at the time of the encounter. However, Jesus taught his disciples: *"Ye have heard that it was said by them of old time, thou shalt not commit adultery: But I say unto you, that whosoever looked on a woman to lust after her hath committed adultery with her already in his heart. And if thy right eye offends thee, pluck it out, and cast it from thee: for it is profitable for thee that one of thy members should perish, and not that thy whole body should be cast into hell"* (Matthew 5:27–29 KJV).

Only the Righteous will Enter Heaven

Notice that Jesus was not afraid to tell the people that whoever gives their body and mind to lust, injustice, and unrighteousness, the final destination of their soul is hellfire. He also told them that they need to have their own righteousness and that it should surpass that of the Pharisees to enter heaven. The church of Christ is built on justice and righteousness. Those who enter heaven will be the just and righteous. Of course, when you confess Jesus as Lord and vowed to follow him, you share in his righteousness. But he freed you to develop your own righteousness under his umbrella. This is why he told the Jews that if their righteousness does not surpass that of the pharisees, they will not enter the kingdom of God. He also told them the following: *"From the days of John the Baptist until now, the kingdom of heaven has been subject to violence, and the violent lay claim to it"* (Matthew 11:13 BSB). The Christian can rely on Jesus' righteousness only to use it as a model to develop their own. The Christian should be perfect in love, holiness, justice and righteousness.

Today, church members avoid telling people that there is a hell and that they will end up there if they do not repent of their sins. The church is also full of the customs of man and ignores justice and righteousness. Why? They don't have the Holy Spirit, the Spirit that was in Jesus Christ. If one talks like Jesus did today in a church, they would call him a radical. But do you know that if you are not a radical for Jesus, you cannot serve him? The members of the church are not being taught these fundamentals because the Holy Spirit is partially absent.

However, for the sake of these few who are sincere in calling the name of Jesus, the Holy Spirit stays present among them and sporadically moves them to repent and appreciate the love of God. While he was with them, Jesus confirmed the presence of the Holy Spirit among his disciples. He said, *"If you love me, keep my commands. And I will ask the Father, and he will give you another advocate to help you and be with you forever, the Spirit of truth. The world cannot accept him, because it neither sees him nor knows him. But you know him, for he lives with you and will be in you" (John 14:15–18).* This prophecy was fulfilled on the day of Pentecost in the upper room, where the Holy Spirit came to live in them.

CHRISTIAN ONLY IN NAME

The churches today are only full of Christians in name. They are not benefiting from this prophecy. They don't know the Holy Spirit; therefore, he cannot fully inhabit them as he did for the disciples. He stays in their midst because he must fulfill the promise made by Jesus, who stated that whosoever calls on his name will be saved. Or, as John put it, *"Just as Moses lifted up the serpent in the wilderness, so the Son of Man must be lifted up, that everyone who believes in Him may have eternal life. For God so loved the world that He gave His one and only Son, that everyone who believes in Him shall not perish but have eternal life" (John 3:16 BSB).*

But those who don't believe, who don't take him at his words to obey his commands, do not have the Holy Spirit inside them. They are therefore in danger of losing their souls. They are like the five virgins without oil in their lamps. They are playing a Russian Roulette game with Satan. It will be almost impossible for them to overcome and receive the reward from Jesus or even make it into heaven. I made such a statement for this reason.

Christians that don't have the Holy Spirit can't resist sin, and they are constantly struggling with it. They frequently sin during their days because their minds are set on things of earth, not of heaven. They do not have the spirit of heaven. And so, they fall and get up and fall and get up and fall and get up. If they are lucky before they die, they will ask for forgiveness for their sins, but if they die in sin in any sudden death, Satan wins their souls.

These Christians never make any progress, for they've never known God. They know about him, but not him. They are victims of the big business mindset. The Holy Spirit gets replaced by the spirit of profit and prosperity. Instead of learning about how to serve God, the spectators learn about how to become better citizens of earth and how to profit. They don't know how to pray. They don't know how to worship. They don't have time to consecrate themselves to God. Some blame the children while others blame their work, etc. Either way, they can't mature in the faith. They don't have oil in their lamps. They become reprobates.

Elder Paul says, *"And even as they did not like to retain God in their knowledge, God gave them over to a reprobate mind, to do those things which are not convenient" (Romans 1:28 KJV)*. This statement can be translated to say that since they did not see fit to acknowledge God (or I should say, since they did not have time for God, to fellowship with him, to give him the glory he deserves), he gave them up to a depraved mind, to do what ought not to be done. Instead of progressing, they regress.

Elder Paul said that they would be filled with every kind of wickedness, evil, greed, and hatred. They would be full of envy, murderous intentions, strife, deceit, and malice. They would be gossipers, slanderers, God-haters, insolents, arrogant, and boastful. Moreover, they would be senseless, faithless, heartless, and merciless. If you believe that Elder Paul was addressing the world, you must reconsider. Elder Paul was describing the atmosphere of the average Christian church of today. The people who have known God but rejected the knowledge.

Today's church congregation is full of people eligible to become sons of God but failed to follow through. These are people who had been elevated to a higher state of consciousness but reversed back to their original state, hence they are reprobates. Paul was referring to the apostate church of today—the virgins without oil in their lamps.

CHAPTER 21

Apostasy in the Old and New Church

The trends of the apostasy that we read in Chapter 14 are not new. They existed even in the time of the apostles. During the first harvest, elder Paul battled several of them introduced in the church by the gnosis and the Jews of the synagogues of Satan in Israel. However, as the church population grew, more false doctrines crept into the church silently because the presence of the Holy Spirit among them had become a relative idea instead of remaining the core of their beliefs.

After the apostles were slaughtered worldwide,—some by the Romans, some by the Jews, some in foreign lands,—the church became the prey of charlatans, demon-inspired individuals, and so-called apostles. They infected the church and encouraged it to give the Holy Spirit the boot. He was not fully removed but put aside. The churches started to become autonomous. They wanted self-governance instead of that of the Holy Spirit, just like Israel rejected the rule of God for that of Saul.

In the book of Revelation, the Lord Jesus had already begun to deal with an overwhelming number of problems appearing within the churches. And since elder Paul was no longer alive to write to them and confront them, the Lord himself did it through John. This revelation was to show John that the apostasy had started. The churches had already begun to lose their ground in the war way before Satan hijacked the Word and locked it away in the library of Constantine's church, known today as the Catholic Church.

Some of them have even started to compromise the teachings of the apostles. Consequently, the church was infiltrated by the agents of spiritism, the gnosis, and the members of the synagogues of Satan who wanted to derail the gospel of Christ. The letter of Paul to the congregation in Galatia serves as a suitable example. Paul confronted the Galatians when they switched their whole devotions to honoring some days of the week and other observances Jesus did not establish.

The great falling away had begun even during the life of John, who was the last apostle left alive. Because the church had become incredibly materialistic, they started to identify themselves with their surroundings. The Lord was outlining his reproaches to the churches of Asia Minor. The seven churches that the Lord addressed in Revelation represent the types of churches on earth at that time. Jesus talked to the churches through the Spirit. The warnings came from the Spirit, the Holy Spirit. They were just like the warnings given to Israel by the prophets that if they did not abide in the way of the Lord, he would reject them.

The Holy Spirit took notes then, and He is also taking notes now. Starting with the church of Ephesus—the church that lost their love because of what they have endured—Jesus says, *"I know thy works, and thy labor, and thy patience, and how thou canst not bear them which are evil: and thou hast tried them which say they are apostles, and are not, and hast found them liars: And hast borne, and hast patience, and for my name's sake hast labored, and hast not fainted. Nevertheless, I have somewhat against thee, because thou hast left thy first love. Remember therefore from whence thou art fallen, and repent, and do the first works; or else I will come unto thee quickly, and will remove thy candlestick out of his place, except thou repent. But this thou hast, that thou hate the deeds of the Nicolaitans, which I also hate. He that hath an ear, let him hear what the Spirit saith unto the churches; To him that overcomes will I give to eat of the tree of life, which is in the midst of the paradise of God"* (Revelation 2:1–7 BSB).

Now, the deed of Nicolaitans is the practice of hierarchy that has existed among the Jews, where the doctors of the law lorded over the population. The hypocrisy of the leadership system that concocted religious burdens to assign to the people, while the leaders exempted themselves from practicing them. Jesus despised the hypocrisy of rank among brothers so much that he ordered his disciples to avoid it in their congregations. He still holds the same sentiments today. While on earth, Jesus instructed his disciples on this issue in these terms, *"Then Jesus spoke to the multitudes and to His disciples, saying: 'The scribes and the Pharisees sit in Moses' seat. Therefore, whatever they tell you to observe, that observe and do, but do not do according to their works; for they say, and do not do. For they bind heavy burdens, hard to bear, and lay them on men's shoulders; but they themselves will not move them with one of their fingers. But all their works they do to be seen by men. They make their phylacteries broad and enlarge the borders of their garments. They love the best places at feasts, the best seats in the synagogues, greetings in the marketplaces, and to be called by men, 'Rabbi, Rabbi.' But you, do not be called 'Rabbi'; for One is your Teacher, the Christ, and you are all brethren. Do not call anyone on earth your father; for One is your Father, He who is in heaven. And do not be called teachers; for One is your Teacher, the Christ. But he who is greatest among you shall be your servant. And whoever exalts himself will be humbled, and he who humbles himself will be exalted'"* (Matthew 23:1–11 KJV).

The same practices of the Nicolaitans are reoccurring in today's church. After they hijacked the gospel of Jesus, the Catholic Church used the ways of the Nicolaitans to have the members of their congregations call the church leaders papa, meaning "father." Their system of the pope, the priest, the deacons, the reverends, and the bishops derives from the Nicolaitans' way of thinking. Besides having a pope, the revised churches that spawned from Martin Luther's movement when the Holy Spirit inspired him to free the church from the bondage of the papacy adopted the same system.

Despite reading that Jesus does not approve of it, the protestant church still has reverends, deacons, bishops, and others. They are carrying this tradition established initially by the Catholic Church. Jesus urged the angel of the church of Smyrna, the champion church, the church that suffered persecution, tribulation, and poverty for the sake of Jesus but stayed faithful, to keep persevering, and to remain faithful unto death through these tribulations. As a result, he will give them a crown of life and keep them from being hurt by the second death.

Did you hear that? The crown of life will be given to those who persevere in faithfulness unto death, not those who compromise. *"He that hath an ear, let him hear what the Spirit saith unto the churches"* (Revelation 2:8–12 BSB). To the church located at Pergamum, where "Satan's seat" is installed, the church located in the camp of the enemy, the Lord said, *"I know where you live, where the throne of Satan sits. Yet you have held fast to My name and have not denied your faith in Me, even in the day when My faithful witness Antipas was killed among you, where Satan dwells. But I have a few things against you, because some of you hold to the teaching of Balaam, who taught Balak to place a stumbling block before the Israelites so they would eat food sacrificed to idols and commit sexual immorality. The Lord rebuked those who subscribed to these doctrines and advise them to repent. 'Therefore, repent saith the Lord. Otherwise, I will come to you shortly and wage war against them with the sword of My mouth.' He who has an ear, let him hear what the Spirit says to the churches. To the one who is victorious, I will give the hidden manna. I will also give him a white stone inscribed with a new name, known only to the one who receives it"* (Revelation 2:12–17 BSB).

Notice the reoccurring themes: "'To the one who overcome, to the one who is victorious, I will give…' saith the Lord." He also called all these churches to repent. To Pergamum, Jesus even says he will war against them if they do not repent of their sins. Those who hold the doctrine of Balaam are the profit- and prosperity-minded leaders, who taught the people that they don't need to seek sanctification, that all they need is to seek ways to profit. They refrain from teaching sanctification to the church to keep them from receiving the Holy Spirit of God.

The doctrine of Balaam is the "prosperity and profit" doctrine. Now, Balaam was a prophet in Israel, whose mind was set on profit. He found an opportunity to receive that profit from the king of Moab named Balak. The king offered to reward him greatly, but the catch was that he had to curse Israel. We find the story about Balaam in Numbers 22–25. What is scary about the story is that Balaam was not a false prophet. He was a genuine prophet of God. But greed had gotten the better of him, and he decided to do this deed.

When Balaam realized that he could not curse the people of Israel, because Balaam had no power to curse what God had blessed, he devised a devilish tactic. Balaam wanted the reward, so he advised the Moabites that the only way they could get God to allow him to curse the people was to make them sin. This is the tactic of Satan. Balaam taught the Moabites to entice the people with prostitution and idolatry by sending Moabite women to Israel as prostitutes and also false spiritual leaders.

The Israelites then fell into idolatry and prostitution, and consequently, they brought a curse upon the nation. Balaam was not satisfied with what the Lord gave him. He wanted more, so he went to compromise with the enemy of Israel. Likewise, the Balaams of our time decided to compromise themselves with devils to gain massive profit while hundreds of Christians are falling under the spell of Satan. Later, when they die, they fall into the pit of hell.

There are thousands of Balaams in places of leadership in the churches today. They are prosperity-seeking fellows who couldn't care less about seeking the lost souls. The Lord acknowledges the deeds of the church of Thyatira and their love and faith and service and perseverance and the fact that those good deeds increased with time. However, the Lord didn't like the fact that they tolerated the woman Jezebel, who called herself a prophetess and taught and led his bondservants astray so that they committed acts of immorality and ate food sacrificed to idols. The Lord told her that since she was not willing to repent of her immorality, he would plague her and those who committed adultery with her with sickness and great tribulation. He would make an example of her by killing her children with pestilence for the whole church to witness. *"But I say to you sayeth Jesus, the rest who are in Thyatira, who do not hold this teaching, who have not known the deep things of Satan, as they call them, I place no other burden on you. Nevertheless, what you have, hold fast until I come. He that hath an ear, let him hear what the Spirit saith unto the churches" (Revelation 2:18–29 BSB).*

When the Lord said, "They tolerated the woman Jezebel, who calls herself a prophetess and teaches and leads my bondservants astray so that they commit acts of immorality and eat things sacrificed to idols," he was not talking about an actual flesh-and-blood woman. He meant the spirit that possessed Jezebel, the ex-queen of Israel. This same spirit undoubtedly had some of the women members of the current church claim sacerdotal positions in the church and leadership over the men.

As a human, Jezebel was the daughter of Ithobaal I, king of Sidon, and the wife of Ahab, king of Israel (1 Kings 16:31 BSB). If you don't remember the story, you can read it in the book of Kings. Jezebel, in this story, personifies the evil and wicked spirit who is still acting and possessing women in the world today. It is the spirit that fuels the women's movement in the world. This spirit has infiltrated the church and possessed the women of the church. And because the Holy Spirit is absent in the churches, the teachings of the Jezebel spirit are revamped in the church. This is the spirit that advocates women's dominance over men in the church of Jesus Christ.

It is the spirit that said it is okay to ordain women as pastors in the church. And so, as in the time of Jezebel, the spirit is using the women of the church to undermine the authority of the office of the steward or every man in the church. In most denominations, it is now customary to ordain a woman into the pastorship office of the church when the Lord Jesus opposes this practice. The apostle Paul said it best to Timothy when he stated, *"Let a woman learn quietly with all submissiveness. I do not permit a woman to teach or exercise authority over a man; rather, she is to remain quiet. For Adam was formed first, then Eve; and Adam was not deceived, but the woman was deceived and became a transgressor"* (1 Timothy 2:8–14 BSB).

However, this doctrine suddenly became unacceptable in the churches of today. As the women covet the ministries assigned to men, they find teachers who now disagree with elder Paul and insert their reasoning into the matter as if elder Paul did not know what he was talking about. Or, as some stated, this is no longer relevant in our time. Did the word of God lose its meaning in our time? I know that this statement might offend many women, but I can't help but tell you the truth. Now, if the truth of the Lord Jesus Christ offends you, I cannot help you. I can only remind you of King Saul's fate for performing the duties of the prophet Samuel. Remember how the Lord destroyed his kingdom and lineage and gave his throne to David. You need to pray to Jesus for him to enlighten you on this subject. Everyone has his/her role in the affairs of God. It is wise to stay within one's boundaries.

To the angel of the church in Sardis, write: *These are the words of the One who holds the sevenfold Spirit of God and the seven stars. I know your deeds; you have a reputation for being alive, yet you are dead. Wake up and strengthen what remains, which was about to die; for I have found your deeds incomplete in the sight of My God. Remember, then, what you have received and heard. Keep it and repent. If you do not wake up, I will come like a thief, and you will not know the hour when I will come upon you. But you do have a few people in Sardis who have not soiled their garments, and because they are worthy, they will walk with Me in white. Like them, he who overcomes will be dressed in white. And I will never blot out his name from the Book of Life, but I will confess his name before My Father and His angels. He that hath an ear, let him hear what the Spirit saith unto the churches* (Revelation 3:1–6 BSB).

God selects people who are unworthy in this world to make them worthy through the Holy Spirit. Only the worthy will receive the rewards; so, strive to be worthy. To the angel of the church in Philadelphia write: *These are the words of the One who is holy and true, who holds the key of David. What He opens, no one will shut; and what He shuts, no one will open. I know your deeds. See, I have placed before you an open door, which no one can shut. For you have only a little strength, yet you have kept My word and have not denied My name. Look at those who belong to the synagogue of Satan, who claim to be Jews but are liars instead. I will make them come and bow down at your feet, and they will know that I love you.* <u>*Because you have kept My command to endure with patience, I will also keep you from the hour of testing that is about to come upon the whole world, to test those who dwell on the earth.*</u> *The one who is victorious I will make a pillar in the temple of My God, and he will never again leave it. Upon him, I will write the name of My God, and the name of the city of My God (the new Jerusalem that comes down out of heaven from My God), and My new name. He that hath an ear, let him hear what the Spirit saith unto the churches. (Revelation 3:7–13 BSB).*

Notice that Jesus said those who will be removed from experiencing the great tribulation are those who kept his commands to endure with patience. Those who are like Abraham, Joshua, and Caleb.

To the angel of the church in Laodicea, write: *These are the words of the Amen, the faithful and true Witness, the Originator of God's creation. I know your deeds; you are neither cold nor hot. How I wish you were one or the other! o because you are lukewarm either hot or cold, I am about to vomit you out of My mouth! You say, 'I am rich; I have grown wealthy and need nothing.' But you do not realize that you are wretched, pitiful, poor, blind, and naked. I counsel you to buy from Me gold refined by fire so that you may become rich, white garments so that you may be clothed, and your shameful nakedness not exposed, and salve to anoint your eyes so that you may see. Those I love, I rebuke and discipline. Therefore, be earnest and repent. Behold, I stand at the door and knock. If anyone hears My voice and opens the door, I will come in and dine with him, and he with Me. To the one who is victorious, I will grant the right to sit with Me on My throne, just as I overcame and sat down with My Father on His throne. He that hath an ear, let him hear what the Spirit saith unto the churches (Revelation 3:14–22 BSB).* Here, the Lord talks to the prideful—those who believe they have arrived in the faith. He is talking to those blinded by pride, prestige, and prejudice, pumped by the many accolades they receive from people and this world.

CHAPTER 22

EXAMINE YOUR WALK IN LIFE

Jesus does not want anyone to go to hell. In these warnings, he addressed both those doing badly and those who are his. He urged those who are following the path of hell to repent, and he will save them. Jesus also advised those who are his to stay strong and hold firm to what they have to claim their rewards. To those who overcome, he will give authority over the nations, the bright morning star, a new name, new garments, and the list goes on. The only one who really knows you is you. So, don't play the fool! Stop playing Russian roulette with your soul. Don't be ignorant of where you stand with the Lord. Do you hear the echo? *"He that hath an ear, let him hear what the Spirit saith unto the churches."*

What would the Lord say about your church if he were to send you a letter like this? What does the Lord have against your church? Jesus has not changed. He is examining your church in the same way he examined the churches in Asia Minor. Do you know where your church stands to answer this question? Do you have an ear to hear? Can you hear what the Spirit is saying about your church? Does your church even register on the Lord's radar? If your church has not surrendered to the direction of the Holy Spirit, the answer is a resounding no. The Spirit speaks with spirits, and if yours is not born yet, you cannot hear what the Spirit tells the `churches.

The Tale of Two Churches

If your church does not have the Holy Spirit, it is deaf and cannot hear Jesus to learn where it belongs in these categories. Chances are, if it does not allow the direction and counsel of the Holy Spirit, it is not even in the categories of the churches of God. For instance, do you know if your church is faithful before the God of Jesus? Do you know if your garment is soiled in order to clean it? Do you have an ear? Can you hear the Lord? Be honest in your answer. Your salvation depends on it. Don't wait until it is too late to find out that your garment is not clean.

Many people are waiting for the rapture to go to heaven with Jesus. However, they disregard that if they die today, their rapture just happened. Death is the most certain rapture in a person's life. Can you say with confidence, "I have fought a good fight? I have finished the race? I have kept the faith," as elder Paul said to Timothy in 2 Timothy 4:7, if today was your last day on earth? Or, better yet, where are you in the race? Of the Corinthians, elder Paul asked, "Do you not know that in a race all the runners run, but only one gets the prize?" He asked them this question to help them examine themselves, and then he encouraged them. *"Run in such a way as to get the prize" (1 Corinthians 9:24 BSB).*

Are you running to receive the price? The Israelites, while they were in the desert, were running a race to the promised land. They did not make it because they did not have the mind of a runner. Only Caleb and Joshua had that mind—the mind that was in Jesus Christ. This man was focused. He did not take clothes, house, or any material things to weigh him down. He ran the race to the finish line, focusing on the glory reserved for him at the end. Therefore, he ran the race with faith, courage, and strength—the strength to carry his cross and cope with hunger, rejections, assaults, and everything negative that could be thrown at a man, even the death at the cross, which was reserved for the worst of criminals.

That man received that strength and determination from the Holy Spirit. In fact, he totally depended on the Holy Spirit. And thanks to his determination and focus, those of us who are saved can boast of his victory. Who do you depend on? Yourself? Your friends? Your parents? Your spouse? Your riches? Your fame? Your pride? Your abilities? Your strengths? I have news for you. None of these will be able to help you when it matters! Learn to depend on the Lord. Learn to develop ears to hear the Lord and do his will. Say in your heart, *"Not my will Lord Jesus, but thine be done."*

You cannot focus on this world and Jesus simultaneously. You can only focus on one. As we mentioned above, Jesus said that no man can serve two masters; he must choose one and reject the other. You cannot have Satan's world and God's heaven at the same time. Joshua asked the Israelites to make a choice. *"Choose whom you will serve!" "And if it seems evil unto you to serve the Lord, choose you this day whom ye will serve; whether the gods which your fathers served that were on the other side of the flood, or the gods of the Amorites, in whose land ye dwell: but as for me and my house, we will serve the Lord"* (Joshua 24:15 BSB).

I am asking you to choose whom you will serve in the same manner. Will you serve the Lord or the gods of profit, prestige and fame of this world? I am saying like Joshua. Me and my house, we will serve the Lord. I would advise you to do the same.

THE GREAT DIVIDE: THE TARE AND THE WHEAT

The church of Jesus Christ could be divided into the seven groups upon the characteristics we visited above at the time of John. Still, as people became able to migrate more easily, congregations became more integrated. Today, most churches will have at least a few of these characteristics in one congregation. One cannot say, "This church is like Smyrna," "This one is like Thyatira," "This one is like Sardis," "This one is like Philadelphia," or "This one is like Laodicea." One cannot say that this is a good church because it is in a good region or that this church should be avoided because it is a bad church just by looking at the church.

The distinction is not made based upon physical characteristics, although they are essential elements to consider. The segregation of churches is no longer as clear-cut. But some churches are fully secular (they only focus on material prosperity), while others worship idols and initiate their members into the occult and secret societies. You should avoid these churches at all costs if you want to serve Jesus.

The agents of Satan have infiltrated mostly every church on earth. This is no surprise because Jesus predicted it in Matthew 13:30, saying: *"Let both grow together until the harvest. At that time, I will tell the harvesters: First collect the weeds and tie them in bundles to be burned; then gather the wheat into my barn."* The tares are hard to recognize among the crowd. They are good actors; therefore, you must be careful. People migrate from church to church to mingle, taking their spiritual characteristics with them. And because of this, many factions are fighting inside the churches. In one church, you can find groups that emulate the characteristics of all the seven churches intermingling with one another.

Jesus knew this was going to happen, and that is why he told his disciples about the kingdom of heaven in these words: *"The kingdom of heaven is like a man who sowed good seed in his field; but while men slept, his enemy came and sowed tares among the wheat and went his way. But when the grain had sprouted and produced a crop, then the tares also appeared. So, the servants of the owner came and said to him, 'Sir, did you not sow good seed in your field? How then does it have tares?' He said to them, 'An enemy has done this.' The servants said to him, 'Do you want us then to go and gather them up?' But he said, 'No, lest while you gather up the tares you also uproot the wheat with them. Let both grow together until the harvest, and at the time of harvest I will say to the reapers, "First gather together the tares and bind them in bundles to burn them but gather the wheat into my barn"* (Matthew 13:24–30 BSB).

Notice what Jesus said in this passage. The tares and the wheat would grow together. So, who are the tares, and who are the wheat? The parable is about two groups of Christians growing together in the same congregation. It is about the church of the end-time, where these seven types of churches would become two types. Indeed, today, the church is global. It is no longer centered in Asia Minor. There are multiple churches in every corner of every city of the world. But how does one recognize who is serving Jesus and who is not? How do you distinguish between the tares or the wheat?

Let me explain the parable and who can be considered tares or wheat without going in-depth here. The Lord takes the example of a field of wheat infected with tares to illustrate his people and that of the enemy. In the infancy of the garden, the tares and the wheat so resembled each other and grew so close to each other that it became dangerous to remove the tares. The master told the servants to refrain from touching them. However, the master knew that the wheat tree would mature and produce fruit as they grew, but the tares would not. He told his servants to leave them to grow together.

During harvest time, they would be able to distinguish one from the other and separate the wheat for the barn and the tares for the fire. The good master who sowed good seed in the field is Jesus. Through the inspiration of the Holy Spirit, those men who work for Jesus preach the real gospel to the people, and the people gladly accept it. The men who slept are the hired hands, and the enemy is the wolf and his army of fallen who came and sowed false doctrines in the church.

Therefore, the church is divided into two different sects—the church that serves Jesus Christ and the church that belongs to the lord of this earth. The two are growing together in the same environment. As the time of the harvest approaches, both kinds will show their true colors. The righteous will become more righteous, and the wicked will become more wicked.

THE TARES

The tares symbolize those who have no communion with Jesus. When they first come to the church in their infancy, they behave and act like real Christians and so resemble and grow with Christians to gain their trust and rise into places of authority. Some of them go to theological schools to gain knowledge and become pastors and deacons. To give a clear picture, they are precisely like Judas. Remember Judas? He held the power of the purse among the disciples and sought to control what happened to the offerings given to the group. For instance, he protested against the woman using the perfume to wash Jesus's feet, stating that the fragrance should be sold to feed the poor. He presented his objections in the form of taking care of the poor, but in reality, the poor had nothing to do with it.

Judas' opposition was a way to have his will done in order to exercise power among his fellows. He wanted to keep the money for himself. He tried to change the will of God in the burial of his son. He served as a direct channel for Satan to oppose the will of God in the congregation of the saints. The tares have the same spirit that was in Judas; they are materialistic and focus on the world. They want to be church leaders but don't want the Holy Spirit.

The first category of tares are intellectuals who believe they can do better than the Holy Spirit. They are full of hypocrisy, and their tongues deliver curses. Their confession was a strategic move to identify with the Christians for either personal gain, political affiliation, or business relationships. They received the baptism of water, but their conversion is outward. They are rich or have come to seek riches from God. They have not denied Jesus in words but in compromise. They study about the Holy Spirit but don't believe they need him. They have a great influence on the church they attend to the extent of controlling the pastors and elders employing giving money to the church. They look at occupying the places of preeminence in the church. They love authority and see themselves as chiefs, just like the Pharisees.

The second category is made of those who are neither cold or hot. They believe in the "Once saved, always saved" doctrine. They are involved in all types of compromises with secret societies. They have no time to worship God or pray, which leaves them in a state of perpetual conversion, locked in the vortex of endless repentance, if they repent at all. They don't believe that Jesus is the only way to heaven. They don't believe that the whole Bible is true. They believe that the Bible is not relevant to our time. Their gospel is highly philosophical and barely includes Jesus's death or sacrifice. They believe that people have the power to reach God and that they don't need Jesus. They have been baptized with water and think that this is it—that they need nothing more. They do not want a relationship with Jesus. They do not want to get closer to him. They like feeding their intellectual minds but don't seek any spiritual food or gift. They believe that only God can be perfect and that perfection is too much of a reach. They stay in the comfort of their churches, portraying a form of holiness, but kick the Holy Spirit and his power out of the church. They have no sense of righteousness and justice or respect for the things of God or fear of God.

In the third category, you will find those who are completely confused. They go to church as a tradition. In the United States, where the people believe that every citizen is a Christian, many people believe they've inherited Christianity from their forefathers. Therefore, they think they don't have to make an effort to know Jesus Christ. There are also those who come to church because they believe they can find God, but they are taught human customs and man's doctrines. Their leaders do not instruct them that they've just entered ground zero of a very ancient and deadly war and that they need to equip themselves with the Holy Spirit to fight and be successful.

They are taught that they are ambassadors of God to change the world. So, instead of putting time to pray to be sanctified, they put the glamor of activism and set on to changing the world and making right what they think is wrong. They voice their opinions on the world's affairs and try to influence change, advocate for human rights, etc. Among them, there are those who come to seek a miracle, those who come to network for their businesses, and then those for whom the religious gatherings are just social events. Their church membership is a community affair. They only operate in the flesh.

When I was in college, I remember at one time in the United States when one moved to a different city, the media would advise them that the best way to make friends and avoid bad people was to join a church. Although the influence of the spirit of the Antichrist is greater now, some people still maintain this practice. That is why most people looking for a peaceful place to hang out go to a church when they are in a different city. Theoretically, this sounds like a good idea. However, since the church is no longer engaged in preaching the Christ crucified, these people never hear the true gospel and never come to Jesus. Instead, they subscribe to the philosophy of "Come as you are, and stay as you are."

The Tale of Two Churches

I once saw a church banner that read, "Join us for Sunday service. Come as you are. There is no need to change. You will feel welcome here." Of course, one does not need to change to come to Jesus, but once one comes to Jesus, he/she must go through the change. But that change is not encouraged among the new converts. The churches have no program to help them change spiritually. They encourage them to change socially and economically but not spiritually. When you talk to them, they tell you that their leaders tell them that they are good because they don't steal, they pay their taxes and tithe, and they come to church. It is a misconception because no man is good. Man has some instances of Good in him, but he is evil to the core. Even Jesus himself did not believe man is Good.

In Luke 18:18-25, we read, *"And a certain ruler asked him, saying, Good Master, what shall I do to inherit eternal life? And Jesus said unto him, why callest thou me good? none is good, save one, that is, God. Thou knowest the commandments, Do not commit adultery, Do not kill, Do not steal, Do not bear false witness, Honour thy father and thy mother.* Trying to prove that he is good, the young ruler replied in verse 21, *"All these have I kept from my youth up. Now when Jesus heard these things, he said unto him, Yet lackest thou one thing: sell all that thou hast, and distribute unto the poor, and thou shalt have treasure in heaven: and come, follow me. And when he heard this, he was very sorrowful: for he was very rich. And when Jesus saw that he was very sorrowful, he said, How hardly shall they that have riches enter into the kingdom of God! For it is easier for a camel to go through a needle's eye, than for a rich man to enter into the kingdom of God.* Pay attention to Jesus' words after he heard that the young ruler was walking into the path of righteousness in verse 22. Jesus said you lack love and charity, which completes the path. Go and perform the sacrifice of Charity to prove your love for your fellas, then come follow me.

Since this path is not taught to the new converts in the status quo, they believe that they need to make no efforts to follow Jesus and serve in his congregation. They embrace the material culture of that particular church or denomination, change their wardrobe, and become involved in everything. Before you know it, they are handling music or finances, or they are deacons, and so forth. And as we saw above, they grow with the wheat. They come because the church offers a safe environment for them and their families, and they stay for the community.

There are those for whom attending church is a way to access a higher socioeconomic class, market their products and services, or grow their businesses. Some of them simply need to score a spouse, so they go to church. They know that they can trap a Christian in that position to use and abuse because the Bible forbids divorce. Many women have trapped pastors, evangelists, and deacons in toxic marriages in this manner to hold them hostage. Likewise, many men have enslaved servants of God to use and abuse. There are those who were born in the church. Since their parents were members, they are considered members, and they continue coming to church without ever confessing Jesus to become a disciple and develop a relationship with him. Some of them come to church to create a facade of seriousness, righteousness, and goodness.

While in their inner self, they don't possess any such characteristics. With this conduct, they expect to appear in front of the great white throne to say, "Master, Master, didn't we heal the sick, cast out demons, and prophesize in your name?" The Master will say, "Get out, for I know you not." Notice that Jesus said to the miracle workers that he did not know them. The same people we hold in high esteem on earth. You may ask, how could that be? I explained this in chapter 9, in the quest for the truth.

They were operating with a counterfeit spirit, not the Holy Spirit. Knowing Jesus can only happen in the Holy Spirit. One needs to be born of the Spirit to know Jesus. To be a friend of Jesus, you must be able to relate to him in some way. Many say that they relate to Jesus because he was a man like them. But remember that man died and was buried. He rose from the dead; he was given a new body. His risen body is glorious and is beyond our world.

On a physical level, he is beyond us; he is beyond time. We can only relate to him in the Spirit until we receive our glorious body to be like him. We do not have the same body anymore, but when we are born of the Spirit, we have the same Spirit that was in him, the same sentiments. That's why elder Paul said to the Philippians, *"Let this mind be in you which was also in Christ Jesus" (Philippians 2: 5 BSB).*

THE WHEAT

The wheat symbolizes a group that is not too popular on earth. They are the saints. They are righteous, just, and holy. The army of Satan calls them the traitors. They are a threat to the forces of evil. Just one of them can put a thousand devils to flight, and two of them can send a legion of them fleeing. The human governments and the intellectuals call them radicals. This group stays intimate with Jesus through the Holy Spirit. They have received the baptism of fire and their gifts from the Holy Spirit and are working hard in his employ. They are very few and are in retreat, as they are constantly under attack. They are the target of the enemy, as they pose a threat to the growth of his kingdom wherever they go. They have little in this world as they are being persecuted. They are the overcomers, the ones who are gradually being perfected. They are filled with the Holy Spirit, and he empowers them to fulfill the great commission. They are a close-knit group. They rely on the guidance of the Holy Spirit. They don't just talk the talk, but they also walk the walk. They set time aside to pray and worship. Their interactions with the world are minimal. They have no political affiliations and no great contacts in the government. They are truly like sheep among wolves. They are in danger inside or outside the church.

Satan uses the tares to attack them in the church to try to destroy them. With the anointing of the Holy Spirit, they are as simple as the dove and candid as the snake. They are always looked at as a danger to people even when they have not hurt anyone. They don't have a suitable look, as they are not fashionable or trending. They are simple people who are always prayerful. They are peculiar people. They act in ways the world does not understand. They speak a different language, and their thought pattern is different.

Take a Stand and Repent

There is still time if your conscience convicted you of being among the tares. Don't do the same things the Israelites did when they squandered the grace of God. There is still time for repentance. You can pray the repentance prayer[1] below. There is still provision for grace. To repent of one's sins is like walking out of Egypt, as I mentioned above in the example of the Exodus of Israel. You can repent if you cannot stand the heavy labor, the humiliations, the degradations, and the slavery of sin any longer. You can run to Jesus for freedom. God the honorable, worthy of all glories and blessings, in this age and forever more, will hear your cry for the sake of the blood of his Son, Jesus Christ. He will free you from the bondage of Satan. Don't be stiff-necked like the Israelites, who murmured, complained, and blamed Moses for their troubles and requested to go back to Egypt. Repent and sin no more; wash your robe in holiness to stand for your God.

If you never surrender your heart to Jesus, you can do that now by reciting the sinner's prayer[2]. He is waiting for you. He died for

---

[1] Repentance prayer: *"Lord Jesus of Nazareth, son of God, born of Mary, who was crucified on Calvary, died for my sins and was buried. To you who conquered death and the grave and rose victorious on the third day to go sit at the right hand of the Father of majesty, I address this prayer of repentance. I have sinned against righteousness, justice, and the courts of heaven. I recognize my iniquitous life and the sins that derive from it. I have not strived for righteousness, justice, and holiness. I have not been a faithful servant. I repent of my iniquitous life and ask you to help me change. Please forgive me and restore my first love. Teach me how to be a better servant, a worthy servant. Please help me to sanctify myself and renew the right spirit within me. Lead me in the path of justice, righteousness, and love. Let your Holy Spirit fuse with my spirit so that he can help me overcome the wise of the devil, and seal me for the day of the resurrection of the saints."* If you prayed this prayer, email us at Jesus.saves@bgm.org or visit us at www.bannerofgraceministries.org for support

[2] Sinner's prayer: *"Lord Jesus of Nazareth, son of God, born of Mary, who was crucified on Calvary, died for my sins and was buried. To you who conquered death and the grave and rose victorious on the third day to go sit at the right hand of majesty, I address this prayer of repentance. I acknowledge your sacrifice on the cross to save my soul. I accept your Lordship over my life and to your I surrender all. Please*

you, and he still loves you. If you still breathe on earth, you can be saved. For the sake of Jesus, the Christ, God, the honorable, worthy of all praises and worship, hallowed be his name, can free you from the bondage of sin. Repent of the idolatry, the prejudice, the racism, the greed, the lust, the fornication, the adultery, the stealing, the murders, the lies, the witchcraft, the sorcery, the anger, the greed, the jealousy, and all the human tendencies that are warring with life and sin no more!

---

forgive my sins and wash me clean. Make me a disciple worthy of your name and write my name in the Book of Life. I invite you to come to my heart and change me. Sanctify my spirit soul and body and give me the gift of the Holy Spirit to seal me for the day of redemption". If you prayed this prayer, email us at Jesus.saves@bgm.org for support. Visit us at www.bannerofgraceministries.org

CHAPTER 23

THE POWER OF SIN VERSUS THE PENTECOST POWER

There is power in the blood of Jesus Christ to free all those who call on his name from all bondage. The fight between the kingdom of light and the kingdom of darkness is a deadly fight. It is hard for man to enter the kingdom of light, for this world is shrouded in a web of darkness that is impenetrable without the power of God. In case you ask, the power of God is in the blood and in the name of his son Jesus Christ.

As I mentioned in previous chapters, every human is born in this darkness, and the darkness intends to keep them. The darkness sets up deceptions to dilute the seriousness of its intentions in the form of pleasures, riches, fame, etc. Sin is without doubt the connection between man and the forces of darkness. It is what gives Satan his power over man. Jesus Christ came to destroy the power of sin so that those who believe in him can be set free from the powers of this fallen and his minions. This is a fact.

However, let me remind you that there is no such thing as a Christian sinner. Jesus shows acceptance for the unrepentant sinners because they are in bondage and under the chains of the enemy and cannot reason correctly. That does not mean Jesus condones sinful behaviors once he opens the eyes of a proselyte to repent and recognize the light. One needs to meet his many conditions to become his disciple.

To be a Christian, you need to live in holiness. Hence, you can't live in sin and call yourself a Christian. As it is quoted in the scriptures, *"He that committeth sin is of the devil; for the devil sinneth from the beginning. For this purpose, the Son of God was manifested, that he might destroy the works of the devil. Whosoever is born of God doth not commit sin; for his seed remaineth in him: and he cannot sin, because he is born of God. In this the children of God are manifest, and the children of the devil: whosoever doeth not righteousness is not of God, neither he that loveth not his brother"* (1 John 3:8–10 BSB).

To be righteous is to do what is right at all times and in all things. Do you know that spiritual adultery[3] is unrighteousness? Many Christians would ask, "When have we committed spiritual adultery?" The practice of spiritual adultery which is idolatry is alive and well in this country, and is disguised as tolerance and culture. But it is a sin, and it is of the devil. It has infiltrated the church, and many so-called Christians live in it. It can appear in an innocent form; for instance, some Christians will refer to their children, their wives, their husbands, their diamond ring, and their puppies as adorable.

But do you know that this is a form of idolatry? Only the God of gods is adorable. Many Christians are addicted to football, soccer, basketball, Hollywood entertainment, TV shows, things about their bodies, etc. And they worship those activities to the point that worshiping God takes second place in their lives. Do you know that these also are forms of idolatry?

Any relationship more important to you than your relationship with God, whether with an object or a person, is idolatry (spiritual adultery) and is of the devil. If you worship any graving images, such as the statues, rocks, or sacred animals (such as beasts, dragons, snakes, cows, etc.), it is idolatry, and it is of the devil. If you worship trees, the sun, the moon, yourself, your children, your spouse, your money, your material possessions, your fame, the celebrities, it is idolatry and of the devil.

---

[3] Ezekiel 16: 8-22, Hos. 4:14, James 1: 14

If you are a member of any secret society, you are of the devil. If you are affiliated with any religion against Jesus Christ, you are of the devil. If you practice any type of magic, you are of the devil. If you subscribe to any type of greed, prides, and prejudices, you are of the devil. This is the reason why Elder Paul advised the Colossians to "mortify their members which are upon the earth." He listed these members as fornication, uncleanness, inordinate affection, evil concupiscence, and covetousness. The first member, fornication, refers to sexual immorality. It involves consensual sexual intercourse between two people outside of marriage.

The second member is uncleanness. Here, this word refers to the things that defile the spiritual man. As Jesus explained in Matthew 15:11 (KJV), *"A man is not defiled by what enters his mouth, but by what comes out of it."* The tongue is the instrument used for this defiling as it processes all the unclean thoughts, lies, calumnies, corrupt conversations, and curses and brings them into utterance. In James 1:26 (KJV), Elder James advised that *"if any man among you seem to be religious and bridleth not his tongue but deceiveth his own heart, this man's religion is vain."*

The third member, inordinate affection, occurs when a human develops an uncontrollable love that exceeds reasonable limits: an obsessive attraction to a person, a thing, an animal, etc. The fourth member, evil concupiscence, is at the root of unnatural sexual desires, lust, and uncontrollable passions, such as sexual intercourse between humans with beasts, males with males, and females with females.

The fifth member, covetousness, follows in the same cart with inordinate desires but is the desire for wealth or the need to possess someone else's possession. Covetousness is at the root of all greedy-acquisitive mindsets, grasping, and avaricious tendencies. These members are created and strengthened by an idolatrous mindset. *"For which things' sake the wrath of God cometh on the children of disobedience" (Colossians 3:6 KJV).*

When you practice any type of idolatry in your life, you attract the wrath of God, not his grace. Moreover, many churches practice some form of racism. There are many people who call themselves Christians who identify with racist and discriminatory ideologies.

They act as if they will go to God's heaven to segregate it. If you are a racist, you will not enter the kingdom of God, and this is why. Do you know that this, too, is a sin? The ignorance of racism goes directly against the great commission.

Racism is one of Satan's tactics to divide man to conquer them, to keep them from helping one another. Racism keeps a man from loving his brother; it is hatred. It goes in direct opposition to God's command to "love your brother as you love yourself," which both Moses of the old contract and the Jesus of the new contract reiterated. It is of the devil. Now don't get me wrong; when I say racism, I am talking about discrimination against people simply based upon skin color or ethnicity. I am not condoning those living a life of abomination and corruption.

If one lives in the debauchery of carnal lust, greed, and any form of corruption and abomination, the Bible instructs us not to associate with that kind. We should tell them the truth about their station in life and their destiny in death and urge them to change their ways to save their souls in love. Yet, one should never accept their behavior or behave like them. You might have heard that you cannot live a life of holiness without sin as a human. That is false!

Whenever the Lord asks you to do something, He makes provisions for you to do it well. The Holy Spirit is the provision you need to live a holy life. However, without the Holy Spirit, you don't stand a chance. Sin is not powerless! You cannot fight its fleshly desires without power. Your power is the Holy Spirit. So, beware of the leaders who tell you that you do not need power. This is a watered-down version of Christianity that makes you the prey of the enemy, not a fighter.

THE INTELLECTUAL GOSPEL VS. THE GOSPEL OF POWER

In the theological culture of the current atmosphere in the church, one needs the intellect to preach the gospel. However, in the Pentecostal culture, one needed power to preach the gospel of Jesus

Christ. The enemies of Jesus did not lose their power. The principalities of the air still retain their potency. One needs power to fight against power. Peter had no intellectual training. He was a simple fisherman. But on the day of Pentecost, he was very eloquent in his speech. Thousands of people were able to hear his preaching in their own language.

The Pentecostal culture is a culture of justice, righteousness, and power. There are many people who say that Christ came on earth to give peace to those who accept him. This peace comes with authority and power. Yet, spiritual power seems to be a taboo subject in today's church. But the real church did not and could not start without it. Jesus would not let his disciples go anywhere or talk to anyone about the gospel without it.

During the end of his pilgrimage and training of the disciples, Jesus told them that he was going to the Father but would not leave them without help. In John 14:16 (BSB), he said, *"I will ask the Father, and He will give you another Advocate to be with you forever."* Again, in John 14:26 (BSB), he told them, *"The Advocate, the Holy Spirit, whom the Father will send in My name, will teach you all things and will remind you of everything I have told you."*

Jesus even told them that the Holy Spirit would give them greater insight into who he truly is. In John 15:26 (BSB), we read, *"When the Advocate comes, whom I will send to you from the Father, the Spirit of truth who goes out from the Father. He will testify about Me."* Knowing the strength of the enemy, Jesus urged them to wait until the Father clothed them with power before they proceeded further.

In Luke 10:1–23 (NIV), we read how Jesus commissioned his seventy disciples to go evangelize their neighborhood in Israel. In verse 19, Jesus said, *"I have given you authority to trample on snakes and scorpions and to overcome all the power of the enemy; nothing will harm you."* Ask yourself, "Why did they need authority?"

Jesus knew that they could not face the authority of Satan and his workers with a smile. They needed a greater authority. Furthermore, in Luke 24:49 (BSB), Jesus stated, *"And behold, I am sending the promise of My Father upon you. But remain in the city until you have been clothed with power from on high."* Now ask yourself, "Why did the apostles need to be clothed with power?" If they could complete the mission with their intellect, Jesus would have merely sent them to the best university in town and had them learn theology, and they would be set.

God forbids! They wouldn't last a month. The enemy would have devoured them or compromised them. Let's take Peter for instance. He appeared to be the bravest and most zealous of them all. *"Peter said unto Jesus, though I should die with thee, yet will I not deny thee. Likewise, also said all the disciples"* (Matthew 26:35-34 BSB). Right after that statement, Jesus answered and said, *"Simon, Simon, behold, Satan demanded to have you, that he might sift you like wheat, but I have prayed for you that your faith may not fail. And when you have turned again, strengthen your brothers"*.

Peter reiterated his position and said to him, *"Lord, I am ready to go with you both to prison and to death."* But Jesus, knowing everything, said, *"I tell you, Peter, the rooster will not crow this day until you deny three times that you know me."* And eventually, when Peter faced the music, he folded and denied the Master. Peter was so sure of himself that he remained to see what would happen to Jesus when all the others fled for their lives. However, this confidence led him to deny the very Savior he loved.

Peter had confidence in the flesh but was not ready for a fight with Satan without the Holy Spirit. Keep in mind that the Holy Spirit was also around Peter and the others, as Jesus told them that the Holy Spirit was around them. There is a big difference between having the Holy Spirit around one and having the Holy Spirit in one. Jesus knew that, and he prayed for him that he would make it back to the fold to be filled with the Holy Spirit. And once he was filled with the Holy Spirit, Peter was ready. There were no more doubts or fear.

Keep in mind that Peter was baptized with water for the repentance of his sins at the time of the denial. He was the same Peter whose name the Master had changed from Simon to Cephas, saying, *"And I also say to you that you are Peter, and on this rock, I will build My church, and the gates of Hades shall not prevail against it. And I will give you the keys of the kingdom of heaven, and whatever you bind on earth will be bound in heaven, and whatever you loose on earth will be loosed in heaven" (Matthew 16:18–19 BSB).*

He was the same Peter whom Jesus had empowered to go preach the gospel with the other seventy disciples. He was the same Peter who cast out demons while the Master was on earth. But while the Master was being tested, Peter was no match for Satan without the Holy Spirit. He indeed sifted him like wheat.

But after Peter was baptized of the Holy Spirit, Satan was no match for him. Nothing on earth could annoy him. He was now as powerful as his Master to do the will of God. Without the Holy Spirit, Peter reminds me of the types of Christians one finds today. They are highly intellectual and rely on their own strength. They deny the power of God, meaning they aren't interested in receiving the Holy Spirit. They don't want him to manage their affairs. They just want him around to heal them occasionally. They are independent. Their congregations have the policy of every man for himself. They don't have time for God. They are too busy preparing their members to be patriots of the world. They are brave because they have all the material things they need. Their lives are protected by common laws, and they boast strength in their loyalty to Jesus. However, as he did for Peter, Satan has sifted them like wheat.

These people are about to be checked because these laws in which they put their trust are about to be turned against them. The earthly governments they believe in are about to be turned against them; for Satan is about to demand payment for the good times he provided them. Satan is about to demand allegiance for protecting them. They are about to face what Peter faced. They are about to be given a choice. They will soon have to either deny the Jesus of the Bible or die. Notice that I said "the Jesus of the Bible."

Today, we are witnessing a proliferation of the characteristics depicted by the churches of Sardis and Laodicea in our community of churches. Just like the church of Sardis and Laodicea, the churches of today have a reputation for being alive. Yet, they are really dead. Their deeds are incomplete in the sight of the God of gods. They've forgotten the gospel they'd received for a replacement one, and their teachers teach them that Jesus is not the only way to heaven; that they can join Satan's secret societies and still go to heaven. They teach them more false doctrines that have become prevalent in mainstream Christianity.

These churches are liberal. They are neither cold nor hot. They say that they are rich, that they are wealthy and need nothing—while they are wretched, pitiful, poor, blind, and naked. However, there are still some people among them who have genuine love for God and would like to know God. To those people, I say, "Get out from among them and seek a congregation that embraces the Holy Spirit."

Examine your conscience. Are you a tare or a wheat? This is how we can divide the churches today. Salvation is personal just as one's birth or death. You can't share it with anyone. Therefore, you alone are responsible for yours.

As stated in previous chapters, the body of Christ has slumbered and died spiritually. The gospel of power that Elder Paul preached to the Gentiles has been watered down by philosophy. For centuries now, we have operated without the power that was promised to us by the Master. Countless souls have perished because of that mistake. The theologians believe that we need knowledge to be successful in reaching the world for Jesus. But I say, in order to overcome, we need the Holy Ghost's power.

Jesus ordered the disciples to wait in Jerusalem for the power that should come from heaven before they started any ministry. Hence, we need another Pentecost! We have been blinded by the materials and luxury of this world. Make no mistake about it—there is a war going on. The enemy is armed with cruel hatred against every man; but most importantly, against the Christians, even if you are one by name.

Satan is equipped with all kinds of magical powers beyond this realm and has trillions of fallen angels and billions of demons. He also has billions of humans in his employ, whether voluntarily or involuntarily. His goal is to destroy humanity, and humanity is powerless against him. If the whole of humankind was to wake up from this demonic-induced trance it has been put in, the hypnosis of the television and the media, to combine strength and power to fight the fallen cherub alone, we would not stand a chance of winning—let alone fighting him and his legions individually.

We are nothing but ants compared to the fallen cherub's power. All of us together, we are like sheep compared to Satan and his minions. If anyone told you that you could stand against Satan without the Holy Spirit, they were playing a cruel joke on you—a very cruel joke. Today, the theologians tell people that they are powerful enough to face the dark forces. It is not true. This notion is at the roots of secular humanism. Our only hope is Jesus, the Christ, and the Holy Spirit of God. Only they can fight the fallen cherub and his legions.

You must evaluate where you stand in this world. When the Bible says that Satan is the prince of this world, it means just that. Satan owns this world and everything in and on it for now. The misconception is that we humans are in charge of this world. We are not! However, the clever cherub lets us believe we are.

Meanwhile, he is operating in the shadows, preparing the great deception. In this country, some people would laugh me to scorn if I said that devils and evil spirits are surrounding all of us, manipulating our psyche, our reality, and our very existence. But the same people will believe in aliens. It is amazing how delusional humanity has become. They think that everything is all right and that they are in charge. The reality is that the whole world is under the spell of Satan. The whole world is charmed. The human population is cataloged like cattle and inventoried every single day.

Only about 10 to 20 percent of humanity is free from the control of Satan—the Christians. That is why his whole power is fixated on destroying or converting them. He is using all the fame, wealth, power, and prestige in the world to gain the souls of the Christians. He knows that this world is perishable and that nothing will remain here after the wrath of God passes through.

However, the souls of man are eternal and worth earning. Satan wants to earn the souls of the entire race, to rule supreme on the face of the earth, and bargain with God to change his fate; which is not, wasn't, and will never be in the books. But if he can get all souls on earth to reject heaven, he thinks he can claim the planet as his domain. He is hopeful, and that is how he keeps his followers faithful. For he has promised them that if they can get all the Christians converted or killed, they will inherit the planet.

However, Satan and the fallen angels know that God does not change His mind. Once He pronounces a verdict, it is final! So, they know their fates are sealed. Still, they want man to receive the same punishment as them, suffering the lake of fire. That is Satan's ultimate goal. If no one told you that when you became a follower of Christ, let me tell you that you are in the mind of this cruel enemy. Even if he has neutralized you, he still wants you dead to prevent you from repenting. To do nothing about it is soul-spirit suicide.

You are not without options. The Lord Jesus can provide you with the power to face Satan's assaults as he did for the apostles he trained for his service. That power is the Holy Spirit! He is a gift from Jesus. It is easy to receive help from Jesus. All you must do is call on his name. The Lord will not turn away a human who is perishing and call him for help. But as we mentioned in previous chapters, there are conditions to meet once he saves you.

You must abide by the Word and be sanctified. So, now, how do we sanctify ourselves? There are many steps one needs to take to become sanctified. Many say that when you want to abide by the rules of God, you must pray. But this is half the truth. Praying outside of the will of God will not achieve a thing. If you are praying to ask for forgiveness for your sins, you can present yourself in front of the throne the way you are. But once you have become a Christian, you must abide by the Word. You must do what is right. For it is written, *"He who turns away his ear from hearing the law, even his prayer is an abomination" (Proverbs 28:9 BSB)*.

Following in a similar manner, we read in 1 Peter 3:12 (BSB), *"For the eyes of the Lord are on the righteous and his ears are attentive to their prayer, but the face of the Lord is against those who do evil."* Your prayer is a sacrifice unto the Lord, and the Bible says, *"The sacrifices of the ungodly are an abomination to the Lord; but the prayers of them that walk honestly are acceptable with him" (Proverbs 15:8 BSB)*. Honesty and integrity come from righteousness, and righteousness is a side effect of obeying the law.

Now, I know that there are those who will take the statement of "obeying the law" to justify their day-setting habits and other customs. Let me remind you that the Bible said, *"The Law and the prophets were until John; since that time the kingdom of God is preached, and every man presseth into it" (Luke 16:16 KJV).* Jesus fulfilled this physical law, for it was a precursor of the spiritual law as mentioned in Mathew 5:17 KJV. Paul also exhorted the Galatians in these words, saying, *"For you, brothers, were called to freedom; but do not use your freedom as an opportunity for the flesh. Rather, serve one another in love."*

The entire law is fulfilled in a single decree: *"Love your neighbor as yourself" (Galatians 5:14 KJV).* In John 13:34, Jesus said, *"A new commandment I give you, that you love one another; as I have loved you, that ye also love one another."* To the Romans, Paul ordained that they *"Owe no man anything, but to love one another: for he that loveth another hath fulfilled the law. For this, thou shalt not commit adultery, thou shalt not kill, thou shalt not steal, thou shalt not bear false witness, thou shalt not covet; and if there be any other commandment, it is briefly comprehended in this saying, namely, thou shalt love thy neighbour as thyself. Love worketh no ill to his neighbour: therefore, love is the fulfilling of the law" (Roman 13: 8–10 KJV).*

Beloved, know that Paul was fighting the same false teachings we are encountering today. Hence, they are not new. Therefore, I exhort you, brothers, to be aware of the counterfeit. Satan will disguise his servants as angels of light to send them your way. In fact, this is how his Antichrist will charm the whole world. He is going to come to perform miracles. He is going to show that he has power.

Now, this is not something that is to come. The trend is already here, and it is on your TV screen every day. There is a growing number of magicians that Satan is giving power to in order to attract the masses. *"Just as Jannes and Jambres opposed Moses, so also these men oppose the truth. They are depraved in mind and disqualified from the faith" (2 Timothy 3:8 BSB).*

People love to see miracles. However, the miracles that are from the Holy Spirit are done in the name of Jesus Christ, for he says, *"And these signs will accompany those who believe: In My name they will drive*